DEADLY
AIM

Railroads crisscrossed the eastern United States. Federal and Confederate forces used them to transport troops and supplies.

[Library of Congress]

DEADLY AIM

THE CIVIL WAR STORY OF MICHIGAN'S ANISHINAABE SHARPSHOOTERS

SALLY M. WALKER

HENRY HOLT AND COMPANY
NEW YORK

Henry Holt and Company, *Publishers since 1866*
Henry Holt® is a registered trademark of Macmillan Publishing Group, LLC
120 Broadway, New York, New York 10271 • mackids.com

Library of Congress Cataloging-in-Publication Data
Names: Walker, Sally M., author.
Title: Deadly aim : the Civil War story of Michigan's
Anishinaabe sharpshooters / Sally M. Walker.
Description: First edition | New York : Henry Holt and Company, 2019. |
Includes bibliographical references and index.
Identifiers: LCCN 2018038286 | ISBN 9781250125255 (hardcover)
Subjects: LCSH: United States. Army. Michigan Sharpshooters Regiment, 1st (1863–1865).
Company K—Juvenile literature. | Ojibwa Indians—Michigan—History—19th century—
Juvenile literature. | United States—History—Civil War, 1861–1865—Participation,
Indian—Juvenile literature.
Classification: LCC E99.C6 W35 2019 | DDC 973.7/474—dc23
LC record available at https://lccn.loc.gov/2018038286

Our books may be purchased in bulk for promotional, educational, or business use.
Please contact your local bookseller or the Macmillan Corporate and Premium Sales Department
at (800) 221-7945 ext. 5442 or by email at MacmillanSpecialMarkets@macmillan.com.

First edition, 2019 / Designed by Kay Petronio

Printed in the United States of America by LSC Communications, Harrisonburg, Virginia

1 3 5 7 9 10 8 6 4 2

In honor of the past, present, and future ogitchedaw *and their sacrifices to protect their country and people*

CONT

FOREWORD

THE CIVIL WAR is often remembered for the massive number of lives lost, the fight to end slavery, and the issues surrounding states' rights. It's a part of American history that still provokes strong feelings, especially depending on where you live in the country. This was made evident by the protests in 2017 for and against Confederate war monuments, many of which were taken down across the Southern portion of the United States. The Civil War reverberates like few other historical moments can for Americans today. But lost in these ripple effects is what the Civil War meant for Native populations and, more precisely, the effects it had on Native communities who saw their young men fight in this terrible war.

It is estimated that over twenty thousand Native men fought in the Civil War, for both the North and the South. In this fighting body of Native warriors was a distinct group from Michigan: Company K. Company K, of the First Michigan Sharpshooters, was the largest all-Native company in the Union army east of the Mississippi River. These men were from the Odawa, Ojibwe, and Potawatomi tribes of Michigan. The vast majority of them were from the Lower Peninsula of Michigan. Many were farmers or carpenters and carried on their lives much like their settler neighbors.

But in many regards, the men of Company K led lives completely different from those of their Euro-American neighbors. Natives were not U.S. citizens at the onset of the Civil War, and the Michigan tribes had suffered great losses at the hands of the federal government in the decades leading up to the war. Some tribal communities were hunted down and forcibly relocated to Kansas in the 1830s. Diseases brought by settlers in the 1830s and '40s devastated villages. The tribes had also ceded over 90 percent of their ancestral homelands to the United States in treaty negotiations, thus setting the stage for future loss of resources.

This painful history raises the question of why the men of Company K enlisted in the Union army. Perhaps this is the most compelling part of Company K: their decision to fight. Was it their warrior spirit? Was it to avoid slavery? Was it to help obtain equality—socially and legally—in America? Was it to avoid violence that western tribes experienced, such as the Sand Creek massacre and the Lakota war?

We will never know the definite answer, but maybe it's some or all of the above. The stories of Company K are about more than the battles they fought or the number of men they lost. Company K is a reflection of the complicated world the Anishinaabek lived in during the 1800s and how they navigated other wars to protect their homes and their people. Many Michigan Odawas, Potawatomis, and Ojibwes can trace back their ancestry to the soldiers who fought in Company K. They have a great sense of pride knowing their relations fought in this terrible war, as well they should. And it's not only the descendants who have this pride. Company K can make all Anishinaabek proud today.

Eric Hemenway

Director of Repatriation, Archives and Records
for the Little Traverse Bay Bands of Odawa Indians;
Michigan Historical Commission member

Note to the READER

WHENEVER POSSIBLE, the specific name of a group of people is used: for example, Odawa, Ojibwe, Potawatomi, or Cherokee. When referring collectively, in a general sense, to the many peoples indigenous to North America, I have used *American Indians*. I use *Europeans* similarly when referring collectively to colonists and those immigrants who came from countries such as England, Germany, and France.

In quotations from historical documents, the spellings are left exactly as they appear, for example, *Ottawa* and *Chippewa*. Otherwise *Odawa* and *Ojibwe*, the preferred spellings by members of the bands today, are used. Punctuation was used sparingly in many diaries and letters. I have added some periods and capitalized words at the beginning of a sentence if needed for clarity.

Language is an important part of any culture. Anishinaabemowin is the traditional language of the Anishinaabek—the Odawa, Ojibwe, and Potawatomi. The language among these groups has many similarities, but there are variations. For uniformity, Anishinaabemowin words in this book are spelled in keeping with spellings used in the exhibits at the Ziibiwing Center, in Mount Pleasant, Michigan, or with the Ojibwe People's Dictionary, which can be found online at ojibwe.lib.umn.edu/.

Whenever possible, I spell a person's name the same way the

person signed it. Otherwise, for uniformity, I use the primary spelling as it appears in *Who Was Who in Company K*, by Chris Czopek, which is often how the name appears on the soldier's pension record. Czopek's book includes a list of the many ways each man's name appears in a variety of documents.

MUSTER ROLL

Lieutenant General Ulysses S. Grant—general-in-chief of the Armies of the United States

Major General George Meade—commander of the Army of the Potomac

NINTH CORPS (1864–1865, AS PART OF THE ARMY OF THE POTOMAC):

Major General Ambrose Burnside (April 1864–August 1864)

Major General John Parke (August 1864–April 1865)

Brigadier General Orlando Willcox—division commander

Colonel Benjamin Christ—brigade commander

Colonel Ralph Ely—brigade commander

FIRST REGIMENT, MICHIGAN SHARPSHOOTERS, SECOND BRIGADE, THIRD DIVISION, NINTH CORPS

Although nearly a thousand soldiers enlisted in the regiment, this book focuses primarily on Company K. The men listed here, most of whom are Anishinaabe, are prominently featured.

Colonel Charles DeLand—commander of regiment

Lieutenant Edward Buckbee—adjutant, later major

COMPANY B FIRST MICHIGAN SHARPSHOOTERS

William Duvernay   John Kedgnal

COMPANY K FIRST MICHIGAN SHARPSHOOTERS

Edwin Andress—captain (July 22, 1863–July 26, 1864)

James DeLand—first lieutenant (June 20, 1864), captain (November 20, 1864)

William Driggs—first lieutenant (July 22, 1863–July 6, 1864)

Garrett Graveraet—second lieutenant (June 9, 1863–July 10, 1864)

Charles Allen	Louis Miskoguon
George Ashkebug	William Mixinasaw
Amos Ashkebugnekay	Daniel Mwakewenah
Louis Genereau Jr.	William Newton
Joseph Gibson	Marcus Otto
Henry Graveraet	Jacko Penaiswanquot
Benjamin Greensky	Antoine Scott
John Jacko	Thomas Smith
Thomas Kechittigo	Joseph Wakazoo
Amable Ketchebatis	Thomas Wesaw
James Mashkaw	Payson Wolf
John Mashkaw	

July 30, 1864—Petersburg, Virginia

DAWN WAS STILL HOURS AWAY, yet few men in Company K slept.

Hours earlier, the Anishinaabe company of the First Michigan Sharpshooters, the only company in the Union army east of the Mississippi River whose enlisted men were solely American Indians, had moved into position behind the earthworks. The soil ridges shielded them from enemy fire. The federal soldiers prayed that they would survive the coming attack—that they would defeat the Confederate soldiers who hunkered within their own earthworks along the top of a low rise of land several hundred yards away. Colonel Charles DeLand and his officers advised the men in hushed tones to rest while they awaited orders. Nervous energy made that impossible.

Twenty-three-year-old Antoine Scott examined his rifle, making sure the ramrod was in place. By then, he was so familiar with the rifle that even in the dark, he could tell if all its parts were assembled and ready to use. He loaded the square case belted around his waist with gunpowder-filled paper cartridges and double-checked that he had plenty of bullets. Amable Ketchebatis filled his canteen to the brim. The past few days had been scorching hot. He knew there would be little or no chance to refill his canteen in the coming hours.

The Sharpshooters sipped hot coffee and ate a meal of dry biscuits called hardtack. It would be their last meal for many hours.

By 2:00 a.m., Company K had quietly moved forward to within half a mile of the enemy's lines. Only scattered trees and open fields lay between them. The men knew a major assault on Confederate lines would soon begin, and waiting for orders was nerve-racking. However, orders to advance wouldn't be given until 3:30 a.m., after a small group of soldiers had completed an underground mission to break the enemy's battle line. So Company K waited.

Watch hands ticked past 3:00.

Then 3:30.

4:00.

Nothing happened. Still darkest night.

Using the fastest communication available, officers telegraphed: Why the delay?

Soldiers, with hushed voices, wondered too.

And waited.

4:30.

The woods were quiet. Daylight crept into the sky. A slight mist grayed the air.

Fifteen more minutes ticked by.

Then . . . suddenly . . . a mighty explosion!

Scott, Ketchebatis—everyone in Company K—ducked at the roar. The earth shook. Less than half a mile away a massive column of dirt blasted into the air. Within minutes, the men heard the crack of gunfire and the thunderous boom of cannons.

DeLand rallied the Sharpshooters and commanded: "Forward!"

The battle had begun.

The Confederate artillery guns that fired on Fort Sumter on April 12, 1861, heralded the start of the Civil War.

CHAPTER 1

A Broken COUNTRY

★ ★ ★

COMPANY K WAS ONE OF MANY companies that fought on July 30, 1864. The battle in Petersburg, Virginia, was one in a four-year war that had been ignited by decades-old disagreements. Arguments about African American enslavement raged: between states, between groups of people and political parties, even between family members. By the end of the 1850s, opposing views on slavery and its expansion had reached a fever pitch. While the federal government still sanctioned and upheld the slavery that existed in Southern states, the states in the Northern part of the country did not support slavery. In fact, they had already abolished it. The governing bodies of these states and the federal government did not want slavery permitted in any new states that joined the nation. States in the South permitted slavery—their economy was based on it. Their governing bodies favored the continuation of slavery and its expansion into new states.

In November 1860, Abraham Lincoln, who did not support the expansion of slavery, was elected president. Simmering tensions heated to a full boil. By the time Lincoln was inaugurated, in March 1861, seven states—South Carolina, Mississippi, Florida, Alabama, Georgia, Louisiana, and Texas—had seceded from the Union, tearing the country in two. With their secession, these states declared they were no longer part of the United States of America. They set up their own government, with its own constitution. They named their new country the Confederate States of America and chose Jefferson Davis as its president.

Soon after, the Confederacy established a volunteer army. Before dawn on April 12, 1861, in Charleston Harbor, South Carolina, Confederate artillery began a steady bombardment of the Union's Fort Sumter. After thirty-four hours, the fort's commander surrendered.

For many people in Southern states, the election of Abraham Lincoln as president of the United States was the last straw.

[National Archives]

Determined to preserve the United States as one country, President Lincoln responded. He issued a proclamation on April 15 that asked the militia of the United States to enroll seventy-five thousand men "in order to suppress" the rebellious action taken by the states that had seceded.

The situation worsened. By the middle of June, four more Southern states had joined the Confederacy. The Union and Confederate armies tested each other's mettle in a series of small, scattered skirmishes. But on July 21, they clashed in a large battle at Bull Run, near Manassas Junction, Virginia. After that, there was no turning back. Civil war embroiled the country.

UNEXPECTED SOLDIERS

As the war intensified, Union and Confederate armed forces aggressively recruited new soldiers. Men enlisted for many reasons. Some wanted to abolish slavery; others wanted to maintain it. Some men fought to preserve the United States as one country; others fought to keep the seceded states separate. And because soldiers received regular pay, some men enlisted for the money. At the beginning of the war, men enlisted voluntarily. Later, as wounds, death, illness, and desertion reduced the ranks, men had to register for a draft, which is a system for required military service. But if he could afford it, a man could avoid military service by paying another man to serve in his place.

Some men who wanted to fight for the Union offered their service to the federal government within weeks of the war beginning. In May 1861, George Copway, an Ojibwe missionary and writer, wanted to form a company of "Indians of Michigan." Backed by members of the Michigan Legislature, Copway proposed the idea to President

Lincoln. Copway wrote that he would hand-pick the men and enlist them as scouts and messengers. They would be armed only in a way to provide for their self-defense. He added, "They will be young men, inured to hardship, fleet as deers, shrewd and cautious, and will doubtless prove of great service to the army." The federal government turned down Copway's proposal.

On October 30, 1861, Dr. G. P. Miller, an African American who lived in Battle Creek, Michigan, wrote a letter to Simon Cameron, President Lincoln's secretary of war. In his letter, Miller asked for "the privilege of raising from five to ten thousand free men . . . to take any position that may be assigned us (sharp shooters preferred). We would like white persons for superior officers. If this proposition is not accepted we will if armed & equipped by the government fight as guerillas." Miller added that some people who wanted to enlist with him were of "Indian" ancestry and were "legal voters in the state of Michigan." Miller finished his letter, "In the name of God answer immediately." The War Department wasn't interested in Miller's request, either.

That same year, twenty-five-year-old Tom Kechittigo, another Ojibwe man from Michigan, walked up to the army recruiter's table. Kechittigo had been orphaned as a child. While growing up, he supported himself by fishing and hunting, often accompanied by his friend Bernard Bourassa. Kechittigo—by then an excellent shot—and Bourassa attempted to join the Second Michigan Cavalry. Kechittigo was rejected right away because the army wouldn't "take Indians." He recalled later that the officers told him they were afraid the American Indians would "murder and scalp all the womens and childrens." Unfortunately, racist beliefs like this were commonly held by many white Americans. Somehow, though, Bourassa, also Anishi-naabe, was accepted. Perhaps, to the enlisting officer, Bourassa hadn't "looked" Indian.

Tom Kechittigo was rejected along with Copway's and Miller's proposals due to one reason: the prejudice of racism. At that time, many people unfairly believed that neither American Indians nor African Americans were trustworthy and that they were incapable of fighting as soldiers in an organized army.

Twenty-three-year-old Joseph Wakazoo, an Odawa, took a different route than Kechittigo. Instead of seeking a recruiter in Michigan, where he lived, Wakazoo traveled to Virginia, where the 16th Michigan Infantry was stationed. On November 8, 1861, Wakazoo enlisted in Company H of that regiment, apparently without any problem. It's possible that he was permitted to do so because he knew one of the regiment's officers.

By 1863, as the war dragged on and the Union needed more men, the federal government had changed its policy regarding the enlistment of African Americans and American Indians. The army went out and recruited African Americans, but segregated them into their own regiments, separate from white soldiers but under the command of white officers. The new recruits were officially labeled Colored Troops. (Today *colored* is not considered an appropriate way to describe African Americans or other people, but it was in common use during the Civil War.) Similarly, American Indians who were initially denied the opportunity to serve were now recruited to enlist.

In total, about twenty thousand American Indians served in the Union and Confederate armies and navies. In fact, two opposing army officers of high rank were American Indians. Lieutenant

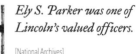

Ely S. Parker was one of Lincoln's valued officers.

[National Archives]

Colonel Ely S. Parker, a Seneca from New York, was General Ulysses S. Grant's adjutant—his right-hand man. He assisted Grant in issuing orders. In 1865, Parker wrote the final draft for the Confederates' terms of surrender at Appomattox. After the war, he was named a brigadier general. Brigadier General Stand Watie, a Cherokee, commanded an American Indian brigade west of the Mississippi. He was the last Confederate general to surrender at the war's end.

Many Choctaws, Cherokees, and Seminoles who lived in Southern states and the Indian Territory (now Oklahoma) enlisted in the Confederate army. Their decision to side with the Confederacy may have reflected their grievances with the federal government, which had forced them from their homelands and broken many treaties. Some members of these nations—Stand Watie among them—owned enslaved people. In 1860, Cherokees in the Indian Territory owned four thousand slaves. Others in the same areas opposed slavery and joined the Union army. A number of battles in the West pitted members of the same community against one another.

About thirty-six hundred American Indians enlisted in the Union army, including the Ojibwes, Odawas, and Potawatomis whose ancestors had lived in the Upper Great Lakes region for many hundreds of years. As a group, these three bands call themselves Anishinaabek. This means "the good, or real, people" in Anishinaabemowin, the traditional language of the Anishinaabek.

For the Anishinaabe soldiers of Company K, a slavery-related reason may have prompted their support for the Union. In July 1863, Ojibwe chief Nock-ke-chick-faw-me gave a passionate speech to a group of young men. He spoke of their people's long tradition as honorable and courageous fighters. He reminded them, "We are descendants of braves, who . . . drove the powerful tribes now beyond the *'great river'* from these *our once beautiful hunting grounds.* . . . If the South conquers you will be *slaves, dogs.*" The chief's words may have caused fear in some of his listeners, given the long history of their mistreatment by the government. If the Confederacy won the war, perhaps they might also be enslaved. On the other hand, slavery was illegal in the North. By supporting the Union cause, they could *avoid* enslavement.

A more pressing reason for the Anishinaabe soldiers was their desire to preserve their homeland. Ever since the Revolutionary War, treaties between the U.S. government and the Anishinaabek had greatly reduced the area of their homeland. Why did the Anishinaabe men support a government that did this? A government whose treaties tried to remove them? As the Civil War began, perhaps the most important reason was to safeguard the right to remain where generations of their ancestors had lived. Unfortunately, the Anishinaabek's fear of losing their land was rooted in a long history of conflict with the federal government.

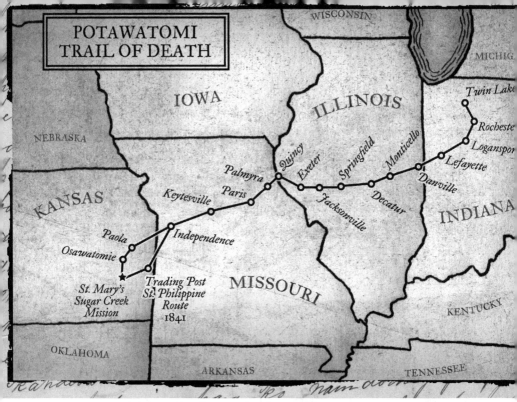

*The forced march from Indiana to Kansas sickened three hundred Potawatomi men,
women, and children and became the death warrant for more than forty.*

[Elisabeth Alba, based on the memorial stone at St. Philippine Duchesne Memorial Park, Kansas]

THE POTAWATOMI TRAIL OF DEATH

On May 28, 1830, President Andrew Jackson signed the Indian
Removal Act of 1830. During the eight years Jackson served as president, he signed almost seventy such treaties, which led to nearly fifty
thousand American Indians being moved from their eastern homelands to Indian Territory.

Michigan gained statehood on January 26, 1837. Until then, the
region had escaped the flood of land-seeking white settlers who had
spread out from the eastern United States. Five weeks later, Martin
Van Buren became the new U.S. president. The Anishinaabek hoped
that he would honor their treaties and leave them alone.

In the autumn of 1838, a band of Potawatomis who lived in part of Indiana had their hopes dashed. Northern Indiana and southwestern Michigan had been the ancestral land of the Potawatomis for many generations. But under terms in the Yellow River Treaty, signed by some Indiana Potawatomis two years earlier, reservation land had been ceded, or formally yielded, to the federal government. The terms of this treaty gave the Potawatomis two years to relocate to territory west of the Mississippi. Some Potawatomi leaders who had signed the treaty had already moved their people.

However, Me-no-mi-nee, the leader of a large Potawatomi community in northern Indiana, had not signed the Yellow River Treaty. On August 6, 1838, Potawatomi leaders, the government's Indian agent Abel Pepper, and white residents of the surrounding area attended a council meeting in Me-no-mi-nee's village. At the meeting's close, Me-no-mi-nee addressed Pepper and the white residents through an interpreter:

The president does not know the truth. . . . He does not know that your treaty is a lie, and that I never signed it. He does not know that you made my young chiefs drunk and got their consent, and pretended to get mine. He does not know that I have refused to sell my lands and still refuse. He would not by force drive me from my home, the graves of my tribe, and my children who have gone to the Great Spirit, nor allow you to tell me your braves will take me, tied like a dog if he knew the truth. . . . I have not sold my lands. I will not sell them. . . . I am not going to leave my lands and I don't want to hear anything more about it.

The government disregarded Me-no-mi-nee's statement. During the weeks that followed, armed troops marched into Potawatomi villages and forcibly removed people from their homes, which the soldiers tore down or burned.

On September 4, 1838, many hundreds of Potawatomi men, women, and children began a two-month march to the Kansas Territory. Provisions, including food, for the trip were "very scarce and of poor quality." Water was equally scarce. Three hundred people sickened with fever. Within a week of departure, six children and one man were dead. By the time the people arrived in the Kansas Territory, on November 4, more than forty people were dead, more than half of them children. Agent Pepper and other officials had promised the Potawatomis that homes would await them in Kansas. None had been built. The people, many ill and weak from the long, harsh march, had to build their own winter shelters.

WE WILL FIGHT

As 1838 drew to a close, the Anishinaabek in Michigan knew what had happened in Indiana. They suspected a similar relocation would be forced upon them, and they were right. In the early 1840s, soldiers with bayonets fixed to their rifles came to southern Michigan and forced a large group of Potawatomi families to leave their homes and land. According to terms in a treaty, they would be sent to the Kansas and Indian Territories. In the confusion, one mother was separated from her baby, a boy named Thomas Wesaw. The soldiers barred her way when she tried to return for him and made her leave with the others. A friend who had remained hidden found the baby and took care of him. Some days later, Thomas's aunt, who had escaped from the soldiers, returned to Michigan and got him from his rescuer. The aunt raised him, and the Wesaw family told this story many times in later years; they knew if it happened once, it could happen again.

In 1855, the Treaty of Detroit stipulated that a number of acres would be selected by Ojibwes and Odawas who signed the treaty. Adult heads of households were to receive more acreage than children. At first, it seemed as if this would end the threat of forced removal. But more settlers and land speculators moved to Michigan, and the land grab spread. Many of the promised lands were never granted due to governmental mismanagement, illegal sales, and outright fraud. By the time the Civil War started, the Anishinaabek again were worrying that their homeland was in jeopardy.

About thirty-nine hundred Odawas and Ojibwes lived in Michigan in 1861. Some Anishinaabe men may have hoped that if they enlisted in the Union army, the federal government would honor their loyalty and service by not forcing them off their land.

Whether the Anishinaabek enlisted to abolish slavery or to safeguard their homeland—or for a combination of other reasons—they did so to uphold their convictions. Who were their ancestors, the men and women who instilled in their descendants such a strong connection with the land?

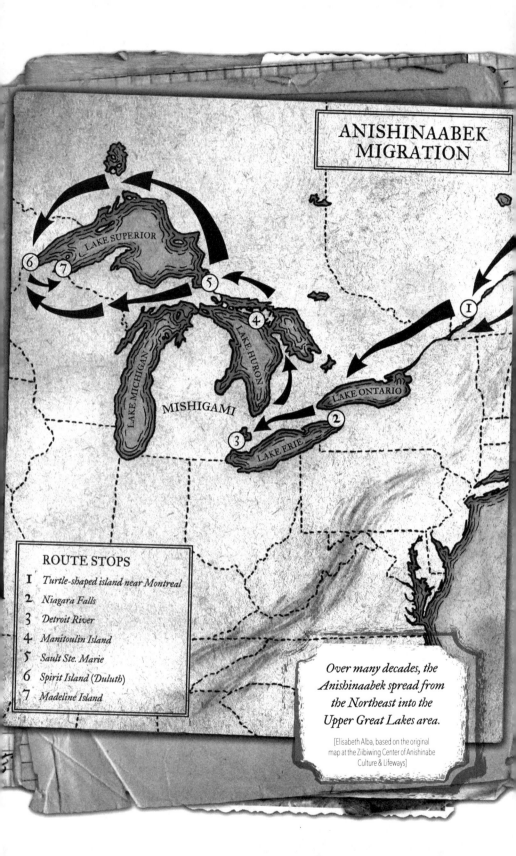

ANISHINAABEK MIGRATION

LAKE SUPERIOR

LAKE MICHIGAN

LAKE HURON

MISHIGAMI

LAKE ONTARIO

LAKE ERIE

ROUTE STOPS

1 — Turtle-shaped island near Montreal
2 — Niagara Falls
3 — Detroit River
4 — Manitoulin Island
5 — Sault Ste. Marie
6 — Spirit Island (Duluth)
7 — Madeline Island

Over many decades, the Anishinaabek spread from the Northeast into the Upper Great Lakes area.

[Elisabeth Alba, based on the original map at the Ziibiwing Center of Anishinabe Culture & Lifeways]

CHAPTER 2

CHI MAAWONIDIWIN

(the Great Walk)

★ ★ ★

MORE THAN ONE THOUSAND YEARS AGO, the Anishinaabek set out on Chi Maawonidiwin (the Great Walk). Guided by a prophecy that told of seven stopping places, they left the Northern Atlantic coast and followed the path of the setting sun. The prophecy foretold their final destination as the place where "food grew on the water."

No one lived through the duration of the whole journey. The entire trip lasted longer than the combined lifetimes of a woman and a man; their children, grandchildren, and great-grandchildren; and the many generations of children that followed.

In *wiigwaasi-jiimaanan* (birchbark canoes), the Anishinaabek paddled southwest on the Saint Lawrence River and traveled into the

Great Lakes. On their generations-long journey, they rested at seven main stopping places, where some people remained. Some left and traveled north, to the area now called Ontario, Canada. Others traveled south. But most continued west.

During Chi Maawonidiwin, three groups formed within the people. One group—the traders and protectors—provided the people with food and other supplies. This group called themselves the Odawas.

The second group, the Ojibwes, were keepers of the faith. They preserved the Anishinaabek's sacred scrolls made of *wiigwaas* (birchbark). The scrolls were inscribed with images about the Anishinaabek's history and beliefs. The Ojibwes also cared for the *mitigwakik dewewigan* (water drum), which held spiritual teachings and songs. The scrolls and the water drum helped religious leaders and elders teach Anishinaabe cultural beliefs, songs, and ceremonies to younger people.

The third group, the Potawatomis, cared for the Sacred Fire. While on Chi Maawonidiwin, they carried the Sacred Fire's burning coals, always protecting them so the fire never burned out.

Over time, Anishinaabemowin, as it was spoken when all the Anishinaabek lived in the Northeast, changed slightly. Each group developed its own dialect. But they could still understand one another. Some customs changed slightly, as the groups became more distinct. Despite these changes, the groups remained close. In fact, they formed an alliance called the Three Fires. United by the alliance, the Ojibwes, Odawas, and Potawatomis vowed to support one another politically to protect their territory and keep the Anishinaabek spiritually strong.

Chi Maawonidiwin ended when the Anishinaabek reached the lands that surround the Great Lakes. In areas now called Michigan, Wisconsin, Minnesota, and Ontario, the Anishinaabek found *manoomin* (wild rice), an aquatic grass that produces long brown grains, fulfilling the prophecy of a land where food grows on water.

Some of the Anishinaabek made their homes in Mishigami. The name, a two-part Ojibwe word, described the area's primary geographical feature: *mishi* (big) and *gami* (lake). And the lake was gigantic. French explorers later called it Michigan.

Widespread forests shaded Mishigami. Aspen, birch, black ash, cedar, hickory, oak, and pine were just some of its species of trees, many of which had trunks five feet wide, or even wider. The trees provided the Anishinaabek with a rich source of materials that helped them survive. Over time, the Anishinaabek established a network of forest paths that stretched north, south, east, and west.

Steep bluffs and the sandy or cobblestoned beaches of three great lakes and several bays fringed Mishigami. Their waters supplied the Anishinaabek with a wide variety of life-sustaining plants and animals. Rivers offered similar bounty but were important in another way too: They crisscrossed the countryside and were water highways for *wiigwaasi-jiimaan* journeys.

Mishigami was a good place to live and raise families, and it was a good place for elders to share Anishinaabe creation stories that told of how Gitche Manido (the Great Spirit) created Earth and everything on it.

To bring strength and order to Anishinaabe lives, the Great Spirit gave them the Odoidaymiwan, a clan system that served as the framework for their government. The clan system of kinship provided leadership in all areas of life: It guided occupations, spiritual teachings, marriages, and relationships between different Anishinaabe bands. Originally, there were seven *odoidayiwug* (clans): Loon, Bear, Deer,

Fish, Bird, Marten, and Crane. Clan members served their community in special ways. For example, members of the Bear Clan were protectors and healers; chiefs belonged to the Crane and Loon Clans; and members of the Bird Clan led the people spiritually. The Anishinaabek added new clans as the years passed and needs changed.

Elders showed the sacred scrolls to the youth and spoke the pictures' stories. They beat rhythms on the water drum and sang. The stories and songs reminded the listeners that everything on earth contained a spirit. The words reminded them that the Anishinaabek were made from Aki (Mother Earth). Because this was so, the Anishinaabek were connected to all living things, and life was a never-ending circle. Above all, the teachings of the elders reminded the Anishinaabek to respect the earth and all her children. Many diverse Anishinaabe stories, songs, and ceremonies celebrated and honored the relationships among people, animals, plants, land, and water.

LIFE AND LAND: AN INSEPARABLE BOND

For countless generations, the cycle of seasons guided the ebb and flow of Anishinaabe life and the places where the people camped. The Anishinaabek celebrated the arrival of *mnookimi* (spring) with ceremonies that welcomed the renewal of life.

Year after year, Anishinaabe families left their winter lodges and traveled to *ziisibaakodokaaning* (sugar bush), the large stands of maple trees. They collected the trees' sap and made maple syrup. They gathered spring plants for cooking and medicinal use. They stripped bark from cedar and basswood trees and made bags and mats. Throughout their work, men, women, and children were mindful of Anishinaabe beliefs: They took only what was needed for survival and no more.

Wiigwaas *sheets layered over the top of a lodge kept it snug and dry.*

[Sally M. Walker, courtesy of Ziibiwing Center of Anishinabe Culture & Lifeways]

Niibing (summer) was a time of plenty and of planting. Families loaded their belongings into long *wiigwaasi-jiimaanan* and paddled to their summer camps. Extended families and friends gathered together and shared news. They built large dome-shaped lodges roofed with sheets of *wiigwaas*. Respecting the birch trees' gift of shelter, men peeled the *wiigwaas* from the trunk in a way that did not kill the tree.

Thick walls made of bundled reeds shielded a lodge's dwellers from wind and weather.

[Sally M. Walker, courtesy of Ziibiwing Center of Anishinabe Culture & Lifeways]

Men hunted and fished, while women and children planted corn, beans, and squash in family gardens. Year after year, families sowed *manoomin* in the shallow waters that nurtured the wild rice.

Niibing was a time for planning ahead. Women smoked fish and dried berries to preserve them. Families harvested *manoomin* and prepared the grains for winter storage. Winter preparations were time-consuming, but the Anishinaabek always made time to hold ceremonies and sing songs in remembrance of the long-ago prophecy that had told them of food that grew on the water. Their songs honored the grain and gave thanks for the land's bounty.

In *digwaagi* (autumn) the Anishinaabek's close relationship with nature and the land continued. Men hunted animals such as bear, elk, and moose. They were skilled hunters, expertly using spears and arrows tipped with stone points and blending with their surroundings

Men used a rock to roughly shape the stone points for spears, arrows, and axes similar to these. They used bone and antler tools to finely chip the sharp edges of the points. Grinding produced the stone ax's smooth surface.

[Sally M. Walker]

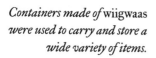

Containers made of wiigwaas *were used to carry and store a wide variety of items.*

[Sally M. Walker, courtesy of Ziibiwing Center of Anishinabe Culture & Lifeways]

so their prey wouldn't see them. This would become a life-saving skill for the members of Company K. Women skinned and tanned hides to make clothes, blankets, and drum heads. They dried and smoked the meat. The Anishinaabek used all parts of an animal whose life had been given to sustain them. Upholding Anishinaabe beliefs, they wasted nothing.

At the end of *digwaagi*, the Anishinaabek again loaded *wiigwaasi-jiimaanan* and traveled south to the areas of their winter camps, a journey that took several days. Moving to a new place allowed the land that had nourished them during the spring, summer, and fall the time it needed to replenish itself.

The short daylight hours and frigid outdoor temperatures of *boon* (winter) made a *boonishiwaaning* (winter lodge), and its crackling fire, a cozy place. Without outdoor distractions, *boon* was a good time for elders to tell stories.

The oral tradition, passing spoken stories from one generation to the next, was—and still is—an essential part of Anishinaabe culture. People who lived as one with the land, who moved seasonally from one place to another, couldn't haul a large printed library. Instead, elders held the wisdom of past generations in their memories—the creation stories, the whys of customs, the ways to live with proper respect for Aki. Young people listened to the elders, and in this way the knowledge became theirs, ready to share when they became the society's elders. During *boon*, teachers composed and shared songs for the ceremonies the people held during the other seasons.

Boon was a time to prepare for *mnookimi*. Men repaired fishnets and hunting tools. Women stitched clothing. They decorated clothing and baskets with shells and porcupine quills. They crafted all their tools and containers from animals, plants, or stone, which were created by Aki. All things Aki created had a spirit. When an object was made from a natural material, the spirit remained within the object. Because this was so, the Anishinaabek fashioned their work slowly, with great care.

Boon did not last forever. Daytime lengthened, snow and ice melted. *Mnookimi* arrived, and sap again rose in the maple trees. In this manner, the flow of Anishinaabe life moved hand in hand with Aki, Mother Earth. The land sustained the people; they protected it. Years and years of this endless cycle had woven the Anishinaabek and their homeland together in an unbreakable bond.

And then, pale-skinned strangers arrived.

MAYAGWEWININIWAG (FOREIGNERS)

In 1615, French explorer Samuel de Champlain traveled west into the area now called Ontario, where he met the Odawas. The following year he visited a large Odawa winter village and reported, "They gave us very good cheer and received us very kindly." By the late 1600s, the Odawas, Ojibwes, and their allies had become France's main suppliers of furs.

The Anishinaabek also supplied French traders whom they called *mayagwewininiwag*, or foreigners, with goods for long trips: canoes, berries, and fish. In exchange for these supplies and furs, the Odawas and Ojibwes received metal kettles, knives, clothes, blankets, glass and porcelain beads, and other items made in Europe. Anishinaabe women became known for their elaborate beadwork designs.

Many French traders married Odawa, Ojibwe, and Potawatomi women. Many Anishinaabek learned to speak some French, or a mixture of it and words from their own languages.

Unfortunately, European traders carried diseases such as smallpox and tuberculosis to America. Anishinaabe healers treated their people as best they could with traditional medicines, but these illnesses spread like wildfire and often killed everyone in a village. Sometimes, an entire tribe died due to disease.

To meet the ever-increasing European demand for furs, Anishinaabe hunters became lax in following traditional beliefs. Unlike their ancestors, they took more animals than they needed for survival. As a result, some animals became scarce.

Many Odawas who lived in Ontario moved south, into Michigan, to find more animals. Odawa camps dotted Lake Michigan's northeast shoreline. But they established their main village at Waganakising, which means "it is bent." Odawa oral tradition says that the village was named after a tall pine tree that grew on a high bluff and was easily seen from the lake. Its trunk, bent by a spirit, overhung the water. The exact location where the tree grew is unknown, but tradition suggests that it was near present-day Middle Village. (In deference to this, the French called the whole regional shoreline L'Arbre Croche, which means "the crooked tree.") For generations, the Odawas built homes, planted gardens, and remained in and around Waganakising, leaving only to winter farther south. Waganakising bustled with life, and as many as three thousand people lived there.

Meanwhile, other Odawas traveled farther south and west, where they established villages that were often shared with the Ojibwes and the Potawatomis. People from the three groups intermarried and established new kinship ties within and among the communities.

While trading with the French brought a lot of change to the Anishinaabek, even more changes lay in their future.

THE *OGITCHEDAW* (WARRIORS)

The ancient Anishinaabek were known as skilled fishers and traders. Anishinaabe *ogitchedaw*, men who trained to become warriors, fought fiercely and willingly sacrificed their lives to protect their people and defend their homeland from invaders.

The *ogitchedaw* did not begin war without careful consideration. When *ogitchedaw* prepared a war party, they gathered warriors from other villages and explained their mission's purpose. Each warrior willing to go inhaled a puff of smoke from a pipe filled with shreds of *semaa* (tobacco). *Semaa* was a sacred gift, given to the Anishinaabek by Gitche Manido, the Great Spirit. Offered back to Gitche Manido and other spirits, or offered to people, tobacco solemnized a ceremony. *Semaa* is used to communicate with the spirit world and lends power to an offering, prayer, or request. It makes an agreement—such as a treaty—more binding. By smoking a pipe filled with *semaa*, the *ogitchedaw* signaled they were undertaking solemn, serious actions that needed spiritual support.

Before the *ogitchedaw* left for war, their community held ceremonial dances and sang songs. The dances and songs spiritually prepared the warriors for the coming ordeal and protected them during battle. Each departing warrior would have worn a small hide pouch filled with the four sacred Anishinaabe medicines: *semaa* for prayers and offerings, *wiingash* (sweet grass) for strength and kindness, *mashkodewashk* (sage) for healing, and *giizhik* (cedar) for purification and protection from harmful energy. After the fighting ended, different ceremonies that healed the spirit and mind welcomed the returning *ogitchedaw* home.

But *ogitchedaw* were more than warriors. They helped people in their communities who were experiencing difficult times. Selflessly, they often gave their possessions to those in need. The Anishinaabek valued and highly respected the *ogitchedaw*.

As England established colonies in America, its colonists clashed with the French, the Anishinaabek's allies. From 1754 to 1763, war raged between French and British forces. Pontiac, an Odawa war chief, believed that a British victory would allow settlers to deprive his people of their traditional hunting grounds. He united many Anishinaabe bands with other American Indians to protect their homeland. After the French were defeated in 1763, the united *ogitchedaw* launched their own campaign to expel the British. The effort ultimately failed, but Pontiac and his coalition made them realize that their presence in the Great Lakes region depended to a large degree on the goodwill of the Anishinaabek.

To protect their land once again, Anishinaabe *ogitchedaw* allied with the British during the Revolutionary War and the War of 1812. The Anishinaabek believed England would be less likely to take their land than the United States, a newly established nation eager to expand westward. Their fears proved correct. U.S. settlers soon began moving west into the Northwest Territory, an area that encompassed Anishinaabe ancestral homelands.

PROMISES MADE, PROMISES BROKEN

The Anishinaabek's many creation stories connected them spiritually and physically with the land. Gitche Manido intended people to share the land and its bounty. Because everything in nature was interconnected, the Anishinaabek understood that the land was a gift from the Great Spirit to be used wisely and safeguarded for future generations. The Anishinaabek did not believe that any one person could "own" the land. A man or woman could no more claim land than he or she could claim the water or the air.

American colonists, their descendants, immigrants from Europe, and the U.S. government had a very different view: They believed that countries and individual people could buy, own, and sell land. The U.S. government sought to obtain land for these people through treaties with American Indians.

A treaty depended on each party upholding its part of the agreement, on keeping one's word on many issues. The Anishinaabek took the treaties seriously, as they held "the word" in special reverence, believing that "keeping word was the measure of a person's integrity." However, this integrity was not always upheld. Interpreters had to translate Anishinaabemowin and English, and sometimes inadequate interpretation unintentionally misled one party or the other. Other times, the misinterpretation was deliberate, and the U.S. government took advantage of the Anishinaabek. And as Chief Menominee would state in 1838, there were many times when white agents gave Anishinaabe negotiators liquor to cloud their judgment.

In four treaties negotiated between 1807 and 1836, the Anishinaabek on Michigan's Lower Peninsula—the part shaped like a mitten—ceded enormous amounts of land to the federal government. Within these lands, the U.S. government set aside reservations where the Anishinaabek would live. The Anishinaabek received yearly payments for ceding their land, but unscrupulous traders often swindled them and robbed them of the payments "in exchange for intoxicating drinks."

The Anishinaabek insisted on certain articles, or terms, that stated they kept the right "to enjoy the privilege of hunting and fishing on the lands ceded." Another treaty contained an article that stated the Anishinaabek would "enjoy the privilege of making sugar upon the same land, committing no unnecessary waste upon the trees." Keeping hunting, fishing, and maple sugar–making rights reinforced their ties to the land and enabled the Anishinaabek to maintain some traditional ways. However, additional clauses in both of these treaties stipulated that these rights were retained only as long as the lands remained the property of the United States. If the government sold the land, a new owner did not have to comply with these

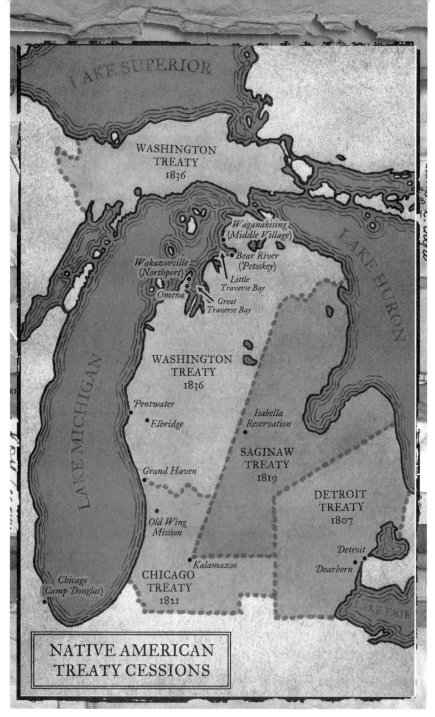

The terms of four major treaties ceded the Anishinaabe homeland,
now Michigan, to the United States.

[Elisabeth Alba, based on Charles Royce Map of Michigan Land Cessions,
Smithsonian Institution]

agreements. Later, when lumber companies purchased lands occupied by Anishinaabek, they did not honor the rights that had been reserved by treaty.

Land wasn't all the federal government wanted. It also wanted to steer the Anishinaabek away from their long-established way of life, to strip them of their culture, their religion, and even their language. It wanted assimilation.

OJIBUE.

SPELLING BOOK.

PART II.

BOSTON:
PRINTED FOR THE AMERICAN BOARD OF COMMISSIONERS FOR
FOREIGN MISSIONS, BY CROCKER AND BREWSTER.
1846.

Some of the lessons that
*Anishinaabe children learned
when they attended mission
schools included reading and
writing English.*

[Sally M. Walker, courtesy of Clarke Historical Library,
Central Michigan University]

CHAPTER 3

Surviving
a Changing
WORLD

★ ★ ★

ODAWA CHIEF JOSEPH WAKAZOO (1805–1845)
knew the arrival of Europeans to Anishinaabe homelands had
brought change. Some of the changes concerned religion. For almost
two hundred years, Roman Catholic and Protestant missionaries had
preached Christianity to the Anishinaabek. Those who converted
often interpreted and incorporated Christian teachings in ways that
harmonized with traditional Anishinaabe beliefs. But after the 1836
treaty was signed, Chief Wakazoo realized that more life-changing
concerns were on the horizon. He knew that their survival as a people
depended on incorporating these new changes into their lives without losing sight of traditional Anishinaabe ways and beliefs.

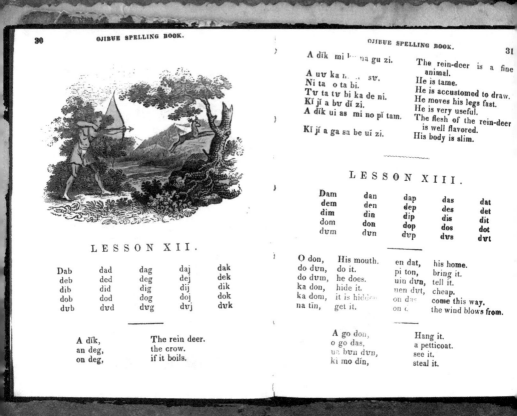

The school-age children of Chief Wakazoo's band received lessons in Anishinaabemowin and English.

OLD AND NEW TRADITIONS

An 1836 treaty between Henry R. Schoolcraft, commissioner, and "the Ottawa and Chippewa nations of Indians" promised "five thousand dollars per annum, for the purpose of education, teachers, school-houses, and books in their own language, to be continued twenty years, and as long thereafter as Congress may appropriate for the object." But the children were also expected to receive some instruction in English. Wakazoo knew that getting a fair deal in legal and business transactions hinged on education. He firmly believed that education was crucial for the future of the children—and of the Anishinaabek.

Other articles in the 1836 treaty pressured the Anishinaabek to abandon the generations-old practice of traveling between summer and winter camps. To achieve this, the federal government agreed in the fourth article to give the Anishinaabek money for "agricultural implements, cattle, mechanics' tools, and such other objects as the President may deem proper." Article seven in the treaty went on to stipulate that "two farmers and assistants" would "teach and aid the Indians, in agriculture, and in the mechanic arts." Considering that the Anishinaabek had successfully raised crops for hundreds of years, this might seem odd. But the government's intent was to encourage the Anishinaabek to abandon their traditional ways of farming—to live and raise crops the same way that Americans whose ancestors came from Europe did.

Chief Wakazoo decided that his people would participate in those agricultural practices. But even as he agreed to make this change, he did not waver in his commitment to remain on Anishinaabe homeland.

Recognizing the need to play by new rules, the Ojibwes and Odawas started buying land in the mid-1830s with the money granted to them under different treaties. Although the Anishinaabek didn't traditionally believe people can own land, the ever-increasing presence of white settlers changed everything. Chief Wakazoo petitioned Congress for permission to buy public land in 1836, but he needed help to make the purchase possible.

In 1837, Chief Wakazoo spoke at a Protestant church meeting and requested a missionary teacher for his people. The Reverend George Smith answered the call. With the support of Smith and his missionary society, Wakazoo obtained permission to buy land.

In 1839, individual families in Wakazoo's band purchased 1,360 acres in Allegan County, along the south branch of the Black River in southwestern Michigan, near their traditional winter camp at Black Lake (now Lake Macatawa). Surely, Wakazoo reasoned, everyone would honor their deeds. Surely the government (or settlers) would not force them off lands they legally owned. (Later, in the 1840s, with the support of the Michigan Legislature, the Anishinaabek petitioned for U.S. citizenship and the right to stay in the state, thus remaining on their homeland. The catch in this approach was that the petitioners had to give up membership in their bands.)

The mission established near Chief Wakazoo's band was named Old Wing Mission, in honor of his recently deceased brother, Chief Ning-wee-gon (the Wing). The mission served about thirty Odawa families, who moved seasonally between their summer camp in L'Arbre Croche and Old Wing Mission for a few more years. The parents wanted their children to attend school, so starting one was a priority.

Within weeks of his arrival, Reverend Smith began preaching and teaching classes. Originally from Vermont, Smith made an effort to learn Anishinaabemowin and eventually taught some lessons in the Odawa dialect. By January 1845, the school had forty-one Anishinaabe students. Among them was young Joseph Wakazoo (named after his uncle and grandfather). Joseph's father, Pendunwan (Peter), was Chief Joseph Wakazoo's younger brother, who succeeded him after the chief's death in 1845.

Young Joseph Wakazoo was independent and adventurous. One day, when he was ten years old, his father sent him to the post office to collect a letter. Wakazoo set off alone—a round trip of twenty miles!

In school, Wakazoo studied arithmetic and reading alongside his older cousin Payson Wolf and Wolf's good friend Louis Miskoguon. When not in school, the boys spent a lot of time together hunting, fishing, doing chores, and, when time permitted, playing games. The three boys knew Reverend Smith's children well. When together, the cousins and the Smith children spoke a mixture of English and Anishinaabemowin, switching from one language to the other without difficulty.

Payson Wolf's home was a short walk from the school. He lived with his mother, Kin-ne-quay, a skilled healer and the sister of Chiefs Joseph and Peter Wakazoo. Payson Wolf's father, Mi-in-gun, died when Payson was a young boy. In his honor, Payson used the name Wolf—the English translation of his father's name.

In his diaries, Reverend Smith regularly wrote about Wolf, Wakazoo, and Miskoguon attending school, church services, or going on hunting and fishing trips. He often stored items that belonged to Wolf's family while they were away. Unlike their grandfathers, who hunted with bows and arrows, Wolf, Wakazoo, and Miskoguon hunted with a rifle. (If, at times, the boys hunted with a bow and arrows, the arrows would have had a metal, not a stone, point.) They became expert marksmen. The skills they acquired during these hunting trips would later play an important role in their lives.

Even as the Odawa at Old Wing farmed and hunted with new tools and weapons, they continued many Anishinaabe traditions. For example, Smith noted on February 22, 1848, that Joseph's and

Payson's families—likely joined by Louis Miskoguon and his family—left the mission. The maple sap was running fast. "All the Indians moved to their sugar camps yesterday."

As their ancestors had, the Old Wing families made a yearly visit to *ziisibaakodokaaning*, the sugar bush. Even though Joseph Wakazoo and Payson Wolf lived in wood houses near the mission, at *ziisibaakodokaaning* they helped set up temporary *wiigwaaman*, where they would live for the next month. Like their ancestors, they tied sap-

lings together and raised them upright into a frame that the men covered with overlapping sheets of *wiigwaas*, which had been removed from birch trees the same way for generations. These dwellings were set up and dismantled without fuss.

Payson Wolf helped his mother, Kin-ne-quay, tap a wooden spout into each maple tree in their stand. They hung a *wiigwaas* container from each spout to collect

Payson Wolf's and Joseph Wakazoo's families sold the syrup they made by collecting maple sap and boiling it.

[Sally M. Walker, courtesy of Ziibiwing Center of Anishinabe Culture & Life ways]

Boiling sap in wooden vats reduced it to syrup.

the sap that dripped out. Kin-ne-quay and her friends boiled the maple sap in either carved wooden vats, as their ancestors had, or in metal kettles—perhaps they used both. They stirred the simmering sap until it became thick syrup. Further simmering reduced some of the syrup to the point where it could be molded into a hard cake.

Money from the sale of syrup and maple sugar cakes was an important source of income for the Old Wing community. In 1845, the families and friends of Wolf, Wakazoo, and Miskoguon produced more than fifteen thousand pounds of maple sugar. They sold it for $1,200 in cash. That was worth what nearly $38,000 was in 2018. Not only did collecting maple sap provide the Anishinaabek with income in their changing world, but it also maintained a tradition of hundreds of years that reinforced the Anishinaabek's bond with their homeland.

MOVING NORTH

After nearly ten years at Old Wing Mission, the Wakazoo, Wolf, and Miskoguon families felt pressure to move. By 1848, Dutch settlers had flooded Allegan County. Tensions about the land and its use grew between the Dutch and the Odawas. At times, violent settlers destroyed Odawa sugar camps. They stole animals and tools. In 1849, Chief Peter Wakazoo and other Odawa leaders began looking for "a place the Dutchman couldn't find." They purchased lakeshore land farther north, on the Leelanau Peninsula, on the western side of Grand Traverse Bay, and sold their southern land to the Dutch. In the spring of 1849, the Odawas and the Smiths packed their belongings, moved north, and established a village named Wakazooville. Later, the area became known as Northport.

As children at Old Wing Mission, Payson Wolf and George Smith's daughter Mary Jane had become fast friends. After the Old Wing community moved

The Reverend George Smith ministered to his congregation at the Old Wing Mission, first near today's Holland, Michigan, and later in Northport. His daughter Mary Jane married Payson Wolf.

to Northport, they spent even more time together. It soon became obvious that they were in love. The couple told their parents that they wanted to get married. By the 1850s, the heritage of many Anishinaabek included a European ancestor, usually French. But many white settlers still frowned on intermarriage. Both mothers objected to the young couple's plans. Neither one wanted her child to marry a person from another race.

However, Reverend Smith's life was dedicated to preaching that in God's eyes all people were equal. Refusing Payson and Mary Jane's request would be hypocritical. At 3:00 p.m., on July 31, 1851, Smith wrote in his diary, "I solemnized the marriage of Payson Wolf . . . and our oldest daughter Mary Jane Smith. All the people of our settlement were present (except Chief and family)—we gave them an entertainment. The occasion was pleasant." Payson was nineteen, Mary Jane barely sixteen.

As the years passed, Wolf often helped his father-in-law tend the farmlands and livestock that they owned. Like his Anishinaabe ancestors, Wolf frequently fished for *adikamegwag* (whitefish), which were a favorite. Mary Jane or Kin-ne-quay often accompanied him.

Every April, Wolf's gun blazed when tens of thousands of passenger pigeons migrated overhead. His daughter Etta later claimed that her father "was the champion hunter and Pigeon shooter of the northland." To support his growing family, Wolf sold pigeons by the barrel-load to buyers from Chicago, promising a specific number of pigeons per barrel. Wolf always erred his count in favor of the buyer. Mary Jane often told him that he cheated himself. And Wolf always replied, "I'd rather cheat myself than anyone else." A hale and hearty man, Wolf was a good provider.

When the Odawa families from Old Wing moved north to their new land on the Leelanau Peninsula, Wolf's young cousin Joseph Wakazoo—who was eleven years old at the time—hadn't been with them. He was 350 miles away. Several times before the mission relocated, Wakazoo had told Reverend Smith that he wanted to go to a bigger school, one where he could learn even more. With Smith's help, he enrolled at the Twinsburg Institute, in Twinsburg, Ohio. Samuel Bissell, the academy's founder, encouraged Anishinaabe students to enroll. At the school, Wakazoo further improved his skills in reading and writing English. During his time in Ohio, Wakazoo and Smith regularly wrote letters to each other. Wakazoo did well at his new school, but in August 1851 he fell ill and decided to return to Michigan. He wrote a letter to Smith saying he was on his way. Payson Wolf took the family's boat, went to Little Traverse, the town where Wakazoo arrived, and brought his cousin home. After recovering from his illness, Wakazoo didn't have enough money to return to the academy that year. (He graduated from the institute in 1861.)

Meanwhile, Wolf's friendship with Louis Miskoguon grew. When Louis married his fiancée, Susan Miscowa Cowt, an Odawa woman, Wolf attended the wedding. He and Mary Jane visited the Miskoguons' home on many occasions. The children in their growing families played together.

DOWN THE ROAD

Not long after Chief Peter Wakazoo's band had resettled on the Leelanau Peninsula, another Anishinaabe community relocated to the area. These families moved from the long, skinny peninsula that splits Grand Traverse Bay.

When Joseph Wakazoo was fourteen years old, he wrote this letter to his teacher Samuel Bissell at the Twinsburg Institute.

[Western Reserve Historical Society, Samuel Bissell papers, Cleveland, Ohio]

Many generations of Odawas and Ojibwes had lived on that sliver of land. With the approval of Anishinaabe leaders, Presbyterian minister Peter Dougherty had established a mission there in 1839. Dougherty lived in a *wiigwaas* house, provided by the chief, and held school in it. After Dougherty's first church service, the chief told him that the people of the village were "at liberty to take" Dougherty's religion if they wished.

As the years passed, the Anishinaabe families replaced their *wiigwaaman* and instead built log homes that they whitewashed on

Singing praises to the Creator was very much in keeping with Anishinaabe spiritual tradition. Singing hymns to God in a Christian church blended well with Anishinaabe customs.

the outside. They listened to Dougherty's religious teachings, but singing hymns captured their hearts. They took "a great interest in learning the hymns in their own language" and crowded Dougherty's home every Friday evening "to sing the praise of the blessed Savior." Customarily, the Anishinaabek sang praises to Gitche Manido, the Great Spirit, so singing praises to the missionary's Creator complemented Anishinaabe religious tradition.

For more than ten years, the mission flourished. However, the state of Michigan still owned the land. There was no guarantee that the peninsula would remain in Anishinaabe hands. The Anishinaabek saw "white men looking about" their land and became "suspicious" that the government would let them settle there. Anishinaabe leaders who lived in Dougherty's mission realized that the only way to guarantee that land would not be taken from them was to buy it. So, using their yearly government payments, they bought land across the western arm of Grand Traverse Bay and moved to the Leelanau Peninsula, about five miles south of Northport.

With the Anishinaabek's support, Dougherty also relocated across the water. By 1852, Anishinaabe men and boys had helped him establish a new mission, near present-day Omena, about a half hour's walk from their homes. Everyone called it the New Mission.

An Odawa man named Naishkaze; his wife, Onjeequa; and their children were among the families that moved to the New Mission. Years earlier, in 1843, Naishkaze was among a group of Anishinaabe men who sent a letter to President John Tyler and the Congress of the United States. In the letter they wrote:

You know that if any thing, as plants or seeds, is taken from one country to a different and distant one, and is there planted, in a different soil not suited to it, it does not grow well, but is weak and sickly; so we think it would be with ourselves and children if we should be removed to a different and distant land. We therefore desire to remain on our Native soil. . . . The desire . . . is that you will allow us . . . to buy the lands where we now live, to become citizens of the state in which we live, and to become subject to and receive the protection of the laws of the American people.

They were asking that the Anishinaabek be treated fairly and with respect.

That same year, Naishkaze and Onjeequa chose to be baptized into the Christian faith and took the names Moses and Emma Allen. When the Allen family moved across the bay, Moses Allen bought forty acres of land not far from the New Mission. On clear mornings, from his property he could watch the sun rise above Grand Traverse Bay. It was a good place for his growing family.

Moses Allen ably tended his farm and raised crops such as wheat, potatoes, and corn until an injury permanently damaged one of his arms. Although he could still hunt and fish, much of the farm's care fell on the shoulders of his eldest son, Charles. Despite his workload at home, Charles excelled in his classes at the mission school. His handwriting was impeccable, and he spoke English fluently. Like Joseph Wakazoo, he too furthered his education at the Twinsburg Institute in Ohio.

Dougherty thought highly of Charles Allen, and by the time Charles was eighteen years old, his language ability was so good that Dougherty hired him to work as an interpreter. The pay from this job—fifty dollars for six months—greatly helped Charles's family. (In 1862, that amount of money would have given him the purchasing power of $1,200 in 2018.)

The Reverends Dougherty and Smith were friends. If Dougherty was away, Smith preached in his church and vice versa. They each came to know Anishinaabe families in the other's congregation. Charles Allen, whose home was only five miles south of Smith's house, knew Joseph Wakazoo, Payson Wolf, and their families very well.

Allen often asked Reverend Smith for advice. He also admired Wolf, who was eleven years older, and may have asked him for advice too.

BEAR RIVER

Instead of buying land on the western side of the bay, some of the Anishinaabek in Dougherty's congregation went north to Bear River, on Little Traverse Bay. Their settlement, later named Petoskey, was part of the larger L'Arbre Croche area, the traditional summer home of the Anishinaabek.

Daniel Mwakewenah and his wife, Catherine, were among those who moved to Bear River. Mwakewenah, an Odawa, was one of the band's leaders. He believed it was important for Odawa youth to be educated and learn English so that they could deal knowledgeably and confidently with government agents. Education gave the Anishinaabek one tool that could help them preserve the claim to their homeland. Mwakewenah and his band sent a letter to the Presbyterian Board of Foreign Missions requesting that it establish a school at Bear River, stating that they didn't want a Catholic mission that would teach classes in Anishinaabemowin. The board approved the request, and Mwakewenah helped build the school. Classes began in 1852.

Like many Anishinaabek, Mwakewenah was deeply committed to staying on his homeland. He had signed the same letter that Naishkaze had in 1843. On January 16, 1855, Odawa and Ojibwe leaders sent a letter to George Manypenny, the commissioner of Indian affairs, in Washington, D.C. Daniel Mwakewenah signed that one too. The letter eloquently stated, "We love the spot where our forefathers' bones are laid, and we desire that our bones may rest beside theirs also."

Several months later, Mwakewenah and fifty-three more Odawa and Ojibwe leaders met with Manypenny in Detroit. They discussed and approved the articles that would be included in the Detroit Treaty of 1855. On July 31, Mwakewenah and the others signed the treaty.

Mwakewenah's leadership inspired many young people in the Bear River band. Joseph Nabawnayasang was one of them. As a child, Nabawnayasang attended Peter Dougherty's mission school, in Omena, where a teacher gave him the English name Joseph Gibson.

By 1850, many Anishinaabe families lived in log houses for their permanent residence, but a wiigwaam *made more sense for their monthlong stay at* ziisibaakodokaaning.

[Wisconsin Historical Society]

Teachers at mission schools commonly gave English names to Anishinaabe students, and Gibson later used his on official records.

Gibson suffered a serious injury when he was about ten years old. School had closed for sugaring season, and he and his family were at *ziisibaakodokaaning* to collect sap. While they were at the camp, Gibson fell and broke the two lower bones in one of his legs. An adult splinted the leg and gave him traditional medicines to dull the excruciating pain. When school reopened after maple sugaring ended, Gibson's mother, Lilla, was determined that her son would not miss classes. She and Gibson's sister took turns carrying him to school on their shoulders.

Gibson's leg healed, and he fished and hunted to feed and support the family. Like Payson Wolf, Louis Miskoguon, and Daniel Mwakewenah, Gibson developed superb marksmanship. Within a few years, the family had moved across the bay and joined the Bear River band, where Daniel Mwakewenah's leadership might have influenced Gibson. By the time Gibson turned twenty-one, the Civil War had started. Maybe his thoughts had already strayed to the army and how it could use his skills; maybe it was admiration for Mwakewenah, who had enlisted on August 15, 1863. Regardless, Gibson enlisted in Company K on September 8.

William Duvernay was determined to enlist in the First Michigan Sharpshooters, but because of his age, he could do so only as a musician.

[Clarke Historical Library, Central Michigan University]

CHAPTER 4

Aim for the BULL'S-EYE

★ ★ ★

ON DECEMBER 4, 1862, there wasn't a net big enough to catch the butterflies fluttering inside William Duvernay's belly. Gray clouds drizzled snow as Duvernay and his mother trudged along the slushy streets of Grand Haven, Michigan. Duvernay was on his way to enlist in the Union army. He knew that Elmer Dicey, a friend of his late father, was recruiting soldiers for Company B of the First Michigan Sharpshooters. Dicey anticipated that he would serve as the company's captain. Duvernay thought he'd be accepted—he was a sure-shot hunter. But he couldn't be 100 percent certain.

William Duvernay's mother, Julia, was Anishinaabe. His father, Pierre, had been a French trader. The Duvernays and their four children were among the first pioneers who settled in Grand Haven, in 1834. Julia and Pierre were known throughout the area for their kindness. Often, they opened their home to care for children whose families suffered from hardship or illness. William, born after the

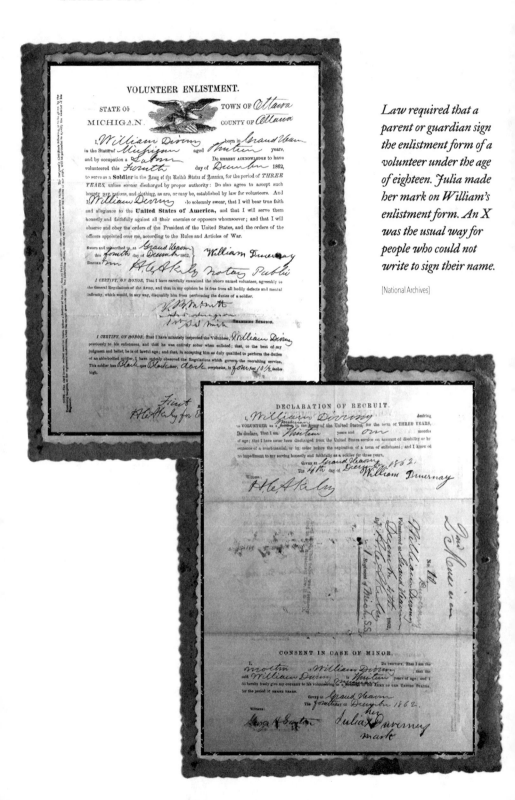

Law required that a parent or guardian sign the enlistment form of a volunteer under the age of eighteen. Julia made her mark on William's enlistment form. An X was the usual way for people who could not write to sign their name.

[National Archives]

Duvernays settled in Grand Haven, always kept a song in his heart. He played the fiddle and the drum. His neighbors often heard him play the violin. And like all drummers, William tapped his fingers on a table or his leg even when he wasn't drumming.

With his older brothers married or living away from home, William became the head of the household in 1862 after his father passed away. Dicey kept in touch with the grieving family, so young Duvernay knew the Sharpshooters were recruiting. The day he went to enlist, Julia had to go with him: Duvernay had just turned thirteen years old. Although Duvernay could have qualified as a Sharpshooter, army regulations required him to enlist as a musician—a drummer—due to his age. Duvernay signed the enlistment form, but his enrollment wasn't legitimate until Julia gave her consent and signed the form.

Within a week, Dicey enlisted another recruit—one of William Duvernay's relatives. Eighteen-year-old John Kedgnal was Pierre and Julia Duvernay's grandson. John's father was Pierre and Julia's eldest son, Charles, who was a sailor. John's mother, Eliza, was Anishinaabe. Eliza was well-known among the Anishinaabek as a doctor and midwife. She treated her patients with traditional medicines.

John Kedgnal was a sturdy, rugged young man, in strapping good health. No one knows why he enlisted, but his descendants speculate that one reason might have been to keep a protective eye on Duvernay.

Unlike George Copway and Thomas Kechittigo, who were barred from joining the army in 1861, Duvernay and Kedgnal had no trouble enlisting despite their Anishinaabe heritage. That may have been because Dicey was a family friend. But it also may have been that Dicey knew the First Michigan Sharpshooters needed experienced marksmen to fill their ranks.

A NEW REGIMENT

Charles V. DeLand despised the institution of slavery. When he was a youth, his father's home, near Jackson, Michigan, had been a stop on the Underground Railroad, a clandestine system that conducted enslaved African Americans to freedom. Later, he became a newspaperman and wrote articles against slavery. DeLand regarded the Southern states' secession as treason and was firmly committed to the Union cause. In 1861, DeLand responded to Abraham Lincoln's call for troops. He recruited a group of men from the Jackson area. They traveled to Detroit, where they enlisted in the Ninth Michigan Infantry. The regiment marched to Kentucky and Tennessee. In July 1862, Confederate troops captured DeLand. He spent the next three months being transferred from one prison camp to another, finally ending up in Libby Prison, in Richmond, Virginia. After his release, DeLand didn't return to his regiment. Instead, he

obtained a commission as colonel and raised his own regiment—the First Michigan Sharpshooters.

A regiment was composed of a thousand soldiers, who were divided into companies. Each company contained a hundred men. Two high-ranking officers, a lieutenant colonel

Colonel Charles DeLand was the commander of the First Michigan Sharpshooters.

[Burton Historical Collection, Detroit Public Library]

and a major, were appointed to DeLand's staff. The regiment also had a surgeon and his assistant; a quartermaster (who took care of arranging transportation and acquiring food, clothing, and material supplies); a chaplain; and an adjutant, who served as DeLand's administrative assistant. In addition to his duties as a soldier, the adjutant's responsibilities included writing reports, maintaining lists of the soldiers, and making sure DeLand's orders were communicated to his troops. By the end of November 1862, Michigan's governor had appointed eighteen-year-old Edward Buckbee as DeLand's adjutant. DeLand soon ordered Buckbee to begin recruiting.

Sharpshooters were often ordered far ahead of the army's main force. They climbed trees and crouched behind rocks. Invisible to enemy eyes, sharpshooters sniped at enemy soldiers. Although it was not considered honorable fighting by old-school officers, they were sometimes encouraged to aim at the enemy's officers. Wounding an officer created confusion by breaking the enemy's chain of command. From a long distance, sharpshooters targeted the artillerymen who loaded and fired cannons. With these men removed, the sharpshooters' comrades could more safely advance against the enemy. But sharpshooters had to always be on special alert: They were the targets of the enemy's sharpshooters, who were equally good marksmen.

Every man who enlisted in the First Michigan Sharpshooters had to prove he had deadly aim. Passing the marksmanship test wasn't easy. The would-be Sharpshooter had to stand between two hundred and three hundred yards away and sight his rifle on a twelve-by-twelve-inch target. He would fire at the bull's-eye, the small circle at the target's center, and reload the rifle, repeating these actions until he'd fired five times. After he finished shooting, someone would retrieve the target and measure the distance from each bullet hole to the bull's-eye. As long as the total did not exceed twenty-five inches, the shooter passed the test. For example, distances from the bullet holes to the bull's-eye might be three, seven, two, ten, and three inches. Added together, that would equal twenty-five inches, so the candidate would qualify. The men who passed the test became soldiers in DeLand's regiment and were ordered to report for duty.

ARMY LIFE AND CULTURE CLASH

William Duvernay and John Kedgnal reported for duty at Camp Chandler, in Kalamazoo, in January 1863. Each received a uniform and other clothes: stockings and shoes, drawers (long underwear), a long-sleeved flannel shirt, trousers and suspenders, a cap, a winter coat.

New recruits were told their daily schedule at first, but after that, all routine parts of the schedule were announced by bugle. The company bugler blew a different series of notes—a call—for every activity, assembly, or order. To avoid getting in trouble, Duvernay and Kedgnal would have quickly learned the calls that governed their new schedule:

> Sunrise: Reveille, the bugle call to get out of bed
>
> 6:30 a.m.: Mess call, used to signal all mealtimes
>
> 7:00: Sick call—anyone who was sick lined up for medical care
>
> 7:45–8:00: Guard mounting calls, to let the guards know the
> shift was changing
>
> 8:30: Officer drill call
>
> 9:30: Company drill call, time for the soldiers to assemble for drills
>
> 11:30: Recall, the end of drills
>
> 12:30 p.m.: Mess call for dinner

William Duvernay would have played a drum similar to the one carried by this unidentified Union drummer.

[Library of Congress]

1:00: Call for general
     police duty
2:00–2:15: Calls for
     field drill
5:00: Dress parade call
6:00: Mess call for supper
8:30: Evening roll call
9:00: Taps. Lights out, go to bed

For the next three months, Duvernay rehearsed on his drum how to beat different rhythmic patterns, what the army at that time called rolls. He learned to hold his drumsticks according to the army's drummer manual. Over and over, he played the rolls notated in the manual until he could perfectly beat any roll his officers ordered. He practiced so much that a callus formed on one of his fingers.

As with the bugle calls, the Sharpshooters learned to recognize Duvernay's rolls. In camp or on the road, they marched slowly or quickly according to the pace dictated by his drum. In battle, Duvernay would be his company's on-field communicator. He would stand close to a high-ranking officer and listen for his order: Assemble. Advance. Retreat. Then he would beat the roll that conveyed the order to the troops. Pressure would be on the boy to make sure his roll was exactly what the officer ordered. Soldiers' lives depended on it. In camp, there was no pressure. Duvernay's steady hands capably controlled the drumsticks. But what about during a battle? Maybe he wondered if he would be so steady under a hailstorm of enemy bullets.

Kedgnal learned different skills. He learned how to march in file and maneuver in strict formations. Day after day, the officers drilled Kedgnal and the other recruits. Drill. Drill. And drill some more. The men lived in close quarters, with little or no privacy. Whether they

Duvernay's drumrolls informed the men of orders and helped them keep pace during a march.

[Library of Congress]

liked it or not, their lives were completely ruled by the army's schedule and its code of behavior. No defacing or destroying public property or the camp's ground. Don't be a nuisance. Don't urinate in public; always use the "sinks," which was the Civil War term for latrines, the area used as a bathroom. (There weren't toilets, just a trench dug in the ground.) There were rules for clothing, rules for eating and sleeping, rules for leaving camp. When smallpox broke out in Kalamazoo, Colonel DeLand ordered that everyone in the regiment be vaccinated. Probably wise, but to some of the soldiers, it was yet another rule.

Some recruits, fed up with army life, deserted. If caught, deserters received jail time. If they'd deserted from the battlefield, they could be executed. In April, Kedgnal was granted a furlough, or permission to leave camp. He left Kalamazoo and returned to Grand Haven to be with his family. When Kedgnal had enlisted, he'd expected the army to use his marksmanship to fight the rebels. To help win the war. To fight for the preservation of the United States as one country. Instead, all he had done was drill in Michigan. Since he had already learned how to do that, returning to camp seemed a waste of time. He decided to stay home until he was needed. Being absent without permission was against army rules. On May 4, he was listed as a deserter.

By that time, the Sharpshooters had left Camp Chandler and were stationed in buildings at the U.S. Arsenal at Dearborn (also known as the Detroit Arsenal), where they guarded a large stockpile of rifles and arrested deserters. Even though duty at the arsenal was more soldierly than drilling at Camp Chandler, more men deserted, depleting the regiment's ranks. And DeLand's recruiters still hadn't filled the regimental roster more than halfway. The colonel decided it was time to try something new.

Two Anishinaabe recruits pledge with raised hands to serve in a Wisconsin regiment. The Company K recruits would have been similarly sworn in to the First Michigan Sharpshooters.

CHAPTER 5

New
OGITCHEDAW

★ ★ ★

AFTER TWO YEARS, the Civil War still raged without hope of resolution. Battles had devastated the countryside around Manassas Junction, Malvern Hill, and Fredericksburg, Virginia. A single battle at Antietam, in Maryland, left more than twenty thousand Union and Confederate soldiers dead or wounded. Two battles in Tennessee—Shiloh and Stones River—added more than forty-seven thousand casualties. In a seemingly endless tug-of-war, both armies suffered victories and losses, back and forth.

In Michigan, Payson Wolf and his Wakazoo relatives had been worried. Wolf's cousin Joseph Wakazoo fought with the 16th Michigan Infantry in battles at Gaines' Mill, Malvern Hill, and Bull Run. He saw hard, bloody combat. In these battles, about three hundred of his comrades had been killed, wounded, captured, or listed as missing in action. Many of the missing were dead. On

August 30, 1862, after the Battle of Bull Run, Wakazoo was reported missing. For weeks, Wolf didn't know if his cousin was alive or dead.

The Union army needed more soldiers, but recruiting volunteers became harder. The federal government implemented two plans to get additional men. First, the United States, along with local and state governments, offered bounties, money to entice men to enlist. Second, the U.S. Congress enacted a military draft. In 1863, Michigan state employees compiled lists of all men between twenty and forty-five years of age who were able to serve. And because the state desperately wanted to enlist more soldiers, it permitted the enlistment of American Indians. Colonel DeLand quickly took advantage of this and ordered officers to recruit Anishinaabe men.

The July day that Chief Nock-ke-chick-faw-me warned his Anishinaabek listeners that they might become "*slaves, dogs,*" he also warned that if the South won, "there will be no protection for us; we shall be driven from our homes, our lands and the graves of our friends." Like their ancestors, his listeners were spiritually connected with the land. It provided them with shelter and medicines. Their homeland sustained them with food—fish, game, vegetables, and syrup. They didn't want to leave.

Despite treaty promises, the parents of many of the Anishinaabe men DeLand sought to recruit feared that the U.S. government would take their land and send them to Oklahoma, where a lot Anishinaabek had already been relocated. They knew that even as the federal government fought Confederate soldiers, it was also waging a brutal war against American Indian tribes west of the Mississippi River.

The Anishinaabek who enlisted may have thought that their

service would safeguard claims to the land they or their parents owned. They hoped that their service would change the state and federal governments' view of the Anishinaabek—that the governments would give them the same rights and treat them the same way as white people.

Many generations ago, when the Odawas, Potawatomis, and Ojibwes formed the Three Fires Alliance, they agreed they would stand together and support one another. Allies fought for one another. Some recruits, particularly those who were band leaders, may have assumed, according to Anishinaabe customs, that fighting for the Union created an alliance between them and the U.S. government. In return for risking, perhaps sacrificing, their lives, surely the government would honor their service as allies by letting them, their children, and their children's children remain on the lands where their ancestors had lived for hundreds of years.

Whatever their reasons, Anishinaabe men were ready to enlist and become their generation's *ogitchedaw*. And Colonel DeLand was ready to add them to his regiment. The men who enlisted would be in Company K. As government policy mandated, the senior officers were white men. But unlike any other company in the Union army, the rest of the company's soldiers were Anishinaabek.

RECRUITING THE ANISHINAABEK

In early May 1863, William Driggs, the company's first lieutenant, set out on a recruiting mission. Because he couldn't speak any of the Anishinaabe dialects, an interpreter accompanied him. In Saginaw County, Driggs met Tom Kechittigo, whom the army had rejected in 1861. On May 3, 1863, under the state's new outlook, Kechittigo

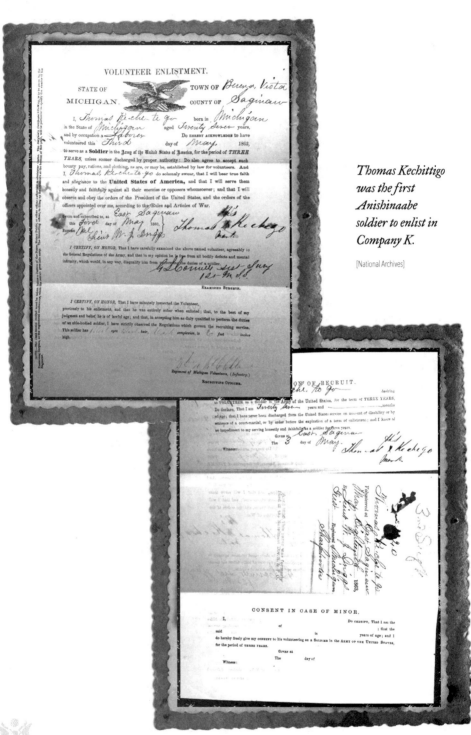

Thomas Kechittigo was the first Anishinaabe soldier to enlist in Company K.

[National Archives]

signed up as the first enlisted soldier of Company K. As a member of the First Michigan Sharpshooters, Kechittigo agreed to the army's terms, which offered a $50 bounty, paid upon being mustered in, a second bounty of $25 when the company was organized, $13 per month pay, and all necessary clothing and food while he was in the army. All the Anishinaabe recruits received these terms, the same benefits offered to white recruits.

Driggs next traveled to Isabella County. Over several days, he spoke about the regiment with the men who lived on the Isabella Reservation. Perhaps he told them about the decisive Confederate victory less than two weeks before, in Chancellorsville, Virginia. He must have convinced them that the Union needed their help: Twenty-one Anishinaabe men agreed to sign up. Two brothers, nineteen-year-old Marcus Otto and his older brother Solomon, enlisted on the same day.

When Thomas Smith stepped up to enlist, Driggs may have raised his eyebrows. The twenty-three-year-old differed from the other Anishinaabe recruits in a way that normally would have disqualified him from service: He did not have a right hand. Born without it, he had learned to cradle his rifle in the crook of his right arm and load it with his left hand. Driggs soon found out that Smith could load and fire as rapidly as any man with two hands. And his aim was spot-on. Driggs wasted no time in getting Smith signed up for Company K.

Two weeks later, Driggs traveled to Northport, where he enlisted forty-year-old Jacko Penaiswanquot, a longtime acquaintance of the Reverend George Smith, Payson Wolf, Charles Allen, and the Wakazoo family. He would prove to be one of the company's oldest recruits.

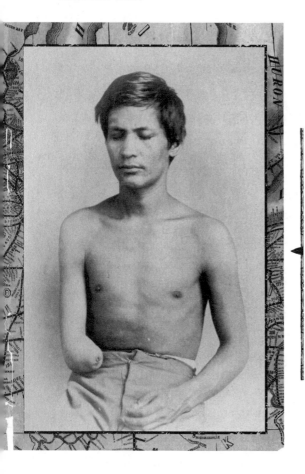

Thomas Smith amazed Lieutenant Driggs with his ability to shoot despite having only one hand. This photo was taken later in the war, when Smith was admitted to a military hospital. The photograph shows his right arm because the doctors mistakenly believed they needed to document an amputation. In reality, Smith needed treatment for severe eye infections.

[Otis Historical Archives, National Museum of Health and Medicine]

Like Daniel Mwakewenah of the Bear River band, Penaiswanquot may have been one of the Anishinaabek who petitioned George Manypenny in 1855 to stay on their homeland. "Pinesiwanaguat" was among the names on the second petition, and since translators spelled Anishinaabe names as they sounded, it's likely the same man. Penaiswanquot may have had several reasons for joining the army. Protecting his land was surely one of them, but an income may have been another. He and his wife, Mary, had eight children. The army's regular pay would have helped the family.

While in Northport, Driggs would have heard about Charles

Allen, possibly from Reverend Smith. As soon as Lieutenant Driggs met the nineteen-year-old, he realized that Allen would be an excellent go-between for regimental officers and the Anishinaabe soldiers who didn't fully understand or speak English. Furthermore, he thought Allen's stellar reading and writing skills would make him a perfect candidate for sergeant. Allen was the forty-third man to enlist in Company K.

Payson Wolf supported the Union from the war's start. In 1850, the Michigan Constitution gave Anishinaabe men the right to vote, *as long as they weren't members of any tribe.* But upstanding Anishinaabe men who were well-known members of their community weren't always closely questioned about tribal membership. Payson Wolf voted in the 1860 presidential election, probably for Abraham Lincoln, as his father-in-law had. In May 1861, Wolf painted the stars on a flag made by his sister-in-law Annie. Wolf and his father-in-law raised it on a pole fastened to their house. Flying forty feet above the roof, the waving Stars and Stripes was impossible to miss. But two years later, when Driggs was in town, Wolf did not enlist. Perhaps it was because his five young children needed him at home. Mary Jane or his mother, Kin-ne-quay, may have urged him not to go. Maybe he knew his father-in-law couldn't harvest their acres of crops alone and planned to enlist after harvest. Whatever his reasons, Wolf did not accompany Charles Allen when he left Northport.

THE MEN FROM ELBRIDGE

Seven hundred miles away, the war continued. Union and Confederate armies clashed around Gettysburg, Pennsylvania, July 1–3, 1863. Although the Union army won, intense fighting left twenty-three thousand Union soldiers dead, wounded, or missing in action. Confederate losses were twenty-eight thousand. Although costly, the battle stopped the Confederates from advancing farther into the North.

Meanwhile, pleased with Driggs's success, Colonel DeLand had already sent Company K's captain, Edwin Andress, on a recruiting mission. Andress had a big advantage over Driggs: He spoke several languages. He had worked as a clerk in a store, where he met many different people. As a result, Andress spoke "German, French and Indian without any training" and was "reported to have talked these three languages one after the other with his customers. He traded for furs with the Indians and added to his vocabulary of the Indian language by making a written note of every new word."

Andress attended the Fourth of July celebrations held at the Elbridge Reservation. He stepped onto a platform and delivered a speech. The Union needs your help, he would have said in a voice loud enough to reach everyone in the crowd. Maybe he mentioned Gettysburg. The First Michigan Sharpshooters need expert marksmen like you, he may have said. Come and join the Anishinaabe men who have already enlisted. He probably added that the army would give them a gun, ammunition, and clothing. Andress could speak Anishinaabemowin, but to make sure that everyone understood all his words, he asked the French trader Louis Genereau to translate. Genereau was married to an Anishinaabe woman and spoke Anishinaabemowin fluently. Reverend Smith often employed him as an interpreter.

After Andress finished speaking, Chief Pay-baw-me, a highly respected member of the community who was known for delivering powerful, convincing sermons, took the platform and encouraged the young men to enlist. Louis Genereau Jr., the interpreter's eighteen-year-old son, led the group of men who stepped forward to volunteer. (Louis Jr. already knew about the First Michigan Sharpshooters; John Kedgnal and William Duvernay were his friends.) Antoine Scott, John Etarwegeshig, John Wabesis, and seventeen-year-old William Newton quickly joined him, as did brothers James and John Mashkaw. Before the day's end, Amos Ashkebugnekay had added his name to the growing list. Ashkebugnekay was one of Company K's older soldiers—thirty-two when he enlisted—but he was a "healthy athletic young man capable of running down a deer every day."

Ashkebugnekay demonstrates one way the Anishinaabek blended with the settlers' society. Although not an Anishinaabe custom, many Anishinaabek started using last names—often an Anishinaabe word or the Anishinaabe name they were already known by. Some translated that name into English. As he stated, "The word Ashkebugnekay is an Indian word and means Green in English. I am called Amos Green by white men and Amos Ashkebugnekay by all Indians." He added that Ashkebugnekay was "the name I wish to be called by when I die." The English names made it easier for white settlers, but among themselves, the Anishinaabe used their true names.

A FAREWELL WALK

Genereau, Scott, Ashkebugnekay, and the other new recruits left for the army from Pentwater, a town on Lake Michigan's eastern shore, where a steamboat waited. It was a momentous day for them and their loved ones. Whether they and their families had converted to Christianity or not, many likely offered prayers to the God of the

Christians or to Gitche Manido, or maybe to both, to keep themselves or their warriors safe.

Families and friends gathered to wave goodbye. But, for them,
waving goodbye involved more than a ten-minute walk to the wharf.
Pentwater was sixteen miles from Elbridge, with no paved roads
there in 1863. For these families, going along to say goodbye was
an all-day or even overnight trip. A wagon could drive to Pentwater
in about three hours; it would have taken those who walked nearly
six. Yet everyone—wives, parents, children, even one mother carrying
her baby in a cradleboard strapped to her back—accompanied their
men to show support and good wishes. Some of the new *ogitchedaw*
may have carried intricately beaded bandolier bags slung across
their chests. Most carried a pair of comfortable moccasins to wear
at the end of day.

Like their *ogitchedaw* ancestors, many of the new soldiers may
have worn a small medicine pouch, probably as a necklace that could
be tucked inside a shirt. The *semaa, wiingash, mashkodewashk*, and
giizhik (tobacco, sweet grass, sage, and cedar) would spiritually
aid and protect them while they were away from home.

Even as Anishinaabe men prepared to risk their lives on behalf of
the United States, white people remained skeptical about allowing
them to fight alongside white soldiers. On July 9, 1863, less than a
week after the Elbridge men enlisted, an editorial in the *Detroit Free
Press* urged the government to "recall white soldiers" who were fighting the Sioux in Minnesota and "send Indians in their stead." The
editorial reasoned, "The Chippewas of Michigan, Wisconsin, and
Minnesota are the hereditary enemies of the Sioux, and would not
only be glad to fight them, but would, with the advantages of

government support, soon reduce them to peace." Furthermore, the editorial suggested, it would save the government money, since the Chippewa, in familiar country, would require "less baggage and provisions than white troops."

AN ANISHINAABE OFFICER

Company K's ranks received another boost when twenty-three-year-old Garrett Graveraet signed on as second lieutenant. Graveraet was the son of Henry and Sophia Graveraet. Henry was a merchant-trader of European and Odawa heritage, and Sophia was the

Second Lieutenant Garrett Graveraet was an officer highly regarded by the other Anishinaabe soldiers in Company K.

[Emerson R. Smith Papers, Bentley Historical Library, University of Michigan]

granddaughter of an Odawa chief. The Graveraets were respected members of their community. Garrett was a musician and a painter, and he'd been employed as a teacher for three years at a government school. Garrett also had an invaluable skill: He spoke English, French, and both the Odawa and Ojibwe dialects. He could communicate with every soldier in the company.

Within two months of Graveraet's arrival, Colonel DeLand sent his new second lieutenant on a recruiting mission to the towns that ringed Grand Traverse and Little Traverse Bays. Sergeant Charles Allen, who had grown up in the area, accompanied him. By the time they reached Northport in August, Allen's friend Payson Wolf had decided that it was his duty to enlist, and Allen added his signature to Wolf's enlistment paper. Together, Wolf and Allen left on a steamboat for Dearborn. Perhaps Wolf hugged his infant son before he boarded. The six-month-old would be baptized Edwin Andress Wolf, in honor of Company K's captain, one month later. Although leaving his family was difficult, Wolf knew that his mother and his in-laws would help Mary Jane care for the children.

Wolf wasn't the only man from Northport to leave for the army that month. Amable Ketchebatis, a family man like Wolf, left behind his wife, Lizette, and their four children when he enlisted. It wasn't long before variations of Ketchebatis's name started to appear in army paperwork. Recording Anishinaabe names in the company letter book, on hospital cards, and on muster rolls confounded army officials. Before European contact, Anishinaabemowin was a traditionally oral language; its speakers never had a need for a written language until white traders and settlers began requiring written documents. As a result, there was no standard spelling of

Anishinaabemowin words. When people wrote Anishinaabe names and words, they transcribed them using their own alphabet. Another stumbling block was that although a number of the men in Company K spoke at least some English, they couldn't read or write it, so they couldn't correct variations. For these reasons, many Anishinaabe names appear several different ways in government and regimental records. Amable Ketchebatis's name, for example, was spelled at least seven different ways!

Graveraet left Northport and took a boat over to Bear River, where he spoke with Daniel Mwakewenah. He may have believed

When Payson Wolf posed for this picture, he wore his uniform. The feather was a distinctive touch that he added on his own.

[Burton Historical Collection, Detroit Public Library]

that if Mwakewenah, who was highly regarded by members of the Bear River band, could be persuaded to join Company K, it would influence others in the area to enlist too. Even though Mwakewenah was forty years old, he did not hesitate to take up arms to defend his homeland for the reasons so eloquently stated in the petition he had signed eight years earlier.

Joseph Gibson followed Mwakewenah's example less than a month later. Gibson's father had left the family the year before and moved to Canada. Gibson, mindful of the care his mother and sister had given him when he'd broken his leg years before, willingly supported them by farming and fishing. After he enlisted, Gibson sold his horse and a small parcel of land that he owned to leave money with his mother.

One of the Odawa men Garrett Graveraet enlisted during his July-to-September recruiting mission was his own father, Henry. At the time, Henry Graveraet was about fifty years old. The Conscription Act capped the maximum age for enrollment at forty-five. But that didn't stop Henry. His father had been a soldier in the War of 1812, and Henry was ready to uphold the tradition. Garrett knew that his father's organizational abilities and his ability to relate well to people would be valuable assets for Company K. Henry boarded the steamboat with Garrett's recruits, who were on their way to the arsenal at Dearborn. When Henry stepped forward to be sworn in, the recording soldier asked his age. Henry said he was forty-five. No one questioned it.

Since both Graveraet men would be away at war, Garrett was concerned about his mother's well-being. Before Garrett left, he bought a small house and a plot of land for her. He and Henry promised to send home most of their pay. Garrett was confident that, with help from friends and neighbors, Sophia and his sister and brother would be fine.

Alone or in groups, the recruits traveled to the U.S. Arsenal in Dearborn. There they were mustered into the army and officially became comrades in arms with the rest of the First Michigan Sharpshooters. By the end of the summer, Company K had 102 men.

Posed in a photographer's studio, the soldier holds his rifle with its bayonet fixed to the muzzle. Company K was ordered into battle with their bayonets fixed several times. The thin rod beneath the muzzle is the ramrod.

CHAPTER 6

Rifles
AND RULES

★ ★ ★

AT THE DEARBORN BARRACKS, the Anishinaabe recruits received uniforms and supplies they would need for battle, among them a cartridge box and belt, a small screwdriver and wrench, a knapsack, a canteen, a bayonet and scabbard. And a rifle.

Most men who qualified for the First Michigan Sharpshooters expected the army to issue them a rifle with a telescopic sight. Instead, they received a Model 1861 Springfield rifle. No fancy sight. Just a long rifle that weighed nearly ten pounds. While some men were disappointed, the Springfield rifle delighted most men of Company K. It was a much newer model than the ones they had at home. The inner surface of the gun's long barrel was rifled, or engraved, with screwlike grooves that controlled a bullet's path in a way that increased accuracy.

During target practice, Thomas Kechittigo had to complete

several steps before he could fire his rifle. First he took a premade paper cartridge filled with gunpowder from his cartridge box. He bit off the top of the cartridge and poured the powder into the rifle's muzzle. Then he dropped a bullet into the barrel. Every Springfield had a thin metal ramrod that fit into a channel along the underside of the barrel. Kechittigo pulled out the ramrod and slid it all the way into the rifle's barrel. This tamped the bullet on top of the gunpowder. He replaced the ramrod. He partially cocked the rifle's hammer. After placing a percussion cap on a small raised bump, called the nipple, Kechittigo fully cocked the hammer. Then he lifted the rifle and braced the butt against his shoulder. Two sights along the barrel helped him zero in on the target. He was finally ready to shoot.

The Springfield rifle's bullets were called minié balls. Each lead

This diagram shows a .58-caliber minié ball (left), that would have been fired by the Model 1861 Springfield rifle, beside a bullet (center) like those used in modern M-16-type rifles. Both could be considered the "workhorse" rifles of their respective armies. A soldier slid a minié ball down the muzzle of the rifle until it rested on top of a gunpowder-filled paper cartridge he had rammed down the rifle barrel. The bullet for a modern rifle (right) is inserted into a metal cartridge filled with explosive powder.

[David A. Walker]

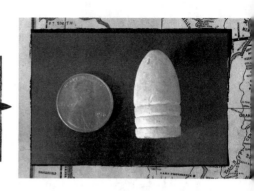

A rifle's grooves sent minié balls spiraling through the air with great accuracy. Hitting a target, the hollow lead bullet would flatten out or splinter, shattering bone and ripping apart soft tissue.

[Sally M. Walker, courtesy of Jack and Pat North]

bullet had three grooves molded around its hollow base. When Kechittigo pulled the trigger, the hammer slammed against the percussion cap and caused a spark. The gunpowder ignited with a small explosion that expanded the minié ball's hollow base as it traveled through the barrel. The expanded bullet caught the spiral grooves, forcing it to spin. A spiraling bullet—like a perfectly thrown spiral pass in football—is more stable and travels farther than a bullet fired from a musket without grooves. With his expert marksmanship, Kechittigo could accurately hit a target (or an enemy soldier) from five hundred yards away. An experienced rifleman like Kechittigo could fire three shots a minute.

Per army regulations, the Anishinaabe men took the same marksmanship test as all other recruits: five shots, with the total distance of the bullet holes from the bull's-eye not exceeding twenty-five inches. On average, most recruits qualified with a score between twenty and twenty-five inches. The Anishinaabe soldiers averaged in the teens.

Over the next weeks, Company K settled into army life. But not all members of the regiment welcomed them. Skeptics didn't think the Anishinaabek would make good soldiers. Some soldiers complained that Company K kept to themselves and spoke Anishinaabemowin. But Company K's soldiers soon proved naysayers wrong as they quickly learned the bugle calls and drumrolls. They marched in formation and obeyed Sergeant Tom Kechittigo's shouted orders during drills.

Charles Allen trained with the men, but paperwork occupied much of his time. As the company's orderly sergeant, he kept the roll book and was accountable for who was present and absent. He wrote requisitions for rations, ammunition, and supplies that would be needed on the march or in camp, such as tents and utensils. Allen called roll at reveille and issued certificates to Company K's men who wanted to apply for leaves of absence. Men who sought a furlough or had to leave the barracks for some reason had to see Allen, who started the paperwork.

Most men had no trouble while they were off the base. But sometimes trouble found them. One day while on furlough, George Ashkebug, William Mixinasaw, Peter Wells, and Charles Allen entered a Detroit tavern. At that time, selling liquor to American Indians was illegal. Saloonkeeper Thomas Fitzpatrick served drinks to Ashkebug,

Mixinasaw, and Wells anyway. Fitzpatrick got caught, and the federal government pressed charges against him. The U.S. District Court scheduled the trial for December.

Although their role at the U.S. Arsenal was important, the Anishinaabe Sharpshooters became frustrated. Guarding a stash of weapons was tiresome. They had enlisted to use their superior marksmanship to fight Confederate soldiers. Instead, Company K practiced drills and shot at targets in Dearborn. Summer's end brought rumors of a new assignment. Company K was ready to fight; surely they would be sent to battle. Instead, the First Michigan Sharpshooters were ordered west to Chicago for more guard duty—this time guarding men, not weapons.

A NORTHERN MISERY

Chicago bustled with activity in the early 1860s. More than 2,933 miles of railroad track touched the city. The Union army quickly

Camp Douglas, located in south Chicago, had barracks for Union soldiers and Confederate prisoners of war. The First Michigan Sharpshooters practiced drills in the open areas.

[Library of Congress]

took advantage of this. It established Camp Douglas, four miles south of Chicago, as a military training camp and staging area for Union troops. As the war continued, it became a prisoner-of-war camp for captured Confederate soldiers. Trains rapidly transported captured soldiers away from the South and brought them to Camp Douglas. Flat, open land surrounded the camp—good visibility in case prisoners tried to escape—and Lake Michigan, only a quarter of a mile away, offered an abundant supply of water.

But it wasn't long before Camp Douglas became a nightmare. When it was established in 1861, no one knew the war would last so long. No one knew that so many prisoners would be sent to Camp Douglas. Overcrowded barracks for prisoners and their Union guards soon led to unhealthy conditions. An inspector in 1862 reported standing water on the grounds, foul sinks (latrines), and crowded barracks loaded with bugs, rats, and rotting garbage. Prisoners sickened, and several hundred died.

In response to the appalling conditions in overcrowded prisons on both sides, the warring governments agreed to an exchange program in July 1862. During the next eight months, the number of Confederate prisoners at Camp Douglas dropped from 7,850 to 332. But problems persisted.

The federal government required paroled Union soldiers to report to parole camps, where they stayed until they were officially declared "exchanged" and could return to duty. Camp Douglas was one of those camps. The Union soldiers stationed there complained that the camp's barracks were disgusting, not even clean enough to house livestock. In protest, some of them set fire to a number of barracks to get rid of the bad housing and call attention to the deplorable conditions.

As the exchanges continued, the camp cleared out. On August 13, 1863, the commander of Camp Douglas informed his superior officer, "Camp Douglas is in good condition to hold 8,000 prisoners." Three days later, the First Michigan Sharpshooters were on their way to Chicago. Being crammed together in railroad boxcars didn't make the most comfortable ride, but it was the fastest way to transport the regiment from Dearborn to Chicago. Shortly after the regiment's arrival in town, Colonel DeLand was appointed the camp's new commander.

DUTY AND DRILLS

When Company K arrived on August 17, it was immediately placed on sentry duty, an assignment regularly rotated among the regiment's companies. When Payson Wolf was on duty, he paced back and forth on a platform that ran along the inside of the camp's tall board fence. Joseph Gibson, Louis Genereau, and the Otto and Mashkaw brothers guarded the prison boundaries, watching to make sure no prisoners attempted escape.

By the time Company K got to Camp Douglas, hundreds of prisoners were arriving daily. It wasn't long before the prison was overcrowded.

[Chicago History Museum]

Before sunset the following day, five hundred prisoners of war arrived, and five hundred more the day after. By then, the prison had become something of a tourist spot. People drove their carriages along the nearby road to see what was happening. On Saturday, August 22, about seven hundred more prisoners arrived. A newspaper reporter approached the prison wall seeking a story. Company K was on sentry duty that day. The reporter shouted questions, perhaps asking the men if they liked being there. One of the soldiers replied, in French, "This business is good for me—I like it very much to shoot a traitor, breaking away."

The next day, another Company K soldier chatted with a Chicago resident visiting the camp. The soldier told the man that he hunted, fished, and sometimes mined for copper. (There were copper mines in Michigan's northernmost region.) "Did you find much copper?" the civilian asked. "Plenty," the Anishinaabe man replied. Then, the visitor wondered, why become a soldier and leave all that copper behind? The soldier chortled and said he'd catch plenty of copper soon—"Copperheads." He ground his foot into the dirt as though crushing a snake and reached out with his hands, miming the capture of an enemy. The Anishinaabe soldier was making a clever pun. Copperheads are venomous snakes, but during the Civil War, *copperheads* was the derogatory name for people, particularly politicians, who lived in the North but opposed the war.

As the men continued to wait for battle, sentry duty and visits from civilians provided a short break from relentless drilling.

Camp Douglas had a large parade ground, and Adjutant Edward Buckbee was determined that his men would be battle ready. Lieutenant Garrett Graveraet and Sergeants Tom Kechittigo and

*The Sharpshooters drilled in formation like this until they
could reliably follow orders as a fighting unit.*

[Burton Historical Collection, Detroit Public Library]

Henry Graveraet were kept busy translating and loudly calling the
officers' drill commands to Company K's soldiers. Day after day, the
entire regiment drilled for hours. DeLand's officers would settle for
nothing less than excellence when it came to battalion maneuvers.

From their barracks, some of the prisoners of war watched
Company K drill. Confederate soldier George Weston wrote in his
diary, "At this place, there are a few companies of 'Chipawa Indians'
who are formed to gather as Guards, calling themselves the 'Michigan
SharpShooters,' as a body they are a desperate set of men, but as we
all know, they only fight from behind trees & bushes." Weston spoke
from prejudice: Neither he nor anyone else had ever seen Company
K's Anishinaabe soldiers in battle, because they hadn't yet had the
opportunity.

Possibly Weston was echoing opinions expressed by British soldiers
who had fought in the French and Indian War, one hundred years

earlier. During the 1700s, European soldiers always proceeded into battle in straight lines. They maintained the lines as they advanced toward enemy fire and broke rank only in hand-to-hand combat. British soldiers scoffed at American Indian guerrilla tactics and deemed this method of warfare dishonorable and inappropriate. But George Washington's Continental soldiers adopted the American Indians' tactics during the Revolutionary War. They realized that soldiers who fought from behind cover had a better chance of living to fight another day. Weston wasn't alone in his derogatory comments about the Anishinaabe company. Many Union soldiers didn't believe the *ogitchedaw* would fight as well as white soldiers.

KEEPING IN TOUCH WITH HOME

While drilling occupied many hours, Company K did have free time. A number of the men were good carvers. Payson Wolf made a rolling pin for his wife, Mary Jane. Its smooth-as-silk surface perfectly rolled dough. Perhaps he was one of the Anishinaabek who whiled away free hours by carving the wooden stocks of their rifles with fish, animals, snakes, and turtles. During free time, they cherished reading letters from loved ones. Friends and family members who could not write often asked people who could to write letters for them. In turn, soldiers read aloud letters received for comrades who were unable to read them. They also wrote their responses for them. Letters from home were lifelines, telling the soldiers they had not been forgotten and filling them in on what was happening at home. Mary Jane frequently wrote to her husband. In a return letter, he wrote, "I just received two letters from you within the last four days. Was very glad indeed to hear from you. . . . You know not dear wife how much I love you, I say the truth I love you."

Occasionally, letters held photos. Photography was a fairly new technology, one that enabled a soldier to carry a photo of his wife or a child. These small reminders of home could be tucked into a pocket or a knapsack. In September, Mary Jane was excited to receive two photos from Payson. They were probably copies of the photo of him in uniform (see page 69). She may have given one to her mother-in-law, Kin-ne-quay. Within days, Reverend Smith treated Mary Jane and her children to having their picture taken. Perhaps she included the picture in one of her letters to her husband, along with one of Kin-ne-quay that was taken at the same time.

Letters contained promises. As the months passed, Joseph Gibson worried that the money from the sale of his land and horse might not sustain his mother and sister. He wrote a letter to merchant Richard Cooper, whose store was near Gibson's home. In it, he asked Cooper to give his family a barrel of flour and half a barrel of pork, and promised, "I will pay you as soon as we are paid."

Letters also contained money, or news about it. Oftentimes, the army was late in paying wages. Wolf wrote to Mary Jane, "One soldier who has been in the field told me that he was not paid for nine month[s] in one time." Gibson and Wolf wrote their letters in English, while Charles Allen usually wrote home in the Odawa dialect. He regretted telling his family, yet again, that he hadn't been paid. But his idea was to send the money, when he finally received it, by steamboat. He was worried that it might get lost if he enclosed it in a letter. Steamboat captains and other representatives frequently carried a soldier's wages to his family.

In another letter, also written in Odawa, Charles Allen shared a "wild story" with his family and friends. It was about an incident in a Detroit bar, where bartender Thomas Fitzpatrick had illegally served liquor to George Ashkebug, William Mixinasaw, and Peter Wells. Allen wrote that the bartender had been arrested and that he and his three comrades had to go to court and testify. At that time, it was highly unusual for an American Indian to testify in court against a white person. But the army issued passes for the four Anishinaabe soldiers and paid for their train tickets to return to Detroit and speak in court. Allen, being an experienced interpreter as well as an eyewitness, may have acted as a translator between his friends and court officials.

At the December trial, Fitzpatrick was found not guilty and released, Allen wrote, "because the Indians he had served were soldiers. If they had not been soldiers . . . it really would have been trouble for him." Although American Indians could not legally be served alcohol, soldiers could. In this case, the judge decided the Anishinaabe men were soldiers first. He ruled that Fitzpatrick could legally serve them.

The men welcomed letters, but a package from home was cause for jubilation. Payson Wolf's family periodically sent treats and supplies: canned fruit, cakes, newspapers, and magazines. The captain of the steamboat *Allegheny* even transported a pair of moccasins and a bucket of whitefish from Kin-ne-quay to her son!

There were reunions at Camp Douglas. Visitors from home were the best. Mary Jane Wolf visited in October. And Kin-ne-quay, who did not speak English, made the trip—alone—in November to bring her son some winter clothes. Her long ride across Lake Michigan on the steamboat *Allegheny* was probably cold and choppy—the boat's

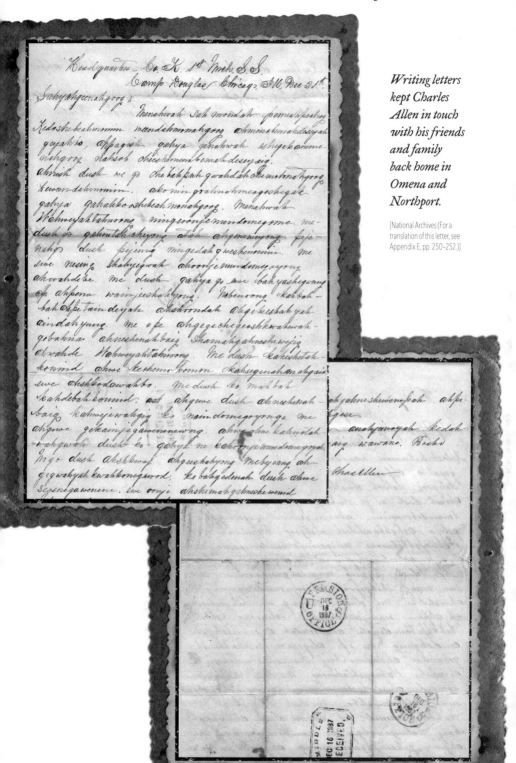

Writing letters kept Charles Allen in touch with his friends and family back home in Omena and Northport.

[National Archives (For a translation of this letter, see Appendix E, pp. 250–252.)]

departure had been delayed overnight due to an icy mix of rain and snow. She returned to Northport on November 22, happy that she'd seen her son and that he was well. The kindly captain did not charge either her or Mary Jane for the trips.

Reunions also occurred among soldiers. John Kedgnal and drummer William Duvernay, from Company B, were glad to see their many Anishinaabe friends. Kedgnal and Louis Genereau had known each other for years. Genereau was soon to be engaged to Kedgnal's sister. When Louis Miskoguon arrived at Camp Douglas in September, he was reunited with his lifelong friend Payson Wolf. Two months later, the two shared an unexpected reunion with someone else.

Wolf's cousin Joseph Wakazoo, reported as missing in action in August 1862, had left his post after the second Battle of Bull Run. On September 9, 1863, the army arrested him in Grand Traverse, Michigan, for desertion, a charge that could be punished by death. Immediately, Wakazoo sent a letter by special messenger to Reverend Smith and asked for help. Smith contacted the man in

Louis Miskoguon

[David Broene]

charge of the arresting police division. He presented the officer with a certificate that he and a number of other community members had signed. It attested to Wakazoo's prior service and noted that he'd left his company in Virginia because he felt isolated, "there being no other Indians" in the regiment. Wakazoo would willingly serve if he could be transferred to Company K. The War Department granted his request in November, and Payson Wolf and Louis Miskoguon were probably glad when Wakazoo joined them at Camp Douglas.

DESERTION, DISEASE, AND DEATH

Company K had troubled times at Camp Douglas. Desertion was a problem. Amos Ashkebugnekay deserted on October 15 and was arrested later that same day. Apparently the incident had been a mis-understanding, because he returned to duty with no further mention. Louis Bennett deserted and went home. In a court-martial hearing, he testified that he left because he didn't see any reason why he should stay in Chicago when he wasn't fighting. The army wasn't using his marksmanship, and things had to be done at home. He rejoined the company when it went to Virginia, when he knew the army needed him to fight. At his military trial, he was told that he would have to make good all the time he had missed and forfeit the pay during his absence. The court's decision stated: "The court is thus lenient for the reason that the prisoner is a member of the Chippaway Tribe of Indian, and at the time of his desertion was unacquainted with the rules and customs of the U.S. Service."

In this instance, the army recognized that the Anishinaabek may have viewed being a warrior differently than soldiers whose roots were based in European tradition. Anishinaabe warriors weren't part of a standing army that drilled skills into them. Their marksmanship—with bows, arrows, and later rifles—was honed by everyday life as hunters. They didn't wait idly for months after a decision to go to war was made.

Some Anishinaabe soldiers got sick while they were at Camp Douglas. Charles Allen had a fever, sore eyes, and a cough. A red rash covered his body, which ached all over. The regimental doctor confirmed what Allen may have suspected: He had measles, which plagued some of the prisoners too. Wolf and Miskoguon had severe colds, but were on the mend. Bitter-cold temperatures in January 1864—minus 38 degrees Fahrenheit on the thermometer—froze the hands and feet of men on guard duty. Citizens of Chicago claimed it was the coldest winter ever.

Sadly, some Company K men died at Camp Douglas. Two died of illness; a third fell sick and died after being sent home. Another was accidentally killed when he was crushed between two railroad cars.

MURDER!

A few times, Chicago newspapers mentioned the company of "Indians" that was stationed at Camp Douglas. But one article reported a very serious incident.

On the night of March 14, 1864, Charles Wabesis and a Company K comrade went uptown to a saloon. John Moynihan, the owner, served the men alcohol. When Wabesis turned to leave, he picked up some money lying on the bar and started for the door, but Moynihan said that Wabesis owed him twenty cents (worth about three dollars in 2018). Wabesis refused to pay, so Moynihan walked around the bar and confronted him with a cane. The two fought, and an eyewitness said Wabesis pulled out a knife, stabbed Moynihan in the chest, and left the saloon. A police officer followed Wabesis, brought him back to the bar, and searched him. Finding the knife in Wabesis's pocket, the officer arrested him and took him to jail. The next morning, Wabesis pled guilty to the charge of "using a deadly weapon with intent to do great bodily injury."

Unfortunately, Moynihan died two days after the fight. Wabesis was then charged with murder. He did not return to serve with the Sharpshooters. (His service records later indicated that he was "confined by civil authorities" from March 15, 1864, to July 28, 1865, on a charge of murder and that "he was discharged on the latter date by reason of the muster out of his company." He went home to Elbridge after his release from jail. The reason why Wabesis was allowed to go home is still unknown.)

Despite misconceptions regarding the army's rules, the discomfort of illness, and the tragedy of death, the Anishinaabe soldiers survived service at Camp Douglas. When they had arrived in Chicago, they were already a community of relatives and friends, old and new. They had a shared heritage and a far-reaching clan and kinship network back at home. During their time at Camp Douglas, they became something more.

Adjutant Edward Buckbee summed it up: "The Indian Company had fine soldiers. By the time [we left Chicago] we had some seven months of drill which was the fact before we were sent to the front. The Indians had learned all the bugle calls, and taking everything together they made the best skirmishers I have ever seen." The soldiers of Company K were their generation's *ogitchedaw*. And they were ready to fight.

CHAPTER 7

The Road
TO BATTLE

★ ★ ★

BY THE END OF FEBRUARY, everyone was antsy. If they weren't going to be ordered east, the soldiers hoped for a furlough so they could visit home. Charles Allen missed his parents and longed to see his brothers and sisters. The last day of the month, he began another letter with the greeting *Suhyahgeenahgoog* (Dear loved ones). If the regiment remained in Chicago, he wrote, "Mother should come here in the spring. . . . I will also try to come visit you all in the spring." Charles knew that maple sap would be running in the trees back home. Perhaps he wished he could be with his family when they went to *ziisibaakodokaaning*, the sugar bush.

Even while the Anishinaabe soldiers may have thought about visiting home, Ulysses S. Grant, commander of all the Union forces, was preparing for a massive campaign in Virginia—an offensive so large that President Lincoln would later issue a proclamation that called for the enlistment of five hundred thousand volunteers.

At last, the day the First Michigan Sharpshooters had been waiting for arrived. On March 17, the regiment left Camp Douglas under orders to head east, to Annapolis, Maryland, where they would become part of the Army of the Potomac. They were so anxious to get under way, Buckbee later recalled, that no one would have needed "any stimulating drinks to make us raise our feet and walk on air." Six new Anishinaabe recruits joined them.

In boxcars, the regiment rode the rails across the Midwest. Rain poured as they crossed Ohio, Companies B and K traveling together. It was still raining two days later when, close to midnight, they arrived in Pittsburgh, Pennsylvania. The next day, citizens greeted the troops. Those who welcomed Company K were surprised to see a company of "Chippewa Indians" and thought they were "splendid-looking fellows, and were very well drilled, and apparently first rate soldiers." That evening, the Pittsburgh Subsistence Committee, a group established to provide meals to soldiers, fed the whole regiment a warm supper.

Rain still fell at the end of March, when the soggy Sharpshooters arrived at Camp Parole, in Annapolis. The camp, a tent city filled with ten to twelve thousand soldiers, sprawled across three to four miles. Soldiers weren't the only residents: Some companies brought an animal mascot with them. An eagle traveled with Company K. Probably captured as a young bird, it was tethered to a platform fixed atop a six-foot pole. Everywhere Company K went, the eagle went too.

The eagle is one of the Anishinaabek's most sacred beings. A story passed along by countless generations tells that long ago the Creator

Trains similar to this one carried the Sharpshooters from Chicago to Annapolis, Maryland, where they encamped at Camp Parole.

believed the Anishinaabek had forgotten their commitment to offer daily prayers; they no longer lived in harmony with others. It was time, the Creator felt, to remove the Anishinaabek from the earth. Eagle flew to the Creator and said he was sure that someone still remembered. He begged for time to bring the Creator proof this was so. The Creator gave Eagle four days. Eagle flew back and forth over the earth until on the fourth day he found a small gathering of Anishinaabek offering *semaa* (tobacco) in a morning prayer fire. Eagle brought a wisp of the smoke to the Creator. Ever since Eagle saved their people, the Anishinaabek have honored and revered the bird.

For many generations, the Eagle Clan had been part of the Anishinaabe clan system. Many of the soldiers in Company K may have belonged to the Eagle Clan. All Anishinaabek knew that the eagle carried prayers to the Creator. Some prayers were offered before battle. Carrying an eagle as the company went to war may have given the men strength and courage. (For more on the eagle, see Appendix D, pp. 248–249.)

While at Camp Parole, some Company K soldiers were given special assignments. Five men, including William Mixinasaw, began permanent guard duty at the general hospital in Annapolis. Marcus Otto and Luther Dutton were assigned to provost guard duty, helping maintain order among the soldiers. Joseph Gibson and four others were detailed on fatigue duty: digging latrines, gathering firewood, policing the camp, loading wagons. While not the most pleasant of assignments, it was work that had to be done to keep the army functioning.

GENERAL GRANT'S PLAN: WIN

Lieutenant General Ulysses S. Grant had one goal for his Union armies' 1864 campaign: batter the Confederacy into submission. Grant began mobilizing his forces in April. Union troops stationed in Texas marched toward Alabama. Major General William Tecumseh Sherman, commander of the Union forces in Tennessee, began a series of marches and battles that would end in Georgia. Troops from all over Virginia squeezed General Robert E. Lee's Army of Northern Virginia. Grant ordered Major General George Meade, the commander of the Army of the Potomac, not to capture Richmond, the capital of the Confederacy, but to pursue Lee: "Lee's Army will be your objective point. Wherever Lee goes there you will go also." Meade assembled his forces.

Ulysses S. Grant became general-in-chief of the Armies of the United States, all the Union armies, in March 1864.

[Library of Congress]

Within a few weeks, at least fifty thousand Union troops had joined the First Michigan Sharpshooters at Camp Parole.

The regiment had been assigned to the Ninth Corps, commanded by Major General Ambrose Burnside. The general commanded forty-five regiments—infantry and cavalry— and fifteen batteries. A battery was a group of artillery and cannons that were arranged together to hammer enemy lines with a barrage of shells

Confederate general Robert E. Lee commanded the Army of Northern Virginia.

[National Archives]

and mortar. Twenty-four thousand soldiers filled the ranks of Burnside's corps. The corps was organized into four divisions, one of which comprised African American soldiers—Colored Troops. The Sharpshooters' regiment belonged to the Third Division.

The Ninth Corps was completely self-sufficient. It had a commissary and two quartermasters, whose job was obtaining food and clothing and dispersing them to the men. Wagon trains carried ammunition and food. The Third Division had fifty ambulances stocked with medical supplies and stretchers to transport the wounded to hospitals.

The corps also had a blacksmith to shoe horses and repair any broken metal parts of ambulances, along with wheelwrights who carried tools to mend harnesses. When the Ninth Corps received its marching orders, it was ready to go.

The Ninth Corps had a train of horse-pulled ambulances ready to carry wounded soldiers to hospitals.

[Library of Congress]

Blacksmiths were important members of the Ninth Corps. They replaced worn horseshoes and repaired broken metal tools and wagon parts.

On April 23, Company K's men rolled their blankets and packed five days' rations. Bugles blared the call to strike tents. Within hours, Companies B and K, again traveling together, were on their way to Washington, D.C. But Payson Wolf wasn't with them. He remained behind, sick with a fever and bad chills, in a hospital. Subjected to poor weather and less-than-sanitary camps, soldiers frequently sickened. Diarrhea was a chronic complaint.

Each Sharpshooter carried sixty rounds of cartridges, an overcoat, a heavy blanket, a poncho, a canteen, rations, portions of a tent, and his rifle and its equipment. Departure day was hot. Sweat-drenched soldiers grew tired; men abandoned things they felt weren't absolutely needed beside the road. Sixteen Sharpshooters collapsed with sunstroke. And that was only the first day of a long walk. In two days, Company K marched forty-four miles.

Just before they marched into Washington, D.C., the entire
Ninth Corps was ordered to stop along the roadside and stack their
rifles. Daniel Mwakewenah and the others in Company K laid
down their gear and spruced up their appearance. Charles Allen
and the Mashkaw brothers scraped dried mud from their shoes.
The Ottos brushed dust from their uniforms. Jacko Penaiswanquot
tidied his gear before he hefted his knapsack onto his back. In
Washington, the Ninth Corps would march in review past President
Lincoln, and officers wanted the men to look sharp. From the bal-
cony of the Willard Hotel, President Lincoln and General Burnside
watched the Ninth Corps, including Company K, march down
Pennsylvania Avenue.

What did Lincoln think when he saw the Sharpshooters? A year
earlier, the president had met with a delegation of Cheyenne, Arapaho,
Comanche, Caddo, Kiowa, and Apache chiefs from the western plains.
He told them:

*There is a great difference between this palefaced people
and their red brethren, both as to numbers and the way in
which they live.... The pale-faced people are numerous
and prosperous because they cultivate the earth, produce
bread, and depend upon the products of the earth rather
than wild game for a subsistence.... You have asked for my
advice. I really am not capable of advising you whether...
it is best for you to maintain the habits and customs of your
race, or adopt a new mode of life. I can only say that I can
see no way in which your race is to become as numerous
and prosperous as the white race except by living as they do,
by the cultivation of the earth.*

Lincoln probably approved of the Anishinaabek who farmed, dressed, and spoke English like white Americans. And he probably appreciated that some Anishinaabe men were fighting for the Union. As a former frontiersman who knew how to use a rifle, he certainly could appreciate their marksmanship. But no one knows what Lincoln was thinking, or if he commented, as Company K marched by. However, William Randall, the lieutenant of Company I, did note

A delegation of American Indian chiefs met with Abraham Lincoln on March 27, 1863. In the front row, left to right, are Cheyenne leaders War Bonnet, Standing in the Water, and Lean Bear, and Kiowa leader Yellow Wolf. Federal troops killed Lean Bear in Kansas fifteen months later. War Bonnet and Standing in the Water were both killed in the Sand Creek Massacre on November 29, 1864, in the Colorado Territory.

[Library of Congress]

the toll of the war on Lincoln, remarking, "The president looked pale and careworn."

As the Union troops marched past, loud cheers greeted the corps's Fourth Division—the regiments of Colored Troops commanded by Brigadier General Edward Ferrero. Ladies waved handkerchiefs, and men shouted, "Remember Fort Pillow." They were referring to a massacre that had occurred two weeks earlier. Fort Pillow was in Tennessee, on a bluff overlooking the Mississippi River. About six hundred Union soldiers were in the fort, half of them African American. A Confederate force of as many as twenty-five hundred overwhelmed the fort, driving the Union troops down the bluff and into a cross fire. Between 47 and 49 percent of the Union soldiers were killed or mortally wounded. Some of them were shot even after they attempted to surrender. More than twice as many African American soldiers died as white Union soldiers, which suggests they were specifically targeted.

After the review, the Colored Troops encamped near the men

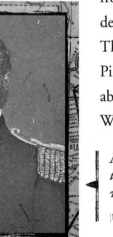

from Michigan. The men of Company K definitely saw them then, if not earlier. They probably had heard of the Fort Pillow massacre, but whether they talked about it with Ferrero's men is not known. What some Company K men must have

Major General Ambrose Burnside commanded the Union army's Ninth Corps. The Sharpshooters were assigned to the Ninth Corps's Second Brigade.

[National Archives]

known was that Anishinaabek with dark complexions often were noted as "colored" in official records. Until African American soldiers proved that they were good fighters, they often were not treated with respect. The Anishinaabek encountered this same prejudice from the skeptics who didn't think they'd be good soldiers.

With the Army of the Potomac, Company K marched across the war-ravaged land of Virginia. At Bull Run, they saw rusted shells, spent shot, and broken pieces of equipment still littering the ground. Lone chimneys dotted the fields, the houses destroyed by artillery fire. Joseph Wakazoo must have thought of the 1862 battle during which he'd seen many of his comrades in the 16th Michigan wounded and killed.

Company K trekked up and down hills and waded through rivers and streams as they marched farther southwest. By May 4, they were camped on a rise a few miles west of the Rapidan River. Confederate troops were encamped on the other side. The night was quiet.

Planks resting on top of a series of boats made pontoon, or floating, bridges that soldiers used to cross rivers.

[Library of Congress]

CHAPTER 8

Into the
WILDERNESS

★ ★ ★

BEFORE SUNUP ON MAY 5, Company K was on the move. After quick cups of coffee and a hurried breakfast, they stuffed clothes, Bibles, and moccasins into their knapsacks and bandoliers. They rolled and stowed blankets. Then they broke camp and marched in step to the Rapidan. Cannons rumbled across the river. Joseph Wakazoo, a veteran of several battles, knew what was coming. Charles Allen, Tom Kechittigo, and the others could only imagine.

Two years earlier, Confederate soldiers had destroyed the wooden bridge that spanned the Rapidan at Germanna Ford. A pontoon bridge bobbed and swayed on the water in its stead. At noon, Adjutant Edward Buckbee skeptically eyed the two-hundred-foot-long bridge. He couldn't believe the Ninth Corps's artillery had successfully crossed it. He saw dismounted officers still leading spooked horses across.

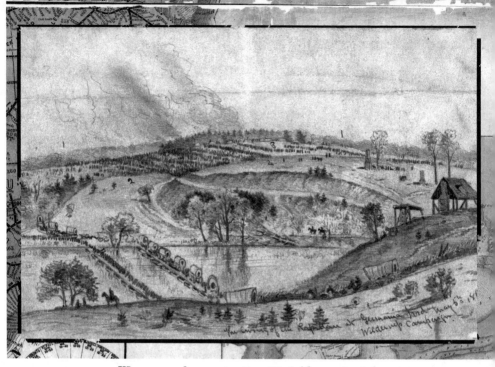

*Wagons crossed on a separate pontoon bridge constructed
alongside the one used by infantry.*

Buckbee, Captain Edwin Andress, Lieutenant Garrett Graveraet, and their comrades—no longer marching in step, which would have aggravated the sway—cautiously made their way across.

They continued up the road for about a mile. Captain Andress led Company K into the woods, where they assumed picket duty. A company on picket ranged as far as five hundred yards in front of an army's main forces, where it acted as a warning system for advancing enemy troops. But no one in Company K saw any rebel soldiers.

That evening, Andress ordered the company back to the road. By nightfall, they saw the "quick bright flash" of artillery fire light up the night sky like an approaching thunderstorm, followed by "the heavy boom" of cannon fire. Byron Cutcheon, the commander of the 20th Michigan Infantry—a regiment that was often positioned near the Sharpshooters—stated, "We slept upon our arms that night," meaning rifles held in hand or close by.

ADVANCE TO THE FRONT

On May 6, at 2:00 a.m., the Sharpshooters led the Ninth Corps as it advanced toward the front. For nearly five miles, Company K snaked its way up a road choked with wagons, troops, and hospital gear. The Sharpshooters finally arrived at the front at 7:00 a.m., where they veered off the road into a large field. The Otto and Mashkaw brothers ate a quick breakfast as Company K awaited orders. Would

In this sketch, drawn in 1864 by Alfred R. Waud, Ulysses Grant writes a telegram advising Union officers that his troops have crossed the Rapidan River. General Ely Parker is standing behind the log, to the left of Grant.

[Library of Congress]

they march southeast, toward the fast and furious gunfire they heard, or somewhere else?

Within the hour, Sergeants Kechittigo and Graveraet called out orders: Advance toward the west, away from the heavy fighting. The Sharpshooters would again be on picket duty. They and several other regiments would march across large fields and align themselves in the woods on the other side. From that position, they could prevent Confederate regiments from circling behind and attacking Union troops already engaged in heavy fighting. Generals Grant and Burnside relied on the Sharpshooters' keen marksmanship to pick off any enemy soldiers leading such an advance.

Tom Kechittigo and Daniel Mwakewenah watched as other companies started across the fields. They noticed that the men's blue uniforms were easily spotted against the plants and soil. Their clothing was going to make them easy targets. Traditional Anishinaabe stories about the *ogitchedaw* said they were smart, savvy fighters and hunters. They concealed themselves from the view of enemies or prey. Using Anishinaabe wisdom, Kechittigo and Mwakewenah scraped up soil and rubbed it into their uniforms.

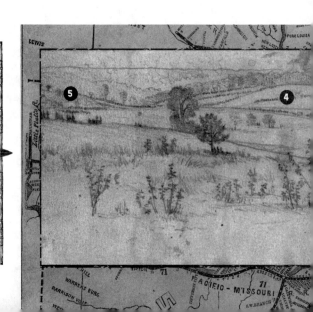

The Sharpshooters crossed the Rapidan (to the far right of this sketch). At 9:00 a.m. on May 6, they had passed in front of the house (2). That afternoon, Company K fought in the woods (3,4) behind the fields. They ended the day in the wooded area on the left (5). The field hospital (1) was ready to care for the wounded soldiers.

[Library of Congress]

Before entering the woods on the other side of the fields, they wedged leaves and twigs into their belts and the straps of their caps. Charles Allen and others quickly copied the hastily made camouflage. At first, soldiers in other companies scoffed, but it wasn't long before they adopted the tactic.

When Company K had practiced drills back at Camp Parole, in Annapolis, their precisely executed maneuvers impressed the officers of other regiments. Maintaining sharp battle lines in the woods was impossible. Branches slapped the men in the face. Tree roots snagged their shoes. Ankles twisted on uneven ground. And, distressingly, some soldiers found human skulls and bones on the forest floor, grim reminders of the Battle of Chancellorsville the previous year. The entire regiment of Sharpshooters abandoned all attempts to remain in battle lines. Instead, they zigzagged from tree to tree. The tangled undergrowth was so dense that Captain Andress and Lieutenant Graveraet lost sight of their men when as little as fifty yards separated them. It was obvious why the area was called the Wilderness.

Canteens swung at the soldiers' sides as they bushwhacked their way into position. Daniel Mwakewenah had tucked a stick about a

foot long and an inch wide into his gear. He planned to notch it with a mark for each rebel soldier he shot. For hundreds of years, American Indian warriors had counted each courageous act, or coup, committed in battle. Such acts included touching or killing an enemy warrior or stealing horses. The number of coups a fighter made increased his prestige. To keep an accurate count, a warrior carried a coup stick and carved a notch into it for each one. Daniel Mwakewenah's coup stick upheld *ogitchedaw* tradition.

Throughout the morning, Charles Allen, the Mashkaws, Joseph Gibson, and their Company K comrades waited in position. The Otto brothers—Marcus and Solomon—tried to stay within sight of each other, as did James and John Mashkaw. Several other Union regiments, also hidden in the woods, waited a few hundred yards to their left. Kechittigo passed Captain Andress's orders to Allen and the others: Fire at will, but don't waste bullets. Don't shoot, Sergeant Henry

A steady rain of bullets and shrapnel from cannons shattered trees throughout the woods.

[Library of Congress]

Graveraet would have cautioned the men, until you see a rebel soldier or, even better, an officer, who would probably be on horseback. Sporadic gunfire peppered the air.

Meanwhile, the battle intensified along a road about a mile away. Confederate armies pressed Union troops in a massive advance. The regiments close to the Sharpshooters retreated and joined the Union troops as they repelled the advancing rebel forces.

That left the First Michigan Sharpshooters alone.

By noon, more than five regiments from North Carolina had moved onto the high ground that faced Company K; artillery batteries blasted them. The 14th North Carolina Infantry moved down into the woods and attacked. Spotting the enemy in the thick undergrowth was hard. Company K's soldiers shot and reloaded as fast as they could. Each time Daniel Mwakewenah—or any soldier— pulled the trigger, the gunpowder inside his rifle's barrel ignited and produced a cloud of white smoke. Hidden momentarily by smoke, he had just seconds to reload. Mwakewenah's nostrils prickled with the sharp odor of burnt gunpowder. Around him, bullets tore through the air, sounding like buzzing bees and whining mosquitoes. Shells chunked into tree trunks and exploded. Splinters of bark rained on the men. Mwakewenah repeatedly reloaded and shot until the barrel of his rifle was hot enough to burn his skin. Mentally, he counted coups.

Not far away, Charles Allen reloaded as swiftly as Mwakewenah. Suddenly, something slammed into the left side of Allen's chest. The force flung him backward, and he fell to the ground. Blood quickly soaked the front of his jacket. Allen's breaths came heavy and hard.

RETREAT

Relentlessly, the 14th North Carolina bore down upon the Sharpshooters. Drummer William Duvernay received orders to beat a retreat. Companies B and K withdrew from their picket positions as quickly as they could. Everyone tried to move quietly, but there was no way George Ashkebug could silence the rattle of bullets in his cartridge box as it bounced on his hip. Ashkebug's knapsack jostled so hard against his back that his skin bruised.

The 14th North Carolina charged after the retreating Sharpshooters. In their haste to withdraw, Company K soldiers abandoned many possessions—moccasins, beaded belts, bandoliers, and Bibles printed in the Ojibwe dialect.

It wasn't until after Confederate troops had secured the area that Thomas J. Watkins, a soldier in the North Carolina regiment, realized he and his comrades had "fought a regiment of Indians." He admired their courage: "As we drove them back one Indian took refuge behind a tree. We saw him and supposed he would surrender. As we moved on he shot our [flag] bearer." The Anishinaabek impressed Watkins by how quickly they navigated the uneven terrain: "The Indians fought bravely in the wood. When driven into the open they did not again fire on us, but ran like deer. We captured not one of them." Whatever preconceptions Watkins might have had about American Indians, his encounter with Company K left him with respect for their ability. He was astonished when he found a bandolier bag beautifully patterned and decorated with thousands of colored glass beads. The bag "was sent home and prized."

The 20th Michigan and 50th Pennsylvania regiments, who were located near the edge of the pine woods, stopped building earthworks and rallied support for the Sharpshooters and other skirmishers in retreat. Their gunfire checked the North Carolinians and other Confederate troops, who moved back through the woods and returned to their own earthworks.

During a battle, many men assisted wounded comrades off the battlefield. Often they stayed behind the lines and didn't resume fighting. To stop this, the army adopted the policy that only stretcher-bearers could remove a wounded soldier from the battlefield. But at the time the battle was fought in the Wilderness, that policy was not strictly enforced. As the Anishinaabe soldiers retreated from their picket line, they may have refused to leave Charles Allen behind. A bullet was lodged in his chest, and his wound was serious. Allen was barely alive. His friends knew that unless he received medical attention soon, he would die.

The Mashkaw and Otto brothers were relieved to find each other alive and unharmed. Following orders, Company K and the rest of

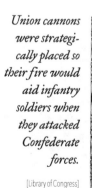

Union cannons were strategically placed so their fire would aid infantry soldiers when they attacked Confederate forces.

[Library of Congress]

the Sharpshooters regrouped and proceeded back through the Wilderness to rejoin the other divisions of the Ninth Corps.

FIRE!

Toward the end of the day, amid the after-battle calm, a different horror began. Sparks from musket and artillery fire smoldered in the dense undergrowth. Tiny flames fed on dry twigs and grew. Within hours, the scattered fires grew into an uncontrollable wildfire. One observer later wrote, "The blaze ran sparkling and crackling up the trunks of the pines, till they stood a pillar of fire from base to topmost spray; then they wavered and fell, throwing up showers of gleaming sparks, while over all hung the thick clouds of dark smoke, reddened beneath by the glare of flames." The men of Company K heard the screams and cries of wounded soldiers

As flames raged through the woods, soldiers raced to carry their fallen comrades out of harm's way.

[Library of Congress]

trapped behind the wall of flames, unable to drag themselves to safety. Two hundred men burned to death.

That night, both armies sheltered behind their own earthworks. Without doubt, Payson Wolf worried about his wounded friend Charles Allen. But he must have been relieved that his friend Louis Miskoguon and his cousin Joseph Wakazoo were okay. Mercifully, no one from Company K had been trapped in the wildfire. But the men were again ordered to sleep on their arms. Before he settled in, Daniel Mwakewenah cut thirty-two notches onto his coup stick. A number of them represented officers.

When Colonel Charles DeLand wrote his report of the battle, he noted that his officers had acted with "conspicuous coolness, courage and gallantry," and "while nearly all did their duty," three men deserved special notice for having done so "nobly." They were Edwin Andress, Garrett Graveraet, and Charles Allen. These men valiantly demonstrated qualities that their *ogitchedaw* ancestors valued and lauded, qualities that wise soldiers of any heritage would admire and respect.

Two days of fighting ended in a draw. Approximately 162,920 men had been at the Wilderness. Both armies had heavy casualties. About 29,800 men were killed, wounded, or missing: 18,400 of them were Union soldiers; 11,400 were Confederates. Rescuing and caring for the wounded took hours.

BLOOD, PAIN, AND PILLS

After the Wilderness battle ended, no one had time to rest. Sharpshooter Lieutenant William Randall of Company I had been assigned ambulance duty. Six hundred ambulances were ready to transport the

Ambulance workers and hospital attendants, aided by soldiers, carried the wounded from the battlefield as quickly as possible, but it still took several days for all the wounded to be removed to hospitals in Fredericksburg.

[Library of Congress]

Union wounded. There were so many wounded that officers assigned musicians, such as drummers, to act as stretcher-bearers and hospital attendants. William Duvernay was probably among them. If so, from late afternoon until 9:00 p.m., he helped men like Randall carry dozens of wounded from the battlefield to the division's field hospital, a tent where their wounds would first be tended. Despite working as quickly as they could, they couldn't transport all the wounded to the hospital at once. At one point during the night, Randall's team of bearers removed nine wounded men who lay within range of Confederate artillery. They carried them to a safer area but had to leave them there to move others out of harm's way. He assured them he would come back for them as soon as he could. Sadly, when he returned in the morning, he found that two of the men had died.

For most Civil War doctors, treating battle wounds was

unfamiliar territory. Of eleven thousand physicians in the North, only five hundred had performed surgeries. Surgeons in blood-soaked aprons did their best. They removed dirt, wood, pieces of cloth, bone fragments, and bullets from the wounds. They amputated feet, legs, hands, and arms. But there was little they could do for the most severely wounded—those shot in the abdomen or the chest. Those men usually died.

Hundreds of incoming wounded overwhelmed the field hospital's doctors and nurses. By the time hospital attendants placed Charles Allen on the wooden operating table, he'd lost a lot of blood. While the surgeon had probably read of the new, specialized technique whereby a doctor transfused stored blood into an injured person, it was rarely done in a field hospital. Allen's condition was serious. He'd been sedated with opium, a narcotic drug used to dull pain. The surgeon probed the wound with his smallest finger, feeling for the bullet. If he was unable to find it, he would have searched deeper with a longer, ceramic-tipped probe. Using at least one of these methods, the surgeon located and removed the bullet lodged in Allen's chest.

Although the surgeon didn't know that bacteria causes infection—the medical field hadn't discovered that yet—he did know that a dirty wound got infected, and when it did, it often led to the patient's death. To reduce the risk of infection, the surgeon removed any bits of cloth, skin, dirt, grass, or leaves that were in or near Allen's wound. A nurse dressed Allen's wound with wet lint, made by scraping and collecting the fibers from linen. A muslin bandage held the dressing in place. After his wound was cleaned and dressed, attendants carried Allen to the area where other wounded men awaited transport to another hospital. He definitely needed more care.

The dead were buried in shallow graves near the battlefield. Wooden boards inscribed with the name of the soldier (*if it was known*) were placed on the graves. At a later date, the soldiers' remains would be reinterred elsewhere. Unfortunately, many of the boards fell or were removed before this happened. Unidentified soldiers were later buried beneath markers that were inscribed *UNKNOWN*.

[Library of Congress]

On May 7, Randall led an ambulance train of seventeen wagons from the field hospital tents, where the wounded were first attended, to Fredericksburg, a town about twelve miles from the Wilderness. Charles Allen lay inside one of them, moaning in pain every time the wheels hit a bump in the pitted road. In Fredericksburg, makeshift hospitals for Union soldiers had been set up in a number of buildings.

Meanwhile, Company K spent the day on the battlefield, where they collected rifles, bayonets, and cartridges that belonged to the wounded and the dead. Exhausted, Wolf, Mwakewenah, Garrett and Henry Graveraet, and their comrades settled in for the night, hoping to get some much-needed sleep.

Earlier in the war, Union generals had been criticized for not pursuing retreating Confederate troops. General Grant, in command of a huge army and an endless supply of ammunition, vowed to beat Lee's army. He wasn't going to wait for Lee to attack. Instead, he planned to lure Lee's troops to a place with more open ground.

At 3:00 a.m., Colonel DeLand roused the Sharpshooters. Still half-asleep, Joseph Gibson and the others struck their tents and packed their knapsacks. Mutterings throughout camp hinted they were on their way to engage the Confederates again. Within a short time, the First Michigan Sharpshooters were marching away from the tangled Wilderness toward a place called Spotsylvania Court House.

They didn't know that Lee and his army were already on the way.

Union troops prepared for battle at Spotsylvania Court House.

[Library of Congress]

Gallantry
UNSURPASSED

★ ★ ★

AT MID-MORNING ON MAY 9, the Sharpshooters and four other regiments—the 60th Ohio, 20th Michigan, 50th Pennsylvania, and 79th New York—arrived at the crest of a gentle hill about two miles north of the small town of Spotsylvania Court House. They stopped short of the Ni River, where a small Confederate picket occupied a bridge. Led by the 60th Ohio—a brand-new, inexperienced regiment—the Sharpshooters and the other regiments splashed across the river. The pickets fled up a slight rise. Unbeknownst to the Sharpshooters, two brigades of enemy soldiers waited just beyond the crest, their weapons aimed directly at the advancing Union soldiers.

Confusion reigned as the rebels attacked. The 60th Ohio folded and retreated, and the Sharpshooters quickly followed. Eventually, Colonel Charles DeLand rallied his troops. Aided by the 20th

Michigan and 79th New York, the Sharpshooters advanced again and drove the enemy back beyond the hill. DeLand later explained his regiment's behavior by saying that misdirected Union artillery shells—friendly fire—had fallen within the Sharpshooters' lines. Also, he maintained, the rebels had quickly taken advantage of the gap left by the fleeing Ohioans and raked the exposed Sharpshooters with gunfire. But, DeLand admitted, the worst offense occurred because an officer—he did not say who—had panicked and without authority had ordered the Sharpshooters to retreat.

The next day, May 10, Confederate skirmishers periodically exchanged gunfire with the Sharpshooters. Captain Edwin Andress was wounded in the right foot. Despite hospital treatment, the injury prevented him from resuming command. He was discharged from the army two months later. A bullet struck Adjutant Edward Buckbee in the head. Fortunately, the bullet was spent, meaning it had lost most of its forward momentum. Stunned, Buckbee collapsed, unconscious. Although blood streamed down his face, the bullet had only grazed his scalp. He returned to duty after an overnight stay in the field hospital. While he was gone, Company K dug earthworks to fortify their position. Rebel forces were equally busy building their own log-and-dirt fortifications.

All was quiet on May 11. Daniel Mwakewenah, Amos Ashkebugnekay, and Louis Genereau waited with the rest of their Company K comrades behind a strong line of earthworks.

It was the calm before the storm.

MAY 12, 1864

Two days of steady rain had turned the countryside into a soggy mess. Rain soaked the Sharpshooters' jackets and trousers and boots. Even their gum blankets, coated on one side with rubber to protect them from muddy ground, were sopping wet. Sharpshooter Amos Farling of Company G complained that it rained so much that it "left us standing in mud and water knee-deep." Just when it seemed as though their situation couldn't get worse, the Sharpshooters heard gunfire to the west. But heavy fog prevented them from seeing anything.

Hours passed—5:00 a.m., 6:00, 7:00, 8:00, 9:00, 10:00, 11:00, noon. Artillery roared. Gunfire was so rapid that the men couldn't distinguish individual shots. Battle smoke, rather than fog, filled the air. Company K restlessly awaited orders.

Telegraph lines provided a crucial communication link between Grant and his officers. Men strung temporary wires on poles. Wagons carried coils of wire and batteries.

[Library of Congress]

Telegraph messages flew back and forth among the Union generals. During the Civil War, sending a telegram was the fastest way to convey information to another location. Hastily set-up electrical wires enabled officers close to a battlefield to communicate with those farther removed. Specially trained operators sent tapped messages in Morse code, a system that assigned each letter of the alphabet a sequence of short and long electric signals. A short signal was written as a dot, the long signal as a dash. A telegraph operator tapped out words in code, sending the signals across the wire to a distant operator. The receiver converted the signals back into dots and dashes and decoded the message.

Shortly after 2:00 p.m., the Ninth Corps received a telegram ordering it to move into battle positions. Brigadier General Orlando Willcox sent the First Brigade of his Third Division across a field, spreading uphill into the woods beyond. The Second Brigade, which included the Sharpshooters, fell into position behind the First.

Confederate artillery pounded the woods with shells. Smoke and the deafening thunder of artillery added to the confusion. Trees and heavy undergrowth blocked the Union soldiers' view. As the First Brigade moved forward, rebel yells pierced the air, and Confederate soldiers seemed to appear out of nowhere. Rifles fired and, with no time to reload, soldiers on both sides began hand-to-hand combat. They bludgeoned each other with rifle butts. Soldiers lashed out with their knives. Those left weaponless probably resorted to rocks and fists. Soldiers cursed and screamed at one another in the free-for-all struggle for survival.

Then the three regiments of the Second Brigade entered the battle. The 20th Michigan, which had aided the Sharpshooters at the Wilderness, occupied the middle of the advance. It charged across open ground that extended right up to the enemy's earthworks. Except for a small rise of land, no higher than a foot, they had no cover. Within a few moments, the regiment lost almost half of its men. On the left, the 50th Pennsylvania advanced. It had also aided the Sharpshooters at the Wilderness. As soon as the 50th Pennsylvania entered a dense pine forest, five North Carolina regiments attacked. The North Carolinians captured about a hundred Pennsylvania men.

William Duvernay pounded rolls on his drum as his Sharpshooter comrades moved into position on the right side of the brigade's advance. A "small, bushy growth of trees" hid them from the enemy's sight, but it also made it difficult for Lieutenant Garrett Graveraet to keep track of his men. Sergeant Tom Kechittigo helped lead the way forward. George Ashkebug and Louis Genereau forged through the wet, slippery undergrowth, weaving and ducking from shrub to shrub. Daniel Mwakewenah, rapidly firing as he had at the Wilderness, shot, reloaded, and shot again. James and John Mashkaw focused on shooting and finding cover. Neither they nor the Otto brothers had time to keep track of each other.

Sergeant Henry Graveraet urged Joseph Wakazoo and the others to keep going. Hearing the whistle of an approaching bombshell, Wakazoo ducked. Soil spattered into the air as the shell hit and exploded.

When the air cleared, Sergeant Graveraet lay on the ground. Wakazoo could see that his sergeant was dead. Wakazoo continued forward, but soon afterward a bullet hit his left hand and injured a finger. Try as he might, he couldn't steady the muzzle of his rifle to aim accurately. While he decided what to do, a piece of shell struck his rifle and smashed it hard into his hip. He collapsed.

Meanwhile, other Sharpshooters and the 27th Michigan Infantry pushed ahead until they were within fifty yards of the Confederate earthworks. There they encountered "a murderous crossfire of shell, grape, and canister." (Grapeshot and canister shot consisted of small metal balls clustered together and shot from a cannon.)

A piece of shell struck George Ashkebug's cartridge box. The cartridges inside exploded. Ashkebug fell, bruising his head and left eye. He bled from his left side.

A bullet thunked into Louis Genereau's leg. He limped toward cover.

Thomas Smith, unhampered by having only one hand, braced his rifle against his right arm, poured powder into the barrel with his left hand, aimed, and took his next shot. Nearby, Daniel Mwakewenah tried to fight. But he'd been wounded three times: in the face, on his head, and finally in his left hand, which had become useless. He could no longer reload his rifle. He could still use his bayonet.

Marcus Otto dropped his rifle when a bullet smashed his right arm. Stunned, Otto cradled his injured arm with his left. The bullet had splintered both bones in his forearm, and blood covered both hands. Otto grimaced; the pain was excruciating.

Colonel DeLand recognized that the Sharpshooters were in dire straits. "Advance was impossible and retreat was difficult," he later wrote. His men were almost out of ammunition, but the two Michigan regiments decided to try to hold the line and hope for aid. DeLand reported: "For a full hour the men [held their position] with a determination and gallantry unsurpassed." Twice the rebels charged and attempted to capture the regiments' flags. The men from Michigan fixed their bayonets and fought face-to-face with the rebels, forcing them back. Finally, the Michigan soldiers heard the bugles call them to retreat.

Stretcher-bearers carried Joseph Wakazoo to the field hospital. Tom Kechittigo walked from the battlefield holding his left arm. It bled from a gunshot wound between his hand and elbow. Fellow Company K soldier John Waubenoo saw Kechittigo sway. Certain that Kechittigo was going to pass out, Waubenoo helped him to a wagon that would carry him to the field hospital.

Colonel DeLand was twice injured, the second time being stunned by an exploding shell. When he recovered his senses and could walk, he rejoined the Sharpshooters, who were re-forming their line back near the woods. Ill with other health problems, DeLand later asked to be sent to the hospital for treatment.

BATTLE CASUALTIES

Field hospitals supplied aid to those with injuries. Surgeons, doctors, and nurses operated or dressed wounds all night and the next day. Once again, musicians were detailed as hospital attendants, so William Duvernay may have offered water to the wounded and brought bandages to the nurses.

Before a wagon transported Marcus Otto to the hospital, someone on the battlefield had wrapped a tourniquet around his right arm to stanch the blood flow. As soon as the surgeon saw the splintered bones of Otto's forearm, he reached for the sharp saw he

Although this photograph of ambulances removing wounded soldiers was taken after the Battle of Fredericksburg, the scene at Spotsylvania would have looked much the same. Tom Kechittigo and Marcus Otto were among those who needed transportation to the field hospital.

[Library of Congress]

used to amputate arms and legs damaged beyond repair. Otto's pain had already been dulled with opium, morphine, or whiskey. Before surgery, the doctor probably anesthetized him with chloroform. A nurse or hospital attendant held Otto's right hand to the tabletop. After the surgeon tied off the blood vessels in Otto's upper arm, he sawed through the bone, just above the elbow. He left a flap of skin below the cut. When the damaged arm was removed, the surgeon folded the flap over the cut bone and stitched the skin closed. A nurse dressed the site. Perhaps William Duvernay was one of the hospital attendants tasked with the grim duty of carrying amputated limbs to the growing pile outside the hospital.

The damage to Daniel Mwakewenah's fingers and hand was beyond repair. A surgeon had no choice but to amputate the hand.

The battles fought at Spotsylvania on May 12 were among the deadliest of the war. One twenty-hour battle occurred at the Muleshoe Salient. A salient is where an army's line bulges outward and can be partially surrounded by the opposition's troops. The Muleshoe was less than a mile from Company K's early morning position. The Sharpshooters had heard gunfire from the Muleshoe before they advanced into battle.

The Muleshoe saw fighting so horrific that one area was called the Bloody Angle. Artillery shells and bullets by the tens of thousands screamed through the air. A large white oak tree grew just

As they had been at the Wilderness, field hospitals at Spotsylvania were soon crowded with wounded soldiers.

[Library of Congress]

behind the salient. Its solid, healthy trunk was about a foot and a half in diameter. Bullets battered the trunk so thoroughly that the tree fell. In steady rain, soldiers bayoneted and clubbed one another until the bodies of the dead lay three and four deep. Blood turned the mud red. One soldier described the fight as a "seething, bubbling, roaring hell of hate and murder."

David Holt, a Confederate soldier in Company K of the 16th Mississippi Infantry, described his company's reaction as it left the battlefield: "We halted in a pasture and broke ranks. . . . All moved by the same impulse, we sat down on the wet ground and wept."

The night after the battle, Payson Wolf, Louis Miskoguon, Amos Ashkebugnekay, and their comrades shoveled dirt and dragged logs into place for new earthworks. Their orders were to resist any enemy attempts to advance. All were exhausted and concerned about their injured friends.

Many wounded men needed care beyond what could be given at

the field hospital. Transporting the Union wounded to hospitals in Fredericksburg and beyond was a nightmare. Poor road conditions slowed the three-to-four-mile-long ambulance trains. Wagon wheels sloughed through mud that reached up to their hubs. The ambulances bumped over roadbeds lined with logs placed side by side to give the wooden wheels traction. Jolts from the wagons' stiff springs during this rough ride sometimes caused wounds to start bleeding. Soldiers yelled with pain. Ambulance drivers prayed that the wounded would survive the trip.

Brompton, the brick mansion owned by John Marye, was used as a hospital for much of the Civil War. The dark marks on the columns are bullet holes. A number of Company K men were treated in Brompton and lay in the hallway just inside the front door.

[Library of Congress]

Several of Company K's wounded were taken to hospitals in Fredericksburg. One of them was in a brick mansion known as Brompton, owned by John Marye, a prominent citizen. In 1864, after the Battle of the Wilderness, rows of wounded soldiers lay on the home's wood floors.

Surgeon William Howell Reed was one of the doctors who worked at the Brompton hospital. The front hall at Brompton was a spacious area. But after the Wilderness and Spotsylvania, wounded soldiers filled the entryway. And that was where Reed found men from Company K: "In a group of four Indian sharpshooters, in one corner of this entry, each with the loss of a limb . . . never was patience

In this photo taken outside Brompton, the photographer identified the men only as "wounded Indians." But they are from Company K. Edwin Andress is probably the man leaning against the tree. The man dressed in white, standing beside Andress, is almost certainly Tom Kechittigo.

[Library of Congress]

more finely illustrated. They neither spoke nor moaned, but suffered and died, making a mute appeal to our sympathy, and expressing both in look and manner their gratitude for our care."

If Reed knew the men's names, he did not give them. But hospital and other records hint at who they may have been. Charles Allen definitely entered a hospital in Fredericksburg after the Battle of the Wilderness; he remained in serious condition in mid-May. He might have been at Brompton. Captain Edwin Andress, shot in the foot on May 10, was probably there too. Marcus Otto, Tom Kechittigo, Daniel Mwakewenah, Louis Genereau, George Ashkebug, and Joseph Wakazoo all needed additional care. John Etarwegeshig may have as well. Brompton was a temporary stopover for most wounded

After he was treated in the field hospital and at Fredericksburg, Louis Genereau was transferred to Lincoln Hospital in Washington, D.C.

[Library of Congress]

soldiers. Many of the Company K wounded men would likely have transferred within days or a couple of weeks to hospitals farther north.

A steamboat carried Genereau to Lincoln Hospital, in Washington, D.C. He remained there several weeks while his leg wound healed.

Mwakewenah had worsened. Angry red lines, the sign of infection, extended up his arm from the amputation site. He too was transferred to a hospital in Washington for more treatment.

The Union army's segregation of Colored Troops from their white counterparts often extended to separate treatment of the sick or wounded. L'Ouverture General Hospital in Alexandria, Virginia, treated African American soldiers. Tom Kechittigo, Joseph Wakazoo, George Ashkebug, and Marcus Otto were sent there. The tone of their skin often subjected them to the same prejudice African Americans faced.

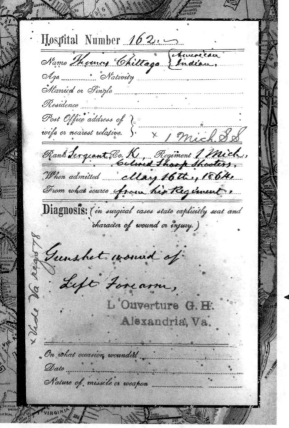

After a short stay at Brompton, Tom Kechittigo was transferred to L'Ouverture General Hospital in Alexandria, Virginia, a hospital designated for Colored Troops.

[National Archives]

In fact, although Kechittigo's hospital record notes he is an American Indian, it lists his regiment as the First Michigan Colored Sharpshooters.

Eventually, Kechittigo's and Ashkebug's wounds healed, and they returned to duty. Wakazoo was in and out of various hospitals for most of the rest of the war.

Marcus Otto's war was over. He was discharged from service in August and sent home. By then his brother Solomon, suffering from the effects of tuberculosis, had been shuttled from hospital to hospital. He was finally released from a hospital in Detroit, but he never arrived home. His family was certain that he died along the way. Where he died and the location of his grave still remain a mystery.

KILLED IN ACTION

Both armies suffered heavy casualties at the Wilderness and Spotsylvania Court House. Approximately thirty-six thousand Union soldiers were dead, wounded, or missing in action. Confederate losses were about twenty-four thousand. Of the First Michigan Sharpshooters, 42 had died, 144 were wounded, and 5 were listed as captured or missing in action. At least 20 of the injured and killed were Company K soldiers.

While Daniel Mwakewenah and the others were on their way to Fredericksburg, their friends said prayers for dead comrades. Nine men from Company K died as a result of fighting at Spotsylvania. Both Mashkaw brothers, James and John, were killed in action. So were Jonah Dabasequam, Benjamin Greensky, Thaddeus Lamourandere, and Samuel Going. The men whose bodies were found and identified were buried in temporary graves. A wooden board, inscribed with the soldier's name, marked the grave. Sadly, rain washed away many names. People removed the boards. The soldiers' remains either still lie buried somewhere on the battlefield or are in graves marked UNKNOWN in Fredericksburg or elsewhere.

Some army records list John Etarwegeshig as killed in action at Spotsylvania. His friend Antoine Scott, who had enlisted with him, saw Etarwegeshig "after he was wounded in the shoulder & body" and believed "he died in a few days thereafter." If Etarwegeshig survived for a few days, as Scott believed, Dr. Reed may have seen him at Brompton. Regardless of the scenario, Etarwegeshig perished from his wounds and is buried in an unknown location.

Months later, when Union remains were removed from the battlefield and taken to Fredericksburg National Cemetery, Samuel Going's remains were reliably identified and reinterred beneath a stone marker. The marker was incorrectly inscribed with the name Samuel Gora.

Just before twilight, after his comrades laid down their rifles to begin other tasks, Garrett Graveraet reported to Adjutant Edward Buckbee. He told him that his father, Henry, had been killed. He asked if a few men from Company K could go with him to search for his father's body. Buckbee went along to help his friend. The men carried Henry's body back behind Union lines. Garrett buried his father near a house owned by the Beverly family and marked the grave with an inscribed board. He carefully noted the location of the house and the trees that surrounded Henry's grave so he could easily find it later. He told Buckbee that he would return after the war, take up his father's body, and bury it in Michigan.

Meanwhile, Charles Allen lay in a Fredericksburg hospital. His chest wound festered with infection. The doctors hadn't been able to stop its spread, and the antibiotics that could have fought it hadn't been discovered yet. Allen, only twenty years old, died on or about May 20. His body was transported to Fredericksburg National Cemetery, where it lies buried beneath one of the gravestones marked UNKNOWN.

The men of Company K mourned the death of every soldier, but none more so than Daniel Mwakewenah, who died from his infected wound in a Washington hospital on June 5. Mwakewenah's leadership, before and during the war, and his courage in battle had earned him special respect. Lieutenant William Driggs's father was a congressman. The company's officers appealed for his help in honoring their fallen friend. Driggs arranged for Mwakewenah's body to be embalmed and placed "in a handsome coffin, with a plate, upon which was inscribed the name of the chief, the cause of his death, the date and name of the battle in which it was received." Sometimes the best tribute is a simple one. One of the Sharpshooters stated, "He was a brave and good soldier."

Earthworks like these at Cold Harbor gave soldiers a degree of protection from enemy fire. But shoveling soil and cutting logs to reinforce them was backbreaking work in hot weather.

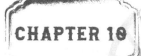

CHAPTER 10

The Continuing FIGHT

★ ★ ★

SKIRMISHING CONTINUED around Spotsylvania Court House for another week. For the most part, the Sharpshooters remained on their arms behind Union earthworks. With Colonel DeLand hospitalized, the Sharpshooters had a new commander, Captain Levant Rhines, previously the leader of Company A.

The last week in May, General Grant ordered the Army of the Potomac to push farther south, toward Richmond, the capital of the Confederacy. During the next week, the Sharpshooters marched more than fifty miles. In a letter to his mother, Adjutant Edward Buckbee complained that he was "profoundly ignorant as to where we are." Furthermore, he wrote, he hadn't had a complete change of clothes in over a month. Many Company K men were sick, especially with diarrhea. They were dirty and exhausted.

But they still were tasked with sharpshooting. One day in late May, the Anishinaabek's distinctive method of camouflage spread beyond their regiment. New Hampshirite Wyman White belonged to the Second U.S. Sharpshooters. On that particular day, he was sent to the Ninth Corps on sharpshooting duty. White hunkered down at the edge of a cornfield. His orders were to cross the field and shoot from the cover of the bushes on the other side, but the young cornstalks were only about two feet high. While deciding what to do, White encountered an Anishinaabe soldier who also had been ordered to cross the field. White observed, "The corn was not large or thick enough to cover us from the view of the rebels." He received unexpected advice: "The Indian said, 'Make self corn. Do as I do.'" The Anishinaabe Sharpshooter cut corn stalks and stuffed them into his clothes and equipment. White did the same, and the two made it safely across the field. After dark, they went their separate ways, "never to meet again." But White always remembered the lesson he had received.

In early June, just outside Richmond, Virginia, at a place called Cold Harbor, the First Michigan Sharpshooters again found themselves in battle. After a barrage of heavy fire, Company K was ordered into a thick pine forest. The Confederate army was preparing to relocate its cannons, each weighing as much as a ton. The Anishinaabe soldiers' mission was to stop the rebels from moving the cannons. They had to target the soldiers who manned the guns and the horses that pulled them.

Antoine Scott, Garrett Graveraet, and Joseph Gibson watched from behind trees, waiting for clear shots. Amos Ashkebugnekay and Jacko Penaiswanquot were ready as well. Whenever rebel gunners

*All soldiers spent a lot of time building forts like this one
to house artillery and protect the troops.*

[Library of Congress]

attempted to move the cannons, shots rang out. Sometimes a rebel
gunner would fall, at other times a horse. All day and through the
night, the men of Company K remained in the woods, shooting
whenever they had a clear shot. In the morning, the regiment found
grim evidence of their comrades' accuracy. Twenty-six horses lay
dead at one of the two abandoned batteries of cannons, thirty-seven
at the other. The loss severely crippled the rebel forces in the area.
Lacking horses to pull the heavy cannons, the Confederates would
have to fight without the support of artillery fire.

By this time, of the more than seven hundred First Michigan
Sharpshooters who had confidently left Camp Douglas in March,
slightly upward of two hundred remained. Battlefield casualties had
taken a heavy toll, but far more were ill and in hospitals. Grueling

weather, poor sanitation, and exhaustion led to various sicknesses. For those who were left, there was no rest. Grant ordered them on to Petersburg.

SNEAK ATTACK

The second-largest city in Virginia, Petersburg was the railroad hub of the Confederacy. During the Civil War, both sides relied on railroads to transport food and supplies to troops as well as civilians. They were lifelines. Grant planned to cut these lines in Petersburg, isolating the Confederate capital in Richmond.

En masse, the night of June 12, the Ninth Corps began the march of more than thirty miles from Cold Harbor to Petersburg. The line of soldiers and wagons stretched for miles, which left them exposed

As the Sharpshooters marched to Petersburg, they had to cross the James River on a pontoon bridge much longer than the one over the Rapidan River.

[Library of Congress]

to fire by enemy pickets and capture. For two days, Company K marched, stopping only for quick meals and cups of coffee. They arrived near the James River the afternoon of June 14. The Sharpshooters were spared major injuries during the long march.

On June 15, the Third Division—which included the Sharpshooters—waited all day for its turn to cross the 2,200-foot-long pontoon bridge over the James River. (For comparison, that's a bit longer than six football fields placed end to end.) By that time, fighting had already started outside Petersburg.

On June 16, Company K marched a few miles east of Petersburg. It stopped less than half a mile from a plantation owned by the Shand family. Confederate forces occupied the large, white two-story home, which stood on a tongue of land where two creeks merged. Each creek flowed in a deep, narrow ravine, one in front of the house and one behind.

To the east, across the ravine in front of the house, the Ninth Corps set up its battle lines. The Confederates had built defensive earthworks along the ravine and placed four cannons in a nearby peach orchard. Farther south on higher ground, two more rebel cannons were poised to fire into the ravine.

Brigadier General Robert Potter, who commanded the corps's Second Division, had a daring plan. That night, he moved his troops down into the ravine within one hundred yards of the enemy. Potter's sneak attack required absolute silence. Officers whispered all commands, which were passed from man to man down the line. Soldiers tucked canteens, tin plates, cups—anything that would rattle—into their knapsacks. No one was to fire his rifle. This charge was bayonets only.

Hours before dawn, his men stealthily moved up the other side of the ravine and huddled just below the bank of sand that formed the Confederate earthworks. The only sound that broke the silence was an occasional shot from a distant picket. Shortly after 3:00 a.m., the Union line rose and rushed the Shand house and the Confederate works. The totally surprised rebels had time to fire only one volley. The Second Division's attack was a complete success: They took control of that portion of the rebel line, capturing four cannons, six hundred prisoners, and about fifteen hundred rifles.

Later that morning, Confederate forces re-formed their line west of the Shand house. Brigadier General Orlando Willcox's Third Division jockeyed into position on ground previously held by the rebels. The Sharpshooters did not participate in the afternoon assaults made by their division and others. Unfortunately, none of the afternoon attacks made further headway against the enemy's line.

Facing the enemy at the end of the afternoon, the Sharpshooters

Cannon fire became a common sound as the siege of Petersburg dragged on.
[Library of Congress]

occupied the very end position, on the extreme left of the Union line. They were the only soldiers from the Third Division in that area. One part of the enemy line bulged outward from the rest. This created a salient—smaller than but similar to the salient the Confederate line had at Spotsylvania. Captain Rhines ordered the men, with bayonets fixed, to charge the salient. The rebel soldiers fled their earthworks, and the Sharpshooters captured the ground without difficulty.

Louis Genereau, perhaps on furlough from the hospital, sat on the ground and rested. Although his skin was almost healed from the gunshot wound he received at Spotsylvania, his lower leg still pained him. Sometimes, he used a crutch to get around. But being with John Kedgnal, William Duvernay, his friends from Elbridge, and officers whom he trusted, such as Lieutenant Graveraet and Adjutant Buckbee, was better than being in a hospital ward.

As the evening wore on, rebels again charged the Sharpshooters, who repulsed them. Suddenly, cannonballs struck their earthworks. Rebel gunners had rolled two cannons onto a railroad cut only half a mile away. Rhines ordered Graveraet and Company K closer to the railroad cut. When a cannon shot, Company K fired heavily into the area where the flash occurred. The cannons soon grew silent. But that didn't put an end to rifle fire. A minié ball seriously wounded Garrett Graveraet in his left arm. After Company K rejoined the regiment, he went to the field hospital. The surgeon could do nothing to save his arm. Later that night, he amputated it.

For a couple more hours, the Sharpshooters held their position. But at 10:00 p.m., Brigadier General Matt Ransom entered the

Rebel forces rolled two large cannons, perhaps similar to this one, into position on a railroad track near the Shand house and fired on the Sharpshooters. Garrett Graveraet led Company K on a mission to eliminate the threat.

[Library of Congress]

field of battle and reinforced the rebels with five regiments from North Carolina. More than five hundred Confederate soldiers swarmed the Sharpshooters' earthworks.

Leverette Case, a Sharpshooter in Company C, recalled that some North Carolinians yelled, "We surrender, don't shoot." Rhines leaped onto the earthworks and told them to lay down their weapons. They didn't. Instead, they pushed forward and through the works. The Sharpshooters realized that surrender was not the Confederates' plan—they were attacking! Simultaneously, soldiers from both sides pulled rifle triggers. A sheet of flame lit the night. The Sharpshooters and Confederates were so close that "the fire from the muskets burned the clothing of the men."

Chaos reigned. Soldiers from both sides hollered "Surrender!" Sharpshooters grabbed Confederates and passed them to the rear as prisoners. North Carolinians grabbed Sharpshooters and did the same. Ferocious hand-to-hand combat followed. Captain Rhines fell, mortally wounded. Adjutant Buckbee stepped forward and rallied his regiment.

In such close quarters, reloading was impossible. Joseph Gibson and Louis Marks may have resorted to bayonets. Jacko Penaiswanquot, Amos Ashkebugnekay, and William Mixinasaw possibly pulled out knives. Louis Miskoguon and Payson Wolf perhaps battered enemy soldiers with the butts of their rifles. The Sharpshooters fought gallantly, but the North Carolina regiments had completely hemmed them in, and no Union troops came to their aid. Escape was impossible. Buckbee wisely realized that further fighting would only lead to senseless loss of life. He ordered the Sharpshooters to stop firing and threw down his sword.

At first light, the North Carolinians herded more than seventy-five Sharpshooters toward Petersburg. Some of the Sharpshooters slipped through the trees and escaped. But at least sixteen men from Company K remained captive and had to surrender their guns. Their captors, soldiers of the 56th North Carolina Infantry, quickly claimed the rifles with the beautifully carved stocks, which they prized highly and carried through the close of the war.

Louis Genereau, Edward Buckbee, and five other Sharpshooters were taken away as a group. Rather than continue to Petersburg in the dark, Genereau's captors locked him and the others in a barn. The three-and-a-half-mile walk to the downtown railroad depot would be much easier in daylight. With their prisoners secured, the guards settled in for a few hours' rest. Although the prisoners didn't have any weapons, they tried to free themselves with something else: a match and a floor strewn with straw! Around 3:00 a.m., they gathered the straw into a big bundle and lit it. When the guards saw the blaze, they threw open the door. Genereau escaped in the confusion and made his way back to the Sharpshooters.

TO PRISON

The morning of June 18, Petersburg schoolteacher Charles Campbell was excited to be downtown. Fellow citizens crowded the streets, hoping to glimpse General Robert E. Lee, who had just arrived in town to coordinate the defense of the city. Lee was conferring with General Pierre Beauregard at his headquarters in the Petersburg customs office.

Approximately three hundred Union prisoners were packed inside an old stone warehouse less than ten blocks away. Fifteen of them were soldiers from Company K. Payson Wolf, Louis Miskoguon, Joseph Gibson, Louis Marks, Amos Ashkebugnekay, William Newton, Jacko Penaiswanquot, and William Mixinasaw were among them.

It was hot and dirty on the third floor of the warehouse. That afternoon, Louis Marks and one of his comrades must have been wary when a guard motioned that they should come with him. On their way downstairs, they must have wondered where they were being taken.

Charles Campbell and his children had come to the warehouse "to see some Indian prisoners." Campbell's children "had never seen one before." Treating the two prisoners as if they were a sideshow exhibit, the lieutenant in charge "brought down 2 of the Indians for us to look at," Campbell later wrote in his diary.

Payson Wolf, Louis Marks, Joseph Gibson, and Jacko Penaiswanquot were among the Company K men imprisoned on the third floor of this building. In years past, it had been a trading post operated by Peter Jones.

[Historic Petersburg Foundation, Inc., owner of the Peter Jones Trading Station, Petersburg, Virginia]

Campbell spoke with the men, who told him "that they were Ottawas, from Michigan & belonged to a Michigan regiment; one [was] named Louis Mark, the other Edward." Campbell couldn't catch Edward's last name, "it being a guttural Indian word."

They were "dressed in Yankee uniform" and refused to answer Campbell's questions about their capture, which made the prison guard laugh. Campbell told them that he supposed they were taken prisoner by accident, something they could not help.

Campbell asked one of the Odawas to remove his cap so the children could see his hair. If this angered the man, he didn't let his face show it. Campbell noted that the two men were "very grave-looking." The only Anishinaabe man who spoke answered one or two questions tersely, and Campbell observed that "the other man . . . did not talk English very well & he had nothing to say."

The Company K prisoners remained in the warehouse for three days. Then all the captives were loaded into boxcars and shipped to prison camps farther south.

Meanwhile, the rest of the Sharpshooter regiment was in tatters. Fifteen men had died near the Shand house. Forty-nine had been wounded; fifteen of them would die later. Dozens of men were prisoners of war. Scarcely a hundred men remained in the regiment's ranks. Leverette Case must have been surprised—and relieved—when Louis Genereau limped into camp. Genereau told Case about his escape from the barn and assured him that their friend and comrade Edward Buckbee was alive and all right the last time he'd seen him.

Because the regiment's ranks were so low, Captain Elmer Dicey of Company B, who was acting commander of the Sharpshooters, combined the men into four companies. Dicey placed Lieutenant William Driggs, who had recruited so many Anishinaabe men for Company K, in command of Company 3, a combination of Companies I and K. Even so, Driggs's new company had only about thirty men. (A company normally had one hundred.)

Lieutenant William Randall of Company I asked to be recalled from ambulance duty. He willingly gave up having a "horse, good tent, plenty of provisions," to be on foot and lying in the trenches with his comrades in Company 3. The men were glad to have him back. One of his jobs was to keep the company's records, a task he didn't find easy because the men from Company K had "some jawbreaking names to write out."

As Lee and his reinforcements arrived to defend the city, Grant's plan to cut off the supply lines to Richmond turned into a siege of Petersburg. The Army of the Potomac dug in. For the next nine months, Grant would concentrate on severing the city's road and rail connections to the South and West. Starved of food, provisions, arms, and ammunition, Lee would have to surrender.

Driggs's company spent the rest of June digging trenches. Confederate skirmishers fired on the Sharpshooters many times. The trenches didn't always provide cover. John Kedgnal, now in Company 4, limped with a minor wound, the result of being hit by a spent bullet. Once a single bullet injured two men. As Asher Huff of Company I was splitting kindling wood, a bullet suddenly tore through the thigh of Anishinaabe soldier John Andrew. It sped on and slammed into Huff's knee. Both men recovered.

SAD NEWS

Garrett Graveraet was not so fortunate. On June 22, from his bed at Armory Square Hospital, in Washington, D.C., he wrote a letter to his mother, Sophia. He told her that his arm had been amputated just below the shoulder and quickly allayed the worry he knew she would feel: "I think I shall be discharged before long and come home if my arm does well. The Dr. thinks it will do well." He regretted having "no opportunity to write about father's death." Graveraet urged his mother not to "be discouraged" about him. "[Your] kind teachings and prayers [were] all that has kept me up. I have thought of these a great deal," he wrote, and added, "This fighting for my country is all right. It has brought me to my senses."

No one knows if he meant fighting for the government, or if

he meant fighting to protect his homeland, his "country." Perhaps he meant both. Fighting alongside soldiers from many different states may have led him to recognize a common cause: All were fighting to save their country. Michigan is part of that country. In a larger sense, Graveraet was fighting for two countries: his homeland and the United States.

Graveraet concluded with his address at the hospital, writing, "A letter from you will do me good. Don't be uneasy. Affectionately, Garret A Graveraet."

William Driggs's father—the congressman—visited Graveraet several times. Sadly, the site of the amputation became infected. By then, Graveraet knew he wouldn't live and asked Driggs to arrange that his body be sent home.

As her son had requested, Sophia sent him a letter. But it arrived too late. Graveraet died on June 30. Returning the letter to Sophia, a hospital ward master named Joseph Finch wrote that the doctors had done everything they could for her son. He told her, "He was a good soldier & was liked by all the men."

Still mourning her husband, Sophia was devastated by the news of Garrett's death. The army notified her that Garrett had $130 among his effects. She asked that the money be used to cover the costs of shipping his body home.

Garrett never had the chance to return to his father's grave and take him home to Michigan. In the months after the war, Henry Graveraet's remains were removed from where they lay near the Beverly house and reburied in Fredericksburg National Cemetery. Garrett's wooden grave marker had remained legible and in place, allowing a white gravestone with Henry's name to be erected on his final resting place.

Expressing his regret at her son's death, Joseph Finch returned the letter Sophia Graveraet had written to Garrett.

No 2

Armory Square Hospital
Ward 2 Washington D C
July 26" /64

Mrs Graveraet—

this letter came hear to the above named Hospital to your Son He Died the 25 of June & I Supposed His Body was Sent to you The Member of Congress from that Congressnal District was here to See Him Several times previous to His Deth & your Son Requested to be Sent Home

Your Son Suffered A good deal we done all we Could for Him it was imposible for him to live His Left arm was amputated near His Shoulder & Mortification Set in & Struck in to His Heart He was a good Soldier & was liked by all the men

in & talked with [   ] before He died [   ] have heard of His Death before this May God give you Grace to bear your afflictions Frient told me that His father was died & he was your only Son it is hard to part with Childern But if we put our trust in God we shall be able to Bear these afflictions Let us be prepared to Die So when the Lord Calls we can go & Meet our Friend that have gon before us

I Close by Sending my Respects to you hoping these lines may find you Enjoying good Helth

Joseph I Finch
asst ward master
of ward B

City Point, a few miles from downtown Petersburg, was the arrival point for ships loaded with supplies for the Union forces. It was also a departure point for steamboats carrying the wounded to hospitals in and around Washington, D.C.

[National Archives]

CHAPTER 11

EXPLOSION!

★ ★ ★

KNOWING THE IMPORTANCE of Petersburg as a transportation hub, the Confederates had dug a ring of defensive trenches around the city in 1863. Along this line they placed fifty-five gun batteries, with walls as high as forty feet. It was a formidable defense, and in 1864 Union forces spent the end of June and the first half of July building their own earthworks and trenches for protection during an ominous waiting game.

No one had any idea how long it would last or how long the soldiers would remain entrenched. The federal government sent a seemingly endless supply of food, ammunition, and other necessities so that its troops could sustain the siege. Yet the camps were uncomfortable, and the heat and oppressive humidity made sleeping difficult. Still, the threat of skirmishes demanded that the men on picket duty stay alert. Everyone was exhausted and edgy.

Illness plagued Company K's remaining soldiers. Thomas Smith was hospitalized, his eyes so inflamed with infection that he was almost blind. No one had privacy, and everyone talked about George Ashkebug's terrible cough. It annoyed them at night. It's possible he tried to treat it with traditional Anishinaabe medicine. Whenever the Anishinaabe men found the familiar plants, they would mash or boil them to treat such symptoms as fevers and coughs.

Amable Ketchebatis, Antoine Scott, and John Wabesis were among the handful of Anishinaabe soldiers who were still reasonably healthy. Lieutenant William Driggs had been discharged for disability, and Lieutenant William Randall, who had been in charge of the ambulance train, now commanded Company K. Colonel Charles DeLand returned to command the Sharpshooter regiment after his release from the hospital.

In the middle of July, the men of Company K saw ripening blackberries. Maybe they dreamed about how ripe berries scented the late-summer air back in Michigan. If they had been home, they and

This interconnected maze of trenches formed part of the Confederate line near Petersburg.

[Library of Congress]

When Company K soldiers were on duty, they spent many hours in the Union trench lines at Petersburg.

[Library of Congress]

their families would have been planning for berry-picking outings. Instead, the soldiers kept their eyes peeled for any berries that grew near camp. The sweet treats were a welcome change from army rations.

Union troops were entrenched in a line almost parallel with that of the Confederates. They dotted the line with forts made of earth, logs, and sandbags. In some areas, open fields separated the opposing lines. Soldiers in these places protected themselves with a network of trenches so deep that a standing man's head was below the ground's surface. These zigzagging "covered ways" were the only safe paths to the front. In other areas, ravines and woods partially screened the combatants from each other's view.

The Sharpshooters were encamped in the woods. Not far from a creek, they'd dug ditches and set up their tents within them.

Ketchebatis, Scott, and Wabesis often heard the howl of artillery shells fired from Union *and* Confederate batteries. Lieutenant Randall noticed that when the shells burst high overhead, the irregular pieces made "a peculiar whirring sound" as they fell. Sometimes chunks of shells landed among the men.

All the Sharpshooters were within range of enemy rifles. So many bullets landed on the ground, Randall noted, that the soldiers could "pick up a hat full of Minnie balls in 15 minutes."

THE MINE

Sniper fire was a particular problem where the Union and Confederate lines came closest together. At a salient fortification about half a mile from the Sharpshooters' encampment, less than five hundred feet separated the two armies.

Here, on the crest of a forty-foot slope, the Confederates had built a fort of logs, earth, and sandbags. Behind seven-foot-high earthworks, nearly three hundred men, mostly from South Carolina, hunkered within mazelike trenches. A battery of four cannons was trained on the Union line. Soldiers of the 48th Pennsylvania Infantry lay in their direct line of fire.

Like the First Michigan Sharpshooters, the 48th Pennsylvania was part of the Ninth Corps, but in the Second Division. Many of the Pennsylvanians were coal miners by trade, and one day their commander, Lieutenant Colonel Henry Pleasants, overheard them discussing the possibility of blowing up the fort by digging a mine shaft under it. Pleasants, a mining engineer himself, discussed the idea with two other engineers. All three believed the plan would work. An enthusiastic Pleasants sought approval up the chain of command:

first Potter, then Burnside, Meade, and Grant. Meade was reluctant, but Grant gave the go-ahead.

On June 25, the 48th Pennsylvania miners began their tunnel in a small ravine shielded from the enemy's sight. At first, only two men worked, one digging the soil, and the other removing it. More men helped as the tunnel lengthened. Secrecy was crucial. The soldiers poured the shoveled soil into sandbags, which were commonly used by both armies to reinforce forts and earthworks. When they ran out of sandbags, they scattered the dirt in the woods, covering it with leaves and shrubs.

Pleasants designed a ventilation system to provide the workers with fresh air. The miners shored the tunnel walls and ceiling with timbers. The project mushroomed until all four hundred of the regiment's soldiers were helping.

Each soldier carried on his shoulder two small kegs of gunpowder that had been stuffed into a sack. The soldiers placed the kegs into the mine's two side tunnels.

[Library of Congress]

Union soldiers from other regiments knew something was happening. Men from the 20th Michigan Infantry, positioned nearby, had started calling the rebel salient "the mined fort."

By July 17, the 511-foot-long tunnel ended directly beneath the Confederate fort. Outstretched arms could touch both walls at once. In most places, a man could not stand upright. At the tunnel's end, the men spent another week digging two shorter tunnels that extended to the right and left.

Meanwhile, Confederate officers suspected that Union soldiers were digging a tunnel. They dug countermines to intercept it. But they didn't dig deep enough to find the Pennsylvanians' mine.

By day's end on July 28, the miners had hauled eight thousand pounds of gunpowder into the two side tunnels. They surrounded the powder with sandbags to force the explosion straight up into the

Colonel Pleasants supervised the placement of the powder kegs in the tunnels.
[Library of Congress]

Soldiers in Edward Ferrero's Colored Troops were often used to build earthworks, guard arms and ammunition, and work in supply areas.

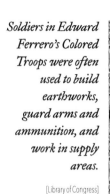

line of cannons. They spliced fuses from each side tunnel into a fuse that led toward the mine entrance. The job was done. Only one task remained: lighting the fuse.

THE PLAN

A week before the attack, General Burnside had set his plan: The Fourth Division of the Ninth Corps, the Colored Troops commanded by General Edward Ferrero, would lead the charge after the explosion.

During the past three months, the Ninth Corps's First, Second, and Third Divisions had fought several major battles. (The Sharpshooters were in the Third.) The men had been confined in trenches that were continually bombarded with shells and raked with musket fire. The soldiers were battle weary and thoroughly exhausted. For this reason, Burnside chose his Fourth Division. It had seen some battle action, but not a lot. For most of Grant's Virginia campaign, the Colored Troops had been assigned fatigue duty: They dug trenches, built earthworks, and guarded ammunition trains. Burnside knew that these men were his freshest soldiers. For a week, Fourth Division companies drilled and prepared to lead the charge.

Burnside planned for the Fourth Division to maneuver past the crater left by the explosion and storm Cemetery Hill, which rose behind the fort. His other three divisions would follow. At the same time, Union artillery would fire on other parts of the Confederate line, weakening it before more Union forces joined the assault. A successful forward push by all regiments should enable the Army of the Potomac to capture Petersburg, less than two miles away.

But on July 28, General Meade nixed Burnside's plan; the Fourth Division couldn't lead the attack. He later said, "They were a new division and had never been under fire, had never been tried, and as this was a operation which I knew beforehand was one requiring the very best troops, I thought it impolitic to trust it to a division of whose reliability we had no evidence." Meade ordered Burnside "to take one of his white divisions that he knew from long service could be relied upon." Burnside objected. They took the matter to General Grant, who sided with Meade.

On July 28, the Sharpshooters welcomed Sergeant Tom Kechittigo back to the trenches. His long hospital stay after being wounded at Spotsylvania was finally over. He was glad to be out. That same day, John Kedgnal and William Duvernay said goodbye to each other.

Kedgnal and his young relative had stuck together as often as possible. But now, perhaps knowing a major attack would soon be under way and the hospital would need extra help, Colonel DeLand had ordered Duvernay and five other Sharpshooters to report for duty at the field hospital, where they would serve as attendants. This placed them out of direct combat. Duvernay had no choice but to obey.

On July 29, the day before the attack, Burnside had to reorganize his battle plan. The commanders of the three white divisions drew lots to see which one would lead the charge. Brigadier General James Ledlie, who commanded the First Division, "won."

As dusk fell, William Randall had already moved the Sharpshooters closer to the front. He figured, "Everything indicates work (the work of death for the morrow)." The men of Company K sat among their Sharpshooter comrades. Randall and his men talked "of the coming storm." Some of them gave Randall messages to pass along to their friends in case they died. Faced with battle's dreadful uncertainty, everyone felt nervous and uneasy.

Within the rebel fort, the South Carolinians settled in for the night. The other regiments in their brigade were spaced to their right and left along the Confederate line.

JULY 30, 1864: THE CRATER

Tom Kechittigo, Amable Ketchebatis, Antoine Scott, and John Wabesis drank their morning coffee hours before daylight. Canteens and cartridge cases full, bayonets fixed, Company K waited less than half a mile from the army's front line. Not long after midnight, the First Division's troops had funneled into the two covered ways that channeled troops to the front. Those at the beginning of the line passed through the covered ways and spread into a ravine. But a logjam occurred in the covered way. The men stood quietly, packed together with no room to sit. By four o'clock, the Sharpshooters, knapsacks left behind, stood ready for DeLand's order to enter the covered way.

At 3:15 a.m., Colonel Pleasants and two assistants from the 48th Pennsylvania entered the main tunnel and lit the fuse. The sizzling flame snaked along. At the tunnel's end, the flame would split and branch into the side tunnels with the gunpowder. Pleasants estimated the flames should reach the gunpowder in about fifteen minutes. He and his men hurried out of the mine.

An hour passed.

No explosion.

The colonel's assistants volunteered to check the fuse. They discovered that it had burned out at a splice. They repaired the splice and relit the fuse.

Hints of dawn lightened the sky. Through the gray morning mist, the Sharpshooters saw the soldiers waiting in the ravine. Behind them, in the woods, soldiers felled trees to give newly placed artillery a clear shot at the enemy. Here and there, a Confederate bugle sounded reveille.

The tension was unbearable. If the sun cleared the horizon, all hope of surprise was gone.

And then, at 4:45, the Sharpshooters felt the earth tremble and jolt. Byron Cutcheon, colonel of the 20th Michigan, was stunned when the salient fort—and the hill beneath it—heaved and lifted: "Then a monstrous tongue of flame shot fully two hundred feet into the air,

After the gunpowder exploded in the mine, the fortifications on the hill above were blown apart. The top of the hill became a crater.

followed by a vast volume of white smoke. . . . [A] fountain of red earth rose to a great height, mingled with men and guns, timbers and planks, and every kind of debris, all ascending, spreading, whirling, scattering and falling with great concussions to the earth once more. It was a grand and terrible spectacle, such as none of us had ever seen. . . . Then a vast cloud of dust and smoke settled over the hill and hid it from view."

Within minutes, Ketchebatis, Scott, and Wabesis heard the crack of gunfire. Bugles sounded the charge. Soldiers yelled. Artillery boomed.

DeLand rallied the Sharpshooters and commanded: "Forward!"

DISASTER AND EXTRAORDINARY COURAGE

From that moment, nothing went as expected. The leading First Division soldiers who'd been in the ravine frantically tried to climb over the Union abatis, a long line of sharply pointed logs arranged to stop advancing rebels. But they couldn't clear the abatis fast enough. The rest of the division had little room to exit the covered ways, and this bottleneck of soldiers slowed the advance. The Sharpshooters had to wait.

Meanwhile, confusion reigned where the fort had been. In its place was a crater 170 feet long, 60 feet wide, and, in some places, about 20 feet deep. Huge chunks of clay studded the crater's steep walls. Broken equipment and bodies lined the bottom. More than three hundred South Carolinians were killed, wounded, or missing after the explosion. Soil from the blast rained down and buried some of them. The disoriented survivors sat stunned or stumbled about. Two of the battery's four cannons lay a hundred yards away near the Union line. The other two remained intact in a small undamaged area.

Ledlie's First Division finally pressed forward into the crater, creating space for the Sharpshooters. However, the First Division did not continue into the network of Confederate trenches or to Cemetery Hill beyond.

Freed from the covered way, the Sharpshooters and two other regiments of the Third Division charged across the field. They leaped into the rifle pits in front of the destroyed fort and captured the men inside.

Meanwhile, the Confederate forces had received reinforcements. Sharpshooter Amos Farling of Company G recalled what happened next: "We started on the double quick for the rebel's works, and were nearly there when we were met with such a murderous fire that we were forced to again seek shelter behind our works."

Soon after, the Sharpshooters again charged forward. As Colonel DeLand prepared to climb the earthworks, a shell struck the works in front of him. Rocks and dirt pelted him. Leverette Case helped his dazed and bleeding commander to the rear. Elmer Dicey, who had recruited John Kedgnal and William Duvernay into Company B, assumed command.

Tom Kechittigo shouted orders for his company to keep going. Antoine Scott, Amable Ketchebatis, John Wabesis, John Kedgnal, and the other Sharpshooters scaled the earthworks and entered the crater, which was tightly packed with Union soldiers. Chaos surrounded them. Confederate soldiers had regrouped and moved from their trenches. They quickly spread through the fields near the crater to regain their lost ground. Soon they stood on the crater's rim and relentlessly fired on the Union troops below. The men had nowhere to go. In a mad scramble for shelter, the Union troops broke ranks. Officers lost any sense of organization as the companies intermixed. Issuing orders was almost impossible.

The Sharpshooters occupied a position on the left side of the crater, within the fort's ruins, where they discovered the two intact rebel cannons partially buried in the debris. Two Sharpshooters and some artillerymen from the 14th New York quickly righted them and fired against the approaching Confederate forces.

Finally, about 8:00 a.m., Ferrero's Fourth Division of U.S. Colored Troops, four abreast and moving double quick, emerged from the covered way.

The layer of logs covered with soil protected those inside from incoming artillery fire. While General Ferrero's troops were under attack in the crater, he had joined General Ledlie in a bombproof shelter behind Union lines.

[Library of Congress]

Enemy fire raked them as they climbed over the earthworks. Several soldiers shouted to the rebels, "Surrender! Surrender or die!" Forging forward, they ran through the trenches and into the crater.

By then the crater had become a bloodbath. Soldiers from both armies reloaded and fired as fast as they could.

"Every man that was shot rolled down the steep sides to the bottom, and in places they were piled up four and five deep," noted Lieutenant Freeman Bowley, of the 30th U.S. Colored Infantry. Wounded men lay beneath the dead. Uninjured soldiers, desperately trying to survive, sheltered behind bodies as they reloaded their rifles. They grabbed rifles and cartridge boxes from the dead and wounded. General Willcox had already sent in ten thousand rounds of ammunition, but even that wasn't enough. Those without ammunition stabbed with bayonets.

By late morning, a brigade of Alabamans, marching at quick time, had entered the battlefield. Their orders were to take back the crater. Stopping to catch their breath, they heard officers inside the ruined fort encourage their soldiers to "remember Fort Pillow." On the ground outside, the Alabamans found abandoned rifles with fixed bayonets. They heaved them over the earthworks like spears, intending to harpoon the men inside. Before they attempted to climb into the fort, the rebels tested the Union fire by placing their hats on bayonets and raising them above the earthworks. As expected, the hats came down "riddled with bullets." Then Alabamans were ordered over, before the Union soldiers could reload.

As the day wore on, the Sharpshooters repulsed more attacks by the Confederate troops. Ketchebatis, Scott, and their Company K comrades met each advance with a show of "great coolness" under fire. They crawled "to the very top of the bank," and rising just above the top, "they would take a quick and fatal aim, then drop quickly down again." But Company K men used their dwindling ammunition wisely. Freeman Bowley, fighting nearby, noticed that they did "splendid service, but they could not be induced to keep up a fusilade; if a Johnny [rebel] showed himself he was their game, but they would waste no bullets."

Careful and deliberate as they were, death claimed some of Company K's men. Bowley saw four mortally wounded men of the company cluster and cover their faces with their shirts. Together, they sang what Bowley assumed was an Anishinaabe death song.

Alabaman John Featherston later wrote, "The slaughter was fearful. The dead were piled on each other. In one part of the fort I counted eight bodies deep."

By afternoon the heat and humidity were unbearable. Ketchebatis, Scott, Wabesis—everyone—longed for a drink. Canteens were already drained. Mouths were so dry that men had trouble talking. The wounded begged for water. But there wasn't any.

Rebel soldiers hadn't managed to silence the two cannons captured early in the day by the Sharpshooters, but lack of water did. Without water to swab the inside of the cannon barrels, the big guns were unusable. (The interior of a cannon barrel had to be swabbed with a sponge to remove any embers left from the previous shot. Loading gunpowder on top of embers would result in an explosion.)

As the battle raged, Confederate soldiers attacked black soldiers with a particular vengeance, even bayoneting men who were already wounded. As Featherston said, they were enraged by the sight of them and "at the whites for having them there." If the rebels saw any Anishinaabe soldiers and judged them by the color of their skin, they may have perceived them as Colored Troops and attacked them with the same fury.

White officers who commanded Colored Troops knew that the Confederate Congress had passed a resolution stating every white commissioned officer who commanded African American troops that had taken up "arms against the Confederate States . . . shall, if captured, be put to death, or otherwise punished at the discretion of the court." When captured, the officers feared harsher mistreatment by Confederate captors, so they often lied about which regiment they commanded.

A few of the white Union soldiers in the crater feared the rebels would turn their anger toward them, that they would be killed for fighting alongside African Americans. In a devastating act of betrayal, they turned and bayoneted their black comrades, hoping that they would be spared "Confederate vengeance."

The Alabamans' last charge overwhelmed Randall and his men. They had run out of ammunition, and the few remaining officers knew further fighting was pointless. Randall and those of his company still near him—including Amable Ketchebatis—became prisoners of war.

Antoine Scott, however, had eluded capture. By 2:30 p.m., the Union generals had ordered all troops to withdraw. General Meade had already left the area. Union soldiers still in the crater fled at the rebels' sudden, final assault. Tom Kechittigo ordered Company K to retreat. But Scott didn't join the running men. He "stood boldly up" on the crater's rim "and deliberately fired his [rifle] until the enemy was close upon him." His courageous act provided the cover that his friends and many other Union soldiers needed to reach the safety of the Union line. And even when Scott's capture seemed certain, he didn't surrender. Instead, "he ran the gauntlet of shot and shell and escaped."

While Scott was standing firm, William Randall and Amable Ketchebatis walked behind enemy lines. Their captors took everything from them. Randall surrendered his field glass, pocketbook (wallet), and knife—and even his hat. But he refused to give up his boots. He and Ketchebatis spent the night in a field about three miles from the crater. The next day, they were on the way to prison.

AFTERMATH

At a field hospital, William Duvernay aided the incoming wounded, who started arriving within an hour of the explosion. He gave them water, covered them with a blanket, and did whatever the medical staff asked him to do. The wounds he saw and the screams he heard in the hospital were beyond imagination.

A steady exchange of bullets throughout the night prevented both

After the battle was over, survivors gathered within their earthworks and regrouped. These African American soldiers fought gallantly, only to be horrified by the actions of some Union soldiers.

[Library of Congress]

sides from gathering their wounded from the battlefield. Midday, a Union soldier waving a white flag of truce approached the battle-field. Two officers followed him. Confederate officers responded with their own flag of truce. Both armies were given time to bury the dead and remove the wounded. Hundreds of wounded soldiers already filled the field hospitals. The additional wounded over-whelmed them.

William Duvernay must have warily approached every new hospital arrival, fearing he would find Kedgnal. How long would he wait before he received the news that Kedgnal was alive and safe?

The Battle of the Crater was a disaster for the Union army. Burnside's Ninth Corps suffered 3,828 casualties: 2,089 killed or wounded, 1,739 missing. Three men from Company K died in the crater; a fourth died of his wounds a short time later. Two men were missing. Amable Ketchebatis was one of them. The other, Jackson Narwegeshequabey, was never seen alive after the battle. Either he died on the field and was buried in an unmarked grave, or he died in a prison camp.

By August 5, Colonel DeLand had sent a letter to General John Robertson in Michigan, requesting more men. Company K's ranks were badly depleted. When the Virginia campaign began, the com-pany had 101 men, including officers. Of those, 83 were present for duty. (Those missing were on temporary leave or on sick call.) A few days after the Battle of the Crater, the total was 56, and only 10 of them were enlisted men present for duty. DeLand proudly stated, "In every action in the campaign the Indians have stood bravely up to the work & won the admiration of all." So far in the Virginia campaign, Company K had lost 16 killed, 25 wounded, and 17 missing in action. For DeLand, recruiting more Anishinaabe men was essential.

BAD NEWS, GOOD NEWS

Less than a week later, the U.S. War Department notified the governor of Michigan that he had the authority to recruit more Anishinaabe for DeLand's regiment. Fifteen Anishinaabe men responded to the call and enlisted in August and September. One of them was Potawatomi Thomas Wesaw—the baby who had been lost in the confusion twenty-three years earlier when soldiers drove his family from their home and refused to let his mother return for him.

Even as Wesaw and the other new recruits made their way to Virginia, the siege of Petersburg continued. Smarting from his defeat at the Crater, General Grant renewed attacks on Petersburg railroads. This kept Lee's forces in constant motion, as they shifted right and left to defend the vital connections.

At the end of August, the Sharpshooters were a few miles south of Petersburg, at Ream's Station. Yet again, William Duvernay drummed as he and his comrades marched into battle. The Sharpshooters pried up the iron tracks of the Weldon Railroad and hacked apart the wooden ties. They burned the ties in bonfires and threw sections of track on top. With the iron heated, they hammered and twisted it out of shape to prevent its reuse. Confederate troops raced to the railroad. Company K's Samuel Chatfield was killed during the two-day battle.

Another battle, near Ream's Station, was fought on August 25. The next day, William Duvernay received very upsetting news: John Kedgnal was missing.

In September, Antoine Scott was promoted to sergeant, and Company K welcomed a new lieutenant, James DeLand, the younger brother of the regiment's colonel. But later that month, Company K was discouraged when three Anishinaabe soldiers, new Lieutenant Kirk Noyes, and Colonel DeLand were wounded in battle on a farm owned by the Peebles family. Colonel DeLand was captured and

During the months-long siege of Petersburg, Company K soldiers lived in a tent camp similar to this one.

[Library of Congress]

taken prisoner. The Sharpshooters were relieved to learn that he had not only survived but also been exchanged in only seven days. Still, the war was over for Colonel DeLand. By year's end, the First Michigan Sharpshooters had a new commander, Captain Asahel W. Nichols, who had formerly been captain of Company F.

In October, the men of Company K congratulated Thomas Smith on his promotion to sergeant and were glad when Louis Genereau rejoined the company. After Genereau's amazing escape from the barn fire, his leg had hurt even worse. The fractures had not completely healed, and he'd been furloughed to Michigan for additional recuperation. While home, he married Louisa, John Kedgnal's sister. Doctors finally cleared him for return to duty in November 1864. His friends welcomed him back, but they couldn't help noticing that he limped and often needed a cane.

November brought the excitement of a presidential election. Abraham Lincoln was running for reelection; his opponent was George McClellan, one of Lincoln's former generals. When McClellan commanded the Union troops, he had been heavily criticized for not pursuing the enemy. One soldier, writing after the 1862 battle at Antietam, noted that his regiment was eager to push after the rebels but that their generals would not permit them to do so "for fear We would kill some boddy & End the war." By Election Day, people just wanted the war over, and with Grant's determined campaign, Lincoln seemed equally committed.

Now home in Michigan, Joseph Wakazoo was ready to vote. Back in May, when he was wounded at Spotsylvania, he had no idea that he would spend the next six months in several different hospitals. In November, the hospital in Alexandria sent him home, he believed, "to vote in the presidential election." The army had actually sent Wakazoo home for treatment, but for Wakazoo, being sent to Michigan and voting in the presidential election were forever entwined in his memory. Wakazoo implied that he intended to vote in 1864; there is no reason to think he didn't.

In the Union army, many regiments, including the First Michigan Sharpshooters, offered ballot boxes in camp so that soldiers could vote. Voting was by secret ballot, and no one knew whom anybody voted for, or even if the eligible Anishinaabe soldiers participated. When the regiment's votes were tallied, Lincoln beat McClellan by a three-to-one margin. Lincoln handily won nationally as well and was reelected president.

While the remaining Sharpshooters struggled through several late-summer and autumn battles, their captured Anishinaabe comrades struggled to survive a different sort of hell.

Thousands of captured Union soldiers walked through the gateway into Andersonville. Thousands of them died within its walls.

[Library of Congress]

CHAPTER 12

The Gates *of* **HELL**

★ ★ ★

DURING THE WAR'S EARLY YEARS, prisoners were regularly paroled. A prisoner was released on the condition that he not return to his regiment until a soldier from the opposing army had also been paroled. At that point, the two prisoners were considered "exchanged" and could return to their regiments. Unfortunately, by the time Company K's captured were imprisoned, General Grant had stopped all prisoner exchanges. It was the only way Grant could prevent released Confederate prisoners from returning to the ranks and rejoining the fight. Exchanging prisoners, he believed, would simply result in a war of extermination. Sadly, the change in policy left Union prisoners stranded in Southern prison camps.

By the end of 1863, captured Union soldiers had filled the Confederacy's prison camps beyond the bursting point. Buildings of all kinds—former warehouses, even hospitals—housed prisoners. In an isolated area of Georgia, construction was under way for a new prison that would be 1,620 feet long by 779 feet wide. Enslaved African Americans enclosed the area with a fifteen-foot palisade wall made of pine logs. The men who designed the prison estimated it could hold up to ten thousand men. Officially named Camp Sumter, the prison soon became known as Andersonville, after the tiny town nearby.

Prisoners began arriving in February 1864. Between April 9 and 12, three hundred of them died. Almost daily, new prisoners—"fresh fish" as they were called—funneled into Andersonville through its tall, narrow gates. More than twelve hundred prisoners arrived on June 27. By then, the stockade walls enclosed twenty-five thousand prisoners. By August, more than thirty-two thousand prisoners were crowded together inside the prison, three times the camp's intended population.

UNEXPECTED DANGER

More than fifty First Michigan Sharpshooters—fifteen of them from Company K—arrived at Andersonville in June. Almost certainly they had heard horror stories about Confederate prison camps. At Camp Douglas they had seen how prisoners sickened and died from disease, poor food rations, and dirty conditions. But they didn't know about one particular threat at Andersonville.

A large number of unscrupulous Union soldiers had banded together in a gang known as the Raiders. They ruthlessly preyed on their fellow prisoners. On June 21, prisoner Henry Tisdale wrote in his diary, "Raiders about last night robbing the newly arrived prisoners. Their doings show phases of humanity hard to believe possible." Six days later, prisoner John Ransom wrote in his dairy, "Raiders going on

A small group of prisoners in the foreground are getting water from the stream that ran through Andersonville prison. The tents in the background, most made with blankets, offered minimal shelter from the weather.

worse than ever before. . . . Something must be done, and that quickly. . . . Any moment fifty or a hundred of them are liable to pounce upon our mess, knock right and left and take the very clothing off our backs. No one is safe from them. It is hoped that the more peaceable sort will rise in their might and put them down."

When Company K's "fresh fish" arrived at Andersonville, they didn't give the prison guards the few possessions—watches, rings, or other jewelry—that they still had with them. On the second night after their arrival, the Raiders attempted to rob them. Payson Wolf, Amos Ashkebugnekay, Louis Miskoguon, Louis Marks, and their comrades didn't let the Raiders intimidate them. As fellow

Sharpshooter C. D. Bibbins, from Company E, later recalled, "The Indians, back to back in a bunch, cut and slashed the 'raiders' until they were obliged to quit the fight." The Anishinaabek believed that fighting in a circle created power. The back of every man who was part of the circle was protected. This tactic wouldn't have been effective on a battlefield, since Confederate soldiers would have simply encircled and shot them. But in close quarters, where fists, clubs, and knives were used, it made sense. Strong and fearless, Company K inspired others to resist the Raiders too.

There was at least one other American Indian at Andersonville. John Ransom repeatedly mentions Battese, an "Indian." Battese was from Minnesota, so he may have been Ojibwe. While in prison, he saved Ransom's life more than once. In combating the Raiders, Ransom wrote, "Battese has called his Indian friends all together, and probably a hundred of us are banded together for self protection." Battese's friends were the soldiers of Company K.

Finally, the prisoners demanded that Henry Wirz, the prison commander, do something. On June 28, Confederate guards armed with fixed bayonets arrested some of the Raiders. With this support, prisoners spoke up and pointed out additional members of the gang. Soon "fifty or more were taken to the guard house." Those reported to be the most vicious were kept in jail cells, and the rest were returned to the stockade. Their fellow prisoners were determined to protect themselves and ready to fight. Holding clubs and sticks, they organized a gauntlet and made the Raiders run it. They confiscated everything from the Raiders' tents, "knives, billies [short clubs], and other murderous weapons, watches by the dozens and trinkets of various kinds . . . many of which were identified by their owners." Rumors circulated that two to three thousand dollars had also been found in the Raiders' possession.

Still the Raiders persisted. On July 3, 1864, a huge fight broke out in the camp after they tried to rob yet another group of fresh fish. This time the Raiders won. Again the camp complained to Wirz, who declared he would stop all food until the Raider leaders were arrested and brought to trial. Hundreds of prisoners formed an impromptu police force. Fierce rounds of fighting continued throughout the afternoon. Some of the Raiders were killed. Their leaders and many more were arrested, which brought forth great cheers. By the morning of July 4, the backbone of the Raiders had been broken.

On July 5, Union soldiers held a trial for the arrested men. Many received punishments that included being put in stocks or hung up by their thumbs. But six men—the worst offenders—were sentenced to death for murder. The morning of July 11, a gallows was built near the prison gate. By noon, the six condemned men, hanged by the neck, were dead.

DISEASE

Even though the Raiders had been conquered, Company K's problems were just beginning. There were no shelters built for the prisoners. After heavy rains, the men would have to stand in water and sleep in the mud. Other times, relentless sun scorched them.

Prisoners created their own makeshift shelters by stitching together two blankets. A man who gave up his blanket for shelter shared the blanket of a tent mate who still had one. Payson Wolf had no blanket at all. To keep warm at night, he and his comrades slept tightly against one another, sharing body warmth. Few men had shoes.

Clothes were worn and patched until the patches had patches. Sometimes the only way a man could keep himself clothed was to strip the pants or shirt from the dead. Lack of shelter and protective clothing weakened men's bodies and made them more susceptible to disease. And William Newton had already had a nasty cough by the time he reached Andersonville.

Bugs were everywhere—maggots in the food, flies around the latrines, lice on the men. "Lice by the fourteen hundred thousand million infest Andersonville," John Ransom estimated. They scurried through every man's hair. They crawled beneath his clothes. Females laid eggs on strands of hair and in the seams of shirts and trousers, which became incubators for developing baby lice. Itchy red spots dotted the men's skin. Prisoners even devised a louse game. A man would reach inside his clothing, grab some lice, and then pull out his hand, asking "Odd or even?" The lice were counted, and the man who guessed correctly won. Like every man at Andersonville, Louis Miskoguon and Jacko Penaiswanquot spent hours picking lice from their clothes and bodies.

A foul stream was the only source of water in the camp. Upstream from the prison walls, Confederate soldiers bathed and washed their clothes in it. Their horses and mules drank from it. Dirty dishes, kettles, and pans soaked in the stream. Then the water flowed into the camp, where it was further fouled by the filthy conditions. Other than rainwater, there really weren't other options. Drinking filthy water led to disease.

Food rations were equally poor. Joseph Gibson and William Mixinasaw received no more than a small amount of cornmeal or beans and a few ounces of raw beef or bacon each day. Sometimes

Men crowded around when rations were distributed. Meager though the rations were, no one refused them.

they received boiled rice crawling with maggots, but hungry men ate it anyway. Often the men were without food for two, three, or four days in a row. Payson Wolf saw men grow so weak with starvation that when they did get food, their stomachs couldn't handle it. They would vomit up beans as soon as they were swallowed. And he saw men so hungry that they rushed forward and ate the vomit.

A man from the town of Andersonville was permitted to enter the camp and sell food and other provisions to the prisoners. But unless they received money from family or friends, prisoners seldom had any to buy the overpriced items. Fruit and vegetables were as rare as gold. Poor nutrition led to more disease.

More than a hundred men died each day, their corpses adding to the appalling conditions. "Dead bodies lay around all day in the broiling sun, by the dozen and even hundreds, and we must suffer and live in this atmosphere. It's too horrible for me to describe in fitting language," John Ransom lamented. The tall palisade walls and the trees beyond the prison prevented freshening breezes from blowing away the stench. "We are obliged to breathe and live in it."

During the day, prisoners carried the bodies of their dead comrades to the prison's south gate, where they placed them in a line. At four o'clock each day, a wagon pulled by a team of four to six mules rolled up to the

These men have just completed digging one of Andersonville's burial trenches. The remains of seven men from Company K, including Jacko Penaiswanquot, William Mixinasaw, and Joseph Gibson, were buried in a trench like this. Today, the graves are marked with white headstones.

[Library of Congress]

gate. After receiving a load of twenty to thirty bodies, the wagon moved off to the prison cemetery about a quarter mile away. The bodies were buried in shallow trenches, one hundred in each trench.

By mid-July, many of the Anishinaabe prisoners were sick. Amos Ashkebugnekay's gums hurt, and his lower legs began swelling. Soon he was unable to walk and was in great pain. In his time at the prison, Ashkebugnekay had become friends with soldier Edgar Baker, from Illinois. Ashkebugnekay's new friend and his friends from Company K took turns carrying him to the creek, where they would wash him and carry him back to his blanket shelter. William Newton bathed Ashkebugnekay's legs with water three times a day, trying to reduce the swelling.

Joseph Gibson ached all over and couldn't eat. Louis Miskoguon had seen the prison guards shove him around, but starvation and the constant exposure to weather extremes also weakened him. Perhaps Jacko Penaiswanquot, who had many years' experience as a healer back home in Michigan, tried to treat Gibson with traditional Anishinaabe medicine. He and Battese, the Minnesotan, made the medicines from roots they obtained in and around the camp. Sadly, Gibson did not improve. Unable to help, Louis Miskoguon, who was also sick by that time, could only watch his friend die. On September 3, Gibson's comrades placed his body in the line at the south gate.

Louis Marks's gums bled, and sores on his skin wouldn't heal. He was admitted to the prison hospital in mid-October. By October 20, Amos Ashkebugnekay's legs had swollen so badly that William Newton carried him to the hospital. Twice he visited to see how

Relics of Andersonville Prison from the collection brought from there by Miss Clara Barton and Dorence Atwater, Aug., 1865, and photographed by Brady & Co. for the great National Fair.
Washington, June, 1866.

Brady & Co.   *Washington.*

During the war, Clara Barton risked her life on battlefields to nurse wounded and sick soldiers, who nicknamed her "The Angel of the Battlefield." Authorities at Andersonville asked a prisoner, Dorence Atwater, to keep an official list of the Union prisoners who died in the camp. Certain that the Confederates would not give the federal government the list, Atwater secretly made a copy, which he smuggled out of the prison. After the war ended, the copy was given to the federal government and used by Barton, Atwater, and others to mark graves in the prison cemetery. The "Anderson Dead Line" sign in the photo refers to a line within the perimeter of a military prison's wall. If a prisoner approached the wall and crossed the deadline, he was shot. The deadline was commonly used in Civil War prison camps.

[Library of Congress]

Ashkebugnekay fared. The medicines the nurse gave him seemed to help.

While in prison, Ashkebugnekay became friendly with George Miller. The two made an agreement. If Miller would help feed and care for him, as soon as the weather permitted and they were strong enough to swim across rivers, they would escape together and head north.

William Mixinasaw also developed symptoms similar to those of Marks and Ashkebugnekay. His gums hurt and bled, and several of his teeth had fallen out. As a result of the terrible prison diet, all three men suffered from scurvy, a disease caused by a lack of vitamin C.

In 1863, Mixinasaw had testified in court against a white man. Months later, he courageously faced enemy fire. But he lacked what was necessary to overcome scurvy—fruit and vegetables. Some onions or sweet potatoes, a pickle, even a few teaspoons of vinegar could have forestalled the disease. But neither he nor his friends had them. Mixinasaw died on October 26. His comrades Adam Sawbequom and James Hamlin died from scurvy that month too.

Diarrhea tormented Payson Wolf for two weeks after he arrived at Andersonville. Just when he got that under control, his joints ached. Like many prisoners without shelter, Wolf was exposed to rain many times. Four-inch-deep puddles often covered the ground where he slept. The only way he could keep most of his body off the wet ground at night was to lie on his left side. As a result, his left arm grew weak. The joints of his arms and legs swelled to a monstrous size. He could no longer use his left arm or either leg with any degree of freedom. He lost some fingernails, and a sore on the index finger of his left hand wouldn't heal. He worried that gangrene would set in, which would mean amputation. By then, his gums had been bleeding for some time and he had lost several teeth. He knew he was ill with scurvy. And his good friend Louis Miskoguon had been diagnosed with scurvy too.

Meanwhile, Mary Jane Wolf knew nothing of her husband's whereabouts. In July, the family had received a letter from one of Wolf's Company K comrades, who informed them of Wolf's capture. But since then—silence. If Wolf, a faithful letter writer, mailed any letters from Andersonville, they never arrived. The wives, mothers, and children waiting at home had no idea if their loved ones were dead or alive.

OTHER HELLS

Andersonville was not the only Confederate prison where a Company K soldier was imprisoned.

In August, news about the Battle of the Crater would have found its way to northern Michigan. Lizette Ketchebatis probably heard that her husband, Amable, was missing in action. No one knew his whereabouts. She and Amable had been married for seventeen years. He was a good husband, and Lizette knew he would return home if he could. But as summer ended, all she could do was wait.

Ketchebatis had survived the bloodbath at the Crater, but he'd been captured and shipped to prison. Inside a railroad car tightly packed with prisoners, Ketchebatis jostled for space as he headed for Lynchburg, Virginia. From there he "marched the sixty-five miles over beaten roads and shallow creeks to Danville." The town, located a few miles shy of the North Carolina border, had several empty warehouses that had been converted into Danville Prison.

By that time in the war, prisoners described supper as "a meal of corn and cob ground together from which the careful cook could obtain a johnny-cake four inches long and two inches wide." One prisoner found "rat dung in the rice, pea bugs in the peas and worms in the cabbage soup." Broth was made with river water. Flies buzzed and lice crawled everywhere; most prisoners suffered from diarrhea and scurvy.

Danville's Building 3 housed captured African American soldiers. Except for some wooden boxes, there was no furniture. At one point, the building contained about two hundred men. Some of them died. Others were sent back to their former slave masters or taken out to build earthworks for the Confederate army. By mid-October, only sixty-four men remained in Building 3. They were all men who belonged to Colored Troops.

Before Ketchebatis arrived at Danville, there had been a number of escape attempts. In response, the guards did not allow prisoners to appear at the windows. They shot some of them who did.

In the autumn, Lizette received a letter, in English, from Ketchebatis. Since her husband could not write in English, she knew that he must have asked another prisoner to write it for him. In his letter, dated August 5, he told her, "i am a prisnor and i am well. . . . i am in a good room and well fed and i hope that my 4 little children are well. Dear wife i would like to be with you but i cant very well leave this good place." He told her that she could send him mail at the prison and just address the letter to his building. Since the guards considered Ketchebatis "colored," they imprisoned him in Building 3.

Ketchebatis knew Lizette as well as she knew him. Everything he wrote was meant to ease her worries. In truth, there was nothing good about the place where he was.

At the end of October, Ketchebatis walked out of Building 3. He and his fellow prisoners entered their new jail: Building 6, a place worse than their former quarters, which would now house white officers.

One of the officers who moved into Building 3 collected information about the deaths in Danville Prison that winter. Between November 1864 and January 24, 1865, a total of 375 men died. "The negro soldiers suffered most," the officer found. "There were sixty-four of them living in prison when we reached Danville, October 20, 1864. Fifty-seven of them were dead on the 12th of February, '65, when I saw and talked with the seven survivors." The officer did not mention the names of the seven men who still lived.

No army representatives offered Lizette specific information on her husband's whereabouts. Her hopes for Amable's survival were dashed when she spoke with Louis Shomin, a member of Company K. He told her that he "heard a white soldier" from the First Michigan Sharpshooters say that he and Amable had been captured after the explosion at the Crater and that her husband had died in prison camp on the first day of March 1865. Recent investigations of prison hospital records and at Danville National Cemetery indicate that Ketchebatis died in late February. That means Amable Ketchebatis must have been one of the seven survivors who had spoken with the white officer.

At the end of July, drummer William Duvernay was thankful in one way: His relative John Kedgnal had survived the Crater. But by the end of August, Duvernay was worried again. Kedgnal had been missing since the battle near Ream's Station on August 25. Duvernay didn't want to believe Kedgnal had deserted or, even worse, died.

It would have been difficult for anyone to pinpoint Kedgnal's whereabouts. After his capture at Ream's Station, Kedgnal found himself in a whirlwind of prison transfers that swept him from overcrowded Libby Prison, in Richmond, to Belle Island Prison, which was equally overcrowded, and finally to Salisbury Prison, in North Carolina.

During the early months of the war, few prisoners occupied Salisbury Prison, an old cotton factory. In the early spring of 1862, it was well stocked with provisions. There was plenty of space—enough that prisoners could play baseball every day, weather permitting. Its four-story brick building and the wooden buildings that surrounded it decently housed two thousand men.

Conditions deteriorated rapidly in October 1864. Prisoners arrived by the hundreds; Kedgnal was one of them. He had no blanket, no overcoat, and no shoes. At first, there was no shelter for the men outside. Kedgnal wasn't even given straw to place beneath him on the ground. When it rained, he had to lie in the mud. Union officers estimated how severe the weather had been the previous night by counting the number of men who lay dead in the prison yard. Eventually, the Confederate army delivered tents, but only enough to shelter about twenty-five hundred men. By that time, there were nearly eight thousand prisoners in the camp.

Food rations were as bad as those at Andersonville and Danville. Kedgnal's health failed; he lost weight. Doctors at the prison hospital treated him when he suffered bloody diarrhea. The classic signs of scurvy appeared: His gums ached; several teeth loosened and fell out; scabs formed on his arms and legs. Kedgnal's mother, Eliza, was an experienced Anishinaabe healer who treated patients with medicines she made from various roots and plants. When Kedgnal got a fever or coughed, he remembered the medicine his mother made. He boiled oak bark, perhaps with another ingredient, and made the same medicine that Eliza used when she treated her patients with similar ailments.

One day, the guards told Kedgnal and a group of prisoners to line up near the prison's main gate. They needed a certain number of men for a job and ordered the prisoners to count off. Kedgnal's position in line was immediately behind the last man required, so he wouldn't be needed. The guard shooed the remaining prisoners away. Suddenly, without reason or warning, the guard slammed Kedgnal in the back with the butt of his rifle. In pain, Kedgnal collapsed and had to be carried away on a stretcher. He never knew why he'd been assaulted.

At the beginning of the war, Salisbury Prison was a decent prison camp. Prisoners even had room to play baseball games. By the time John Kedgnal arrived, it was vastly overcrowded and filthy.

[Library of Congress]

For a while, the only bright spot in Kedgnal's life at Salisbury was the company of his uncle Isaac Duvernay, who had belonged to another regiment. Sadly, it wasn't long before his uncle sickened and died.

THE GATES OPEN

For some prisoners, hope was on the horizon. At Andersonville, the prison commander Henry Wirz began transferring groups of prisoners to other camps in early September. No one from Company K was included among the first men transferred, but William Newton went to Camp Lawton, near Millen, Georgia, in late October or early November. The prison, which was in a less remote location than Andersonville, had a good stream whose water ran fresh. Prisoners received two meals a day—of cornmeal and fresh beef—and were given molasses, a sugar syrup that some nineteenth-century doctors believed would ease the effects of scurvy and starvation. At night the

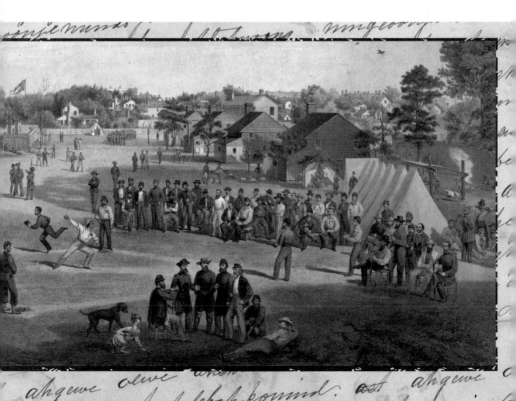

Copied from Confederate Prisoners of War Records, this memo
contains details of John Kedgnal's imprisonment and parole.

[National Archives]

prisoners slept in shanties. Compared to Andersonville, Millen was luxurious. Camp rumors hinted that arriving at Millen was the first step toward parole. Newton hoped to be on his way north soon.

The third week in November, walking on aching legs, Payson Wolf and Louis Marks made it to the train stop outside the Andersonville prison gate. They soon arrived at Millen. Wolf hated leaving Miskoguon behind, but he had no choice: Neither Miskoguon nor Ashkebugnekay was strong enough to walk to the train. Guards didn't let prisoners who couldn't walk leave Andersonville.

On December 15, Mary Jane Wolf received a letter from Payson. Dated two weeks earlier, the letter told her that Payson was well and at Camp Parole, in Maryland. He expected to get a furlough to visit home soon. She and the children were overjoyed. His prayers answered, the Reverend George Smith, Wolf's father-in-law, confided in his diary: "We feared we should never hear of him again." Winter had suddenly become a lot brighter.

Wolf also sent a letter to a good friend in Northport. It contained somber news. He wrote that Jacko Penaiswanquot had died, and so had Adam Sawbequom. He included news about Louis Miskoguon. The last time he'd seen him, Louis was very sick. Wolf feared he was probably dead.

When the news reached Smith, he was saddened. He'd spent many happy times with Louis; his wife, Susan; and their children. And Jacko Penaiswanquot's family had experienced especially hard times since Jacko had enlisted. Mary Penaiswanquot had spoken with Smith about it, and he made sure that friends and neighbors helped her and the children. Now he prepared to comfort them, as he had Charles Allen's family.

On December 28, Mary Jane Wolf and her children received a late Christmas present: Payson Wolf arrived home. But sorrow edged their joy as they grieved with other members of the Northport community. As he told Smith about prison, Wolf would surely have mentioned that William Mixinasaw had died. The Mixinasaws were members of Smith's congregation. Nine years earlier, William and his wife, Mary, had pledged their wedding vows in front of Smith. The Wolf and Smith families certainly comforted Mary Mixinasaw, William's widow. Smith assured Mary Mixinasaw that he would help her with papers that she needed to send the government.

And everyone worried about Louis Miskoguon. Susan Miskoguon and her three children could only hope that Payson Wolf's fears that Miskoguon may have died were wrong.

Head-Quarters Military Division of the Mississippi,

In the Field 186

Savannah, Dec 22 1864

To his Excellency,

    President Lincoln,

I beg to present you as a Christmas Gift the City of Savannah, with (150) *one hundred and fifty* heavy guns and plenty of ammunition, & also about (25000) *twenty five thousand* bales of cotton

        W. T. Sherman
        Maj Genl

For Abraham Lincoln, General Sherman's gift was unusual, but much appreciated. Sherman's telegram to Lincoln stated: "To his Excellency, President Lincoln, I beg to present you as a Christmas Gift the City of Savannah, with 150 heavy guns and plenty of ammunition and also about 25,000 bales of cotton."

[National Archives]

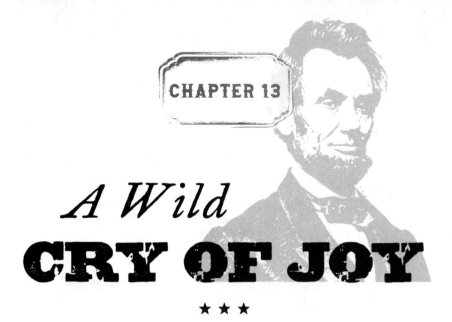

CHAPTER 13

A Wild
CRY OF JOY

★ ★ ★

ONE OF ABRAHAM LINCOLN'S best Christmas gifts of 1864 came from General William Tecumseh Sherman. His troops had stormed across Georgia in a relentless march toward the sea, bringing the Confederate States of America closer to its defeat.

Company K started 1865 entrenched outside Petersburg. By then, the Sharpshooters had been in Petersburg for almost seven months. Although Union army successes elsewhere showed signs that the Confederacy was crumbling—General Sherman's capture of Atlanta, for example—Grant's siege of Petersburg seemed as if it might go on forever.

As 1864 had come to a close, the Sharpshooters had left a reasonably comfortable, battle-quiet encampment about seven miles south of Petersburg. Their new position was along the edge of a ravine, sandwiched between a Union artillery battery across the ravine and the Union's Fort McGilvery. Not more than a quarter of a mile away, two Confederate artillery batteries, cannons aimed and ready, stood between the Sharpshooters and downtown Petersburg. As the Sharpshooters faced the city, the Crater was only a mile to their left.

The Sharpshooters' new position was directly in the line of rebel fire, so Company K picked up shovels and got to work. They reinforced trenches, fortified earthworks, and built bombproofs, shelters that provided protection from cannon fire. Scott, Kechittigo, and the others would have completed a bombproof by shoveling

Occasionally, humor found its way into camp. While at Petersburg, a young man, possibly a relative, came to visit Lieutenant James DeLand. The young artist drew a sketch of DeLand formally presenting him with a pair of white socks, as Company K soldiers (probably chuckling) stood and watched.

[DeLand Family Papers, Bentley Historical Library, University of Michigan]

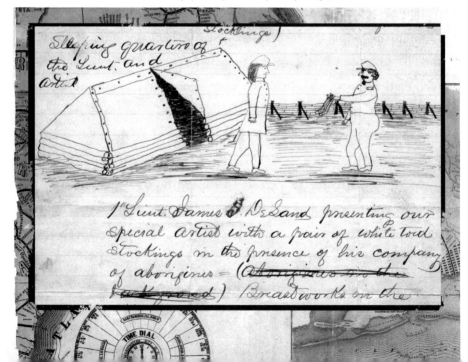

The restaurant sign hung on this bombproof is another touch of soldierly humor that helped relieved tedious days during the long siege of Petersburg.

[Library of Congress]

several feet of soil on top of the roof. It wasn't perfect protection from enemy artillery shells, but it was a lot safer than a tent or an open trench.

In January 1865, the Sharpshooters had a good surprise: Adjutant Buckbee returned. After his capture on June 17 near the Shand house, he'd remained a prisoner until November. Twice during his imprisonment, he'd escaped and been recaptured. But he didn't give up. Aided by African Americans, Buckbee succeeded in his third escape attempt. After a month's furlough in Michigan, he was back on duty at Petersburg and had been promoted to major.

In February, back in Michigan, wives, parents, and children were saying goodbye as more soldiers headed off to join Company K. New recruit John Jacko bid farewell to his mother, Mary Penaiswanquot,

Confederate soldiers captured Fort Stedman before dawn. The Sharpshooters, positioned nearby, had no idea what had happened until cannons in the fort fired on them.

[Library of Congress]

still mourning the loss of her husband. He, along with his brothers, used his father's first name as his last name. Aaron Sahgahnahquato, a close friend of Charles Allen and his family, also headed off, having enlisted the same day as John Jacko.

With his furlough over, Payson Wolf hugged Mary Jane goodbye and left for Camp Parole, in Annapolis, Maryland, where he would wait for news that he too could join his comrades in Company K.

A SURPRISE ATTACK

By the end of March, General Grant's siege of Petersburg seemed to be working. Union troops some miles to the west and north of Petersburg had periodically engaged Confederate forces in skirmishes.

This had prevented them from coming to General Lee's aid in Petersburg. Lee's army had nearly run out of supplies and resources. He knew that if he couldn't overcome the siege, he would probably have to surrender. In a last effort to break Grant's stranglehold, he ordered a surprise attack on Fort Stedman, near the end of the Union line. If his forces captured the fort, he could funnel many hundreds of his soldiers through the Union's ruptured line and end the siege.

On March 25, just before dawn, about three hundred Confederate soldiers captured Union soldiers who were on picket duty in front of the fort. The surprised Union soldiers had no time to fire more than a few shots—nothing more than the number of shots that were routinely heard during any given night. Continuing forward, the Confederates axed through the fort's protective line of chevaux-de-frise. These portable log barriers, usually chained together to prevent dismantling, had sharply pointed ends that made them impossible to

In their successful attack on Fort Stedman, Confederate soldiers moved chevaux-de-frise like these out of their way.

[Library of Congress]

climb. With the chevaux-de-frise out of their way, the rebels climbed the earthworks and entered Fort Stedman. During the fight that followed, the Confederates took command of the fort.

The Sharpshooters, who were several hundred yards to the right of Fort Stedman, had no idea what had occurred. When cannons from inside the fort fired at the Union troops, Major Buckbee first thought that "the soldiers in the fort had gone crazy." As the artillery barrage continued, he realized the fort must have been captured. Under orders, Buckbee advanced two companies of his Sharpshooters to the bottom of the hill near the fort to see if the Confederates had broken the Union line. If enemy soldiers were present, Buckbee and his men were to hold their advanced position. Lieutenant James DeLand, in command of Companies I and K, hurried his men through the dark woods. They settled behind a railroad embankment.

On horseback, Buckbee rode away to get additional orders. Within moments, he encountered a column of soldiers heading toward Companies I and K. In the dark, he mistook them for captured prisoners, or even Union troops. But when one called out to shoot that Yankee on the horse, he realized they were the enemy.

Buckbee wheeled his horse around, swung his hat in the air, and shouted to Company K. Immediately, they rallied to his aid. The formidable rebel battle cry sent chills up the spines of many Union soldiers. But according to Buckbee, Company K "set up a yell that would have frightened Old Nick [the devil] himself and went straight at the Rebs on the run."

The fight around Fort Stedman lasted about four hours. Before morning's end, Companies I and K had captured four rebel officers and fifty enlisted men, and Union troops had regained Fort Stedman.

In all, Buckbee noted, Confederate casualties were "about 2,000 prisoners, a good many wounded, and plenty of dead." From the condition and comments of rebel soldiers who'd surrendered voluntarily, the Sharpshooters sensed that Lee's army couldn't hold out much longer.

On-and-off fighting continued for the next few days, as Grant's army began a major offensive against Lee's forces. During a heavy skirmish on March 29, a piece of shrapnel hit Thomas Wesaw, one of Company K's newest soldiers, on his cheek just below his left eye. Field doctors behind the Union line kept him for almost a week before they sent him to the larger hospital at City Point, about nine miles east of Petersburg.

A DISASTROUS, MIRACULOUS FALL

Grant's commanders assured him that victory was within grasp. One final, relentless push, and Lee's army would fall.

Company K knew something was on the horizon. At ten o'clock the night of April 1, Colonel Ralph Ely, in command of the Second Brigade, ordered Major Buckbee to place his men on picket at the front of the Union line. Minutes after they had dug into position, a hail of cannonballs and other exploding shells fired by Union artillery bombarded the rebel line. Lying inside their shallow trench, Company K shielded themselves from the rain of fire as best they could. After a few hours, they were recalled for a break and some coffee. But by 4:00 a.m. on April 2, they had returned to the front. This time they had new orders: "Take the enemy's line."

Two parallel lines of chevaux-de-frise stretched between Company K and the rebel line. Preliminary scouts examined the sharp works and discovered that the sections had not been chained together. In the predawn darkness, an advance guard of Union soldiers tugged the chevaux-de-frise, pivoting them so they were perpendicular to the Union line. Turned this way, the sections had gaps that opened straight to the Confederate earthworks.

When Buckbee and James DeLand issued the command to charge forward, everyone knew they faced almost certain death. Even though it was still dark, once the enemy heard them coming, nothing would shield Company K from the rebels' direct fire. Antoine Scott, Tom Kechittigo, Thomas Smith, and their comrades summoned courage and ran toward the rebel works. Unbeknownst to any of the Sharpshooters, there was a fairly deep ditch only a few feet behind

The night of April 1, 1865, the Sharpshooters prepared to attack rebel earthworks. They moved into place behind the federal picket line near Fort Stedman and awaited orders.

[Library of Congress]

the disabled chevaux-de-frise. Just as the rebels opened fire, everyone from Company K tumbled into it. Bullets whizzed overhead and missed the men.

A mad scramble followed as the Sharpshooters clambered to their feet, scrabbled out of the ditch, and lunged over the enemy's earthworks. It was a life-or-death race: They had to reach the line before the enemy reloaded.

The Sharpshooters fired into the crowd of rebels, then resorted to bayonets and knives. As he had at the Crater, Antoine Scott fought with courage and might. A bullet smashed James DeLand's left arm and shattered the bone where it joined his shoulder. Jacob Greensky, Cornelius Hall, and Freeman Sutton, who had joined Company K only two months earlier, were also injured.

The Sharpshooters took a number of prisoners and, by themselves, held the line for an hour. At last, another regiment came to their support. Company K and their comrades were ordered toward the rear of the Union line. But Buckbee confidently stated, "We could have held the works if we had been so ordered. . . . The Regiment fought splendidly." Their valor was not without cost. The Sharpshooters lost four men from other companies who were killed in action. In all, eighteen were wounded, two of whom later died.

At the field hospital, doctors bandaged Company K's wounded and said Captain James DeLand's arm would have to be amputated. DeLand absolutely refused. Finally, he allowed the surgeon to try a risky, no-guarantee operation that would remove only a section of the shattered bone. The doctors were sure he would die.

APRIL 3, 1865

In the earliest hours of Monday, April 3, Buckbee received word from Colonel Ely to ready his exhausted men yet again. The previous evening, smoke had billowed high above the city. Antoine Scott, Tom Kechittigo, and Thomas Smith heard the thuds of exploding bombs. Earlier, they'd also heard "the low, distant rumbling of moving artillery and wagon trains."

The 20th Michigan's Byron Cutcheon, whose regiment was positioned near Company K, described the atmosphere in the Union earthworks: "Every nerve [was] strained to its utmost tension, conscious of some great impending event—a rush to death against the forts and breastworks in our front, or a quick march to a bloodless victory—which? No one knew."

Then suddenly, the night filled with "a great mass of flame and smoke . . . followed by a dull roar as of distant thunder." A large Confederate battery, one whose artillery had often shelled Company K, had exploded. Kechittigo and the others realized that the night's sights and sounds were all signs that Lee was evacuating Petersburg. Rather than let artillery guns and ammunition fall into Union hands, the Confederates had blown them up.

Ordered by Colonel Ely, a Union soldier stealthily approached the Confederate line that lay between the Sharpshooters and the city. He reported that all was quiet. In fact, the line seemed deserted. The way to Petersburg seemed clear.

Before the sun rose, Buckbee and a guard of three men cautiously proceeded along Petersburg's dark streets seeking the courthouse, where a Confederate flag had been flying for months. When they arrived, Buckbee entered the building and climbed up its steeple. He

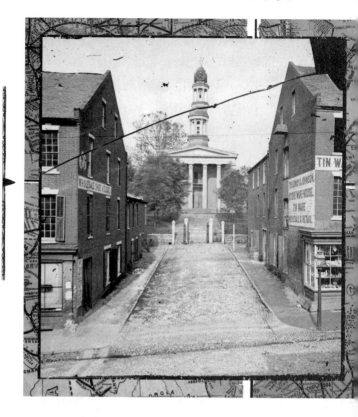

Edward Buckbee climbed to the top of the Petersburg Courthouse and replaced the Confederate flag with the U.S. flag that belonged to the First Michigan Sharpshooters.

lowered and removed the Confederate flag and replaced it with the First Michigan Sharpshooters' Stars and Stripes.

"It was so dark that no one could see it then," Buckbee stated. "But as soon as the sun came up the whole line took up a cheer and oh what a shout." The line of exuberant soldiers flung their caps into the air.

The First Michigan Sharpshooters was the first Union regiment to enter the captured city. Before the morning ended, Generals Grant and Meade were in Petersburg too. Everyone was caught up in celebration. Unbeknownst to Kechittigo, Smith, and their comrades, they had another cause for celebration: For them, the war was over.

VICTORY

Company K and the rest of the regiment remained in Petersburg for two more days, on guard duty to maintain order between the soldiers and civilians. Then the Sharpshooters marched on to investigate and map an area a few miles south of the city.

At Depot Field Hospital, Thomas Wesaw was finally getting treatment for the wound to his face that he had received almost a week earlier. While he was recuperating in the hospital, he had an unexpected visitor: Abraham Lincoln! For several days, Lincoln had been meeting near Petersburg with Generals Grant and Meade. The

On April 8, 1865, when Abraham Lincoln visited General Grant at City Point, he made it his mission to shake the hand of every soldier—Confederate and Union—who was hospitalized at Depot Field Hospital. He shook hands with more than six thousand soldiers that day. Thomas Wesaw, from Company K, was one of them.

[Library of Congress]

Graves near Depot Field Hospital at City Point grimly reminded everyone of the war's heavy toll.

[Library of Congress]

president decided to pay his respects to the wounded. On April 8, Lincoln went to Depot Field Hospital and shook Thomas Wesaw's hand. Lincoln remained at the hospital until he had shaken the hands of all six thousand patients, including Confederate soldiers.

Less than forty-eight hours later, at the Sharpshooters' camp, Company K heard cheering. "What it meant we knew not," Amos Farling, from Company G, stated, "but in half an hour a man on horseback was seen coming out the woods, urging his horse to the utmost, and swinging his hat." The man shouted the best news the men in Company K had heard since their enlistment dates: General Lee had surrendered.

As one, Company K and their Sharpshooter comrades gave a "wild cry of joy." The men cheered, shouted, danced, and cried with happiness.

The war was over!

COURIER---EXTRA.

National Calamity!

Lincoln & Seward Assassinated!!

WASHINGTON, April 15, 1865.

President Lincoln was shot through the head last night, and died this morning.—The Assassin is supposed to be Wilkes Booth the Actor. About the same time a desperado called at Secretary Seward's, pretending to be a messenger from his physician. Being refused admittance, he attacked Frederick Seward, son of the Secretary, knocking down the male attendant, he cut Mr. Seward's throat, the wound was not at first considered fatal. Letters found in Booth's trunk shows that this assassination was contemplated before the fourth of March but fell through from some cause or other. The wildest excitement prevails at Washington. Vice President's and residences of the different Secretaries are closely guarded.

LATER—Seward died this A. M. 9:45.   E. M. STANTON, Sec'y of War.

This sad intelligence falls like a dark pall on the hearts of the people so joyous and hopeful, yesterday, so terribly overwhelmed to-day. What rebels in Richmond dare not do, their accomplices and sympathizes have accomplished in our own capitol.

NOTICE.

All who abhor assassination, deplore murder, and detest the "deep damnation" of the taking off of our Chief Magistrate and Secretary of State, and who sincerely grieve for the great and good men gone are called on to meet

ON THE PUBLIC SQUARE,

AT

3 O'clock, this afternoon, 5.

Lincoln's assassination stunned the newly reunited country.

[Alfred Whital Stern Collection, Library of Congress]

CHAPTER 14

Homeward BOUND

★ ★ ★

ON APRIL 10, 1865, page one headlines in the *New York Times* shouted: "HANG OUT YOUR BANNERS: UNION VICTORY! PEACE!" Beneath the headlines were the texts of Grant's and Lee's notes regarding the terms of the April 9 surrender. Virginia's *Alexandria Gazette* printed the same texts that day on page two. The headline, in regular text size, stated: "Surrender of General Lee and the Army of Northern Virginia."

On April 14, sadness dimmed the jubilation over the war's end. That evening, Abraham and Mary Lincoln attended a play at Ford's Theatre, in Washington, D.C. During the play, Confederate sympathizer John Wilkes Booth entered the area where the Lincolns sat and shot the president in the head. Lincoln died early the next morning.

After Lee's surrender, Lincoln had spoken with Southerners. He expressed sympathy over the many deaths and losses. He indicated that the people of the South would be fairly treated as the country healed and that they would not be persecuted. But his assassination cast uncertainty over how the reunited states would reconcile their differences and reconstruct the South.

But even the terrible news of Lincoln's assassination couldn't dampen the First Michigan Sharpshooters' thoughts of going home. During the next week and a half, they made their way toward Washington, D.C. On April 24, the Second Brigade paraded through Alexandria. The Sharpshooters led the march, preceded only by the brigade's brass band. Exuberant citizens greeted them joyously.

By then, Major Edward Buckbee was the commanding officer of the regiment. Noting that his men were "a tough looking lot," the young commander marveled at their reception: "As we came through the streets I could hear the people all exclaiming, 'Oh my,' 'just look at them!' 'These men have seen hard service.' . . . They cheered us, waved flags, handkerchiefs." For all the Sharpshooters, "it was a proud moment," Buckbee stated. "Leading the 1st M[ichigan] S[harpshooters] was the greatest honor I could have asked."

Four days later, Company K crossed the Potomac River, passed through downtown Washington, D.C., and set up camp outside the village of Tennallytown.

On May 23, William Duvernay, Antoine Scott, Tom Kechittigo, Louis Genereau, John Jacko, George Ashkebug, Thomas Smith, and their company comrades marched with the rest of the Sharpshooters and the entire Army of the Potomac in one last grand review. Mounted cavalry, cannons, and regimental bands all participated in the parade along Washington's Pennsylvania Avenue. They marched past General Grant and Andrew Johnson, the new president of the United States.

After the fanfare ended, Company K returned to camp and, for two seemingly endless months, waited to be mustered out of the army.

During the long wait, Thomas Smith was admitted to Lincoln Hospital. The infection in his eyes had flared with a vengeance, and he was almost completely blind. His arrival at the hospital flustered the doctors. They looked at Smith's right arm, noticed that he did not have a hand, and assumed he was having problems concerning an

The First Michigan Sharpshooters participated in the Grand Review in Washington, D.C., on May 23 and 24, 1865. The Capitol Building is visible in the right background.

[Library of Congress]

amputation. They were stunned when Smith told them that wasn't the situation. Smith spent the next six months being transferred from one hospital to another. Despite many treatments, his sight worsened.

Information regarding Company K's men who had been prisoners of war was a mixed bag. John Kedgnal was back in Michigan. He'd been paroled at Camp Chase, in Ohio, and later transferred to a hospital in Detroit. When he arrived, he was so weak that he had to be carried into the hospital on a stretcher. His father came and stayed with him until he could be brought home to Grand Haven, where his mother cared for him with traditional Anishinaabe medicines.

Payson Wolf spent time at Camp Parole, in Maryland, but was transferred to Camp Chase, where he was released in June and finally sent home to Northport. His father-in-law stated that Wolf "returned home a half killed victim of 'our deer Suthrn brethrens' worse than savage cruelty."

William Newton and Louis Marks, safely back from Andersonville, were eventually reunited with their Company K friends in Washington. During the time that Wolf, Newton, and Marks spent in several different parole camps, they had no idea what had happened to Amos Ashkebugnekay and Louis Miskoguon. When they'd last seen them, the two men had been in the prison hospital at Andersonville.

Miraculously, the two sick men had survived their illnesses at Andersonville. While Company K was fighting the final battles at Petersburg, Amos Ashkebugnekay and Louis Miskoguon were on their way to freedom. They traveled by train, boat, and foot to Vicksburg, Mississippi, where they joined more than five thousand paroled Union prisoners of war at Camp Fisk. They all awaited transportation north on the Mississippi River to Camp Chase, in Ohio, where they would be released to their regiments or receive further orders.

Stronger from weeks of good rations at Camp Fisk, Ashkebugnekay and Miskoguon boarded the steamboat *Sultana* on April 24. More than two thousand paroled men crowded the decks; there was scarcely room to sit and no room to lie down. They heard metallic clanks as one of the boat's iron boilers was being repaired. Ashkebugnekay

When the Sultana *stopped at Helena, Arkansas, the paroled Union prisoners crowded toward the side of the boat nearest the photographer.*

[Library of Congress]

and Miskoguon finally found a spot and settled in. The *Sultana* left Vicksburg later that night.

At 2:00 a.m., on April 27, seven miles north of Memphis, Tennessee, the repaired boiler exploded. Miskoguon and Ashkebugnekay must have thought they were back in the war. Dead bodies and injured people surrounded them. Flames engulfed the boat. Ashkebugnekay and Miskoguon jumped into the river. The swift current quickly separated them.

About twelve hundred men, women, and children died as a result of the explosion. Jesse Huffaker, of the Third Tennessee Cavalry, was one of the lucky survivors. He knew that two of the soldiers onboard were Anishinaabek. After Huffaker was rescued, he heard that one of the two Anishinaabe men was safe. When someone asked the Anishinaabe man if his friend had survived, he replied, "He will be alright." He was correct; both men lived.

Ashkebugnekay, whose name was recorded on the list of paroled prisoners as Amos Green, suffered from chills due to exposure. Louis Miskoguon, listed as Scogen and Scogenes in the records, was bruised but otherwise all right.

Amazingly, Miskoguon arrived at Camp Chase while Payson Wolf was there awaiting discharge. Together, the two friends traveled to Northport, after which Miskoguon continued on to his home. Their families reunited at Reverend Smith's home several weeks later. Smith wrote of the visit in his diary, "Louis Muskoguan [sic] came yesterday [July 25] with his family he was released from Andersonville prison the 26 of March—was on the Sultana when she blew up he seems to have lived thru almost everything it is wonderful that he is alive."

All the Anishinaabek who survived Andersonville were thankful to be alive, but they never forgot their Company K comrades who were left behind, buried in the long trenches outside the prison wall.

HONOR AND LEGACY

Friday, July 28, 1865, couldn't arrive fast enough for the Sharpshooters still encamped on the outskirts of Washington, D.C. On that day, each Sharpshooter there at last received the discharge paper that released him from the army.

Twenty-four hours later, and halfway home, 347 Sharpshooters

Each soldier in the Sharpshooters received a discharge paper that formally released him from service.

[Clarke Historical Library, Central Michigan University]

217

stepped from a train in Pittsburgh, where they again ate a meal. Another train carried them to Cleveland, where they ate and rested in the Soldiers' Home, another stopping place for troops in transit. The Sharpshooters knew they would be in Michigan the next day.

On July 31, the steamboat *Morning Star* arrived at Cleveland's wharf. In scarcely less time than it took to load more coal, the Sharpshooters boarded the boat. Loudly sounding its whistle, the *Morning Star* steamed across Lake Erie to Detroit. From there, Company K's men traveled in different directions as they returned home to their families.

For almost two years, Company K's *ogitchedaw* served the United States of America. Even though they were not considered full citizens of the United States, they did what they believed was their duty. (The 1924 Indian Citizenship Act granted full citizenship rights to all American Indians born within the territorial limits of the United States.) They had upheld *ogitchedaw* tradition as the protectors of their people and of their homeland. They adapted to unfamiliar rules and regulations and fought with weapons and maneuvers very different from those of their *ogitchedaw* ancestors.

One hundred forty-one Anishinaabe men had enlisted in the First Michigan Sharpshooters. Thirteen died in battle. Eight more died from wounds. Another thirteen died of disease or in accidents. Nine died as prisoners of war. They risked and sacrificed their lives in some of the Civil War's fiercest battles with hope that the U.S. government would pay respect to their people: recognizing the Anishinaabek's right to their homeland and its resources and honoring the treaties that the government had signed during the decade before the Civil War.

*The streamers on this banner list the battles in which
the First Michigan Sharpshooters fought.*

[Buckbee family papers, Bentley Historical Library, University of Michigan]

Company K's *ogitchedaw* served to the best of their ability. Did the United States recognize and reward them honorably in return?

Five First Michigan Sharpshooters were recommended for the Medal of Honor, the United States' highest military award for exceptional courage in action. Company K's Antoine Scott was cited for his actions at the Crater and during the assault on Petersburg on April 2, but he did not receive the Medal of Honor. It took thirty years after the war's end for three of the other four Sharpshooters to receive the award. Scott died when he was only thirty-seven years old, in 1878. At that time the Medal of Honor could be given only to soldiers who were still alive. Perhaps that is why Scott didn't receive it. (As of 2019, a group of Anishinaabek and interested historians were attempting to have the medal posthumously awarded.)

For their service and sacrifice, did Company K receive equal rights regarding Anishinaabe land?

Not always. In 1900, white land speculators set their sights on land owned by a group of Anishinaabe families who lived in a village at Burt Lake, Michigan. The Burt Lake band reserved for themselves one thousand acres under the 1836 Treaty of Washington. But to further safeguard their rights, they used the treaty payments given to them between 1845 and 1850 to also buy the land. "On the advice of Federal Indian agents," they placed it in trust with the governor of Michigan.

The Burt Lake band considered it a reservation. As such, it was exempt from taxation. The state, however, taxed the land for many years. The Burt Lake band was not notified that their land could be seized if they didn't pay the tax. Speculators took advantage of this and foreclosed on the homes. One day, while the Anishinaabe men were away at work, speculators forced the women, children, and elders outside. Then they burned the houses and claimed the land for themselves. Simon Sanequaby, Simon Kejikowe, and Charles Porcellay, three of Company K's soldiers, were members of the Burt Lake band.

After the war, enlisted soldiers were entitled to a pension from the army. This was money paid monthly by the government to help them or their dependent family members. A pension was their right as veterans. And as Thomas Eagleson, the First Michigan Sharpshooters' assistant surgeon, declared, "They were good soldiers and should have their rights." But the army made it difficult, sometimes impossible, for Anishinaabe soldiers to receive the pension they deserved.

Because Anishinaabe surnames were often spelled many ways, the soldiers were required to prove their identities when they applied for a pension. Family, friends, and neighbors had to swear in legal documents called affidavits how long they'd known the soldier and state all they knew about the man's army service.

The widows and children of men killed in action or deceased veterans were entitled to certain pension payments. However, many Anishinaabe couples married in traditional ceremonies. Family and friends had witnessed the marriage, but keeping written records was not Anishinaabe custom. Everybody just knew and remembered that the marriage had taken place. Neither did the Anishinaabek keep written records of births, unless it was in a family Bible. Claiming there was no proof of marriage or birth, the army withheld pension monies from Company K widows and young children until ministers, friends, and family provided sworn affidavits. Lizette Ketchebatis not only had to prove she was married to Amable but also had to clarify why his name was listed in different ways. Many widows struggled to feed, clothe, and shelter their families. Some made baskets in the traditional way taught to them by their mothers and grandmothers. Selling baskets was often their only source of income, especially as they aged.

Daniel Mwakewenah's wife, Catherine, died a year after the war ended, leaving their two children orphaned. Collecting pension monies due them was especially difficult for the woman appointed as their guardian.

Many Company K veterans suffered for the rest of their lives from physical problems caused by old wounds or the effects of imprison-ment. These men were war casualties too. The bacteria that causes the disease tuberculosis, which killed so many Anishinaabek after Europeans arrived in North America, can remain undetected and dormant inside a person's lungs for years. But situations that weaken a person's immune system, such as combat stress or war's harsh living conditions, enable the bacteria to become active and thrive. A number of Anishinaabe veterans suffered, and later died, from tuberculosis.

War also took a toll beyond physical problems. The men had survived brutal battles and seen horrific things. These experiences haunted them long after they returned home, making it difficult for them to resume daily life. Today, a soldier suffering this way would be diagnosed with post-traumatic stress disorder and, hopefully, treated. But PTSD had not yet been recognized during the Civil War; a soldier was expected to resume his life as it had been before the war. That wasn't possible for all who suffered in this way.

James and John Mashkaw's remains became lost in the aftermath of battle. Charles Allen died in a hospital and lies in a grave marked UNKNOWN. Amable Ketchebatis, Joseph Gibson, and William Mixinasaw died in prison camps. None of these men came home.

Gibson, Mixinasaw, and five more Company K soldiers are bur-ied at Andersonville National Cemetery, in Georgia. In May 2010, members of the Anishinaabe Ogitchedaw Veteran and Warrior Society, accompanied by descendants of Company K soldiers and Lansing historian Chris Czopek, traveled to Andersonville to honor and send home the spirits of the Anishinaabe men buried there. For four days the *ogitchedaw* and descendants maintained a sacred fire. They sang prayers and gave offerings of *semaa, giizhik, mashkodewashk,* and *wiingash*. The *ogitchedaw* carried the society's staff, adorned with sacred eagle feathers, to honor the service and sacrifice made by Jacko Penaiswanquot, William Mixinasaw, Joseph Gibson, and their four comrades. They sprinkled *semaa* and put soil from the soldiers' Michigan homeland on all seven graves. The Anishinaabe ceremonies released the Civil War *ogitchedaw* so that they could walk on to the spirit world knowing that they had been properly honored and remembered by their people.

On July 30, 2014, the National Park Service held a day of commemorative activities to honor the soldiers who fought at the Crater. Thomas Duvernay, the great-grandson of John Kedgnal and great-nephew of William Duvernay, awoke before dawn to follow his ancestors' footsteps during the same hours at the Battle of the Crater. Eric Hemenway, an Anishinaabe from Cross Village, attended the

After the war, an Anishinaabe skilled in beading—possibly a relative of a Company K soldier—crafted this headband for Colonel Charles DeLand. Company veterans presented it to him as a token of their regard.

[Courtesy of the Charles Meyers family]

Thomas Duvernay (right) visited all the places where his great-grandfather John Kedgnal spent time during the Civil War. He and Eric Hemenway (left) are pictured near the Crater, on July 30, 2014, for the 150th commemoration of the battle.

[Ian Morris, courtesy of Thomas Duvernay]

ceremonies to represent Michigan's Anishinaabek and honor all the Anishinaabe soldiers who served in Company K.

Company K's *ogitchedaw* descended from resilient ancestors who had survived many difficult times. Charles Allen, Joseph Gibson, Jacko Penaiswanquot, Louis Miskoguon, John Kedgnal, Garrett Graveraet, and Payson Wolf had protected their families and their homeland. These are two of many Anishinaabe cultural values that stretch back to their earliest ancestors. These values flowed in the blood of every man in Company K. They still flow in the blood of each new generation. The sacrifices these men made strengthened the resolve of all Anishinaabek to continue the fight for their rights.

Although Company K's Anishinaabe soldiers died many years ago, their descendants are very much alive. They live all over the world, but many, along with thousands of other people with Anishinaabe heritage, still live on Anishinaabe homeland, in Michigan.

Unlike the Company K soldiers, today's Anishinaabek Americans have the right to be citizens of their tribe *and* of the United States. If they choose, they can openly worship according to traditional Anishinaabe spiritual beliefs.

Like the Company K soldiers, they still hold the land sacred. Elders still share Anishinaabe history and beliefs as they tell stories according to oral tradition. Today's Anishinaabek celebrate their heritage with traditional songs and dances.

The Anishinaabek are a vital part of American history, as are Company K's *ogitchedaw*. Remembering their sacrifices and sharing their stories honors the spirits of these courageous men and enriches everyone.

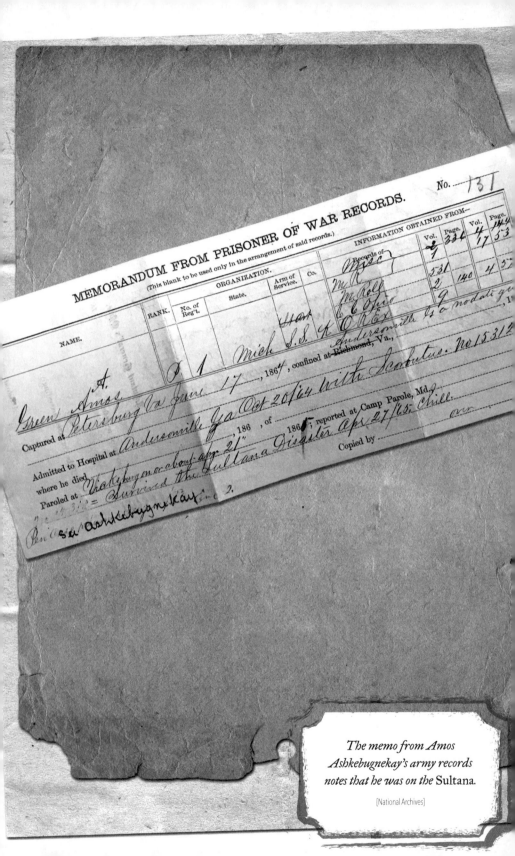

MEMORANDUM FROM PRISONER OF WAR RECORDS.

No. 137

(This blank to be used only in the arrangement of said records.)

NAME.	RANK.	No. of Reg't.	State.	Arm of Service.	Co.	INFORMATION OBTAINED FROM—

Green Amos A.

P 1 Mich S.S. K Andersonville is a nodal ge

Captured at Petersburg Va June 17 , 1864, confined at Richmond, Va.,

Admitted to Hospital at Andersonville Ga Oct 20/64 with Scorbutus. No 15312

where he died Crakybugon or about Apr 21" , 186 , of 186 ; reported at Camp Parole, Md.

Paroled at Survived the Sultana Disaster Apr 27/65. Chill.

Copied by _____

Pen & aahkebygnxkáy ine 2.

AFTER THE WAR, at least thirteen men from Company K joined the Grand Army of the Republic, an organization of Union Civil War veterans. The purpose of the GAR was to regularly reunite veterans, to remind them of their contribution in restoring the country, and to help veterans and their families in need. A post member received a uniform coat, a hat, and a membership medal.

The GAR had many posts throughout the United States. Payson Wolf, William Newton, and Aaron Sahgahnahquato (who married Charles Allen's sister Susan after the war) belonged to the Woolsey GAR Post No. 399 in Northport. Tom Kechittigo was a charter member of Scully GAR Post No. 265 in Omer, Michigan.

George Ashkebug married after the war. He and his wife, Mary, had three children, one of whom died during childbirth. The injuries he received at Spotsylvania troubled him for the rest of his life. The place on his left side that was injured when his cartridge box exploded often pained him. He wore a special belt to support the site of the injury. When Ashkebug died, between 1886 and 1888, his brother-in-law mortgaged his team of ponies so that he could buy a suit of clothes to bury George in.

Amos Ashkebugnekay lived on a farm in western Michigan, north of Elbridge and Pentwater. His neighbors respected him highly. Ashkebugnekay struggled with the effects of scurvy long after his release from Andersonville and his rescue from the *Sultana*. His legs and ankles frequently swelled to the point where his skin split open. Often he was unable to straighten his legs and was confined to bed. It became harder and harder for him to manage the livestock and care for his crops. He was a member of the Haight GAR post 348. When he died in 1906, members of the GAR post attended his funeral.

William Duvernay worked as a sailor for a while. In March 1867, he helped a man dig a water well at Grand Haven. Duvernay held a piece of equipment in place while the other man pounded on it with a sledge hammer. Suddenly, he later wrote, "the man who was sledging, by a mis-blow, struck me on the left hand crushing it so that fore finger was amputated at middle joint while the middle finger is permanently crooked and no power exists in the third finger." By 1881, Duvernay was diagnosed with tuberculosis. He died in the Soldiers' Home in Milwaukee, Wisconsin, in 1893. When death neared, he requested that his body be buried beside those of his parents in Grand Haven. He was granted his wish.

Louis Genereau returned to Elbridge, where he and his wife, Louisa (John Kedgnal's sister), made their home near her parents. The couple had two daughters, both of whom died as infants, and a son, Levi. Eliza Duvernay, Genereau's mother-in-law, attended Louisa at Levi's birth. Genereau's health failed rapidly after the war, and the symptoms of tuberculosis ravaged his body. Just before he died, he said to some close friends, "I am going to die very soon. I hope some of you would be kind enough to look after my bereaved wife, and my poor little boy." Genereau was twenty-six years old when he died. Today, his family treasures the Bible he carried with him as a child and possibly as a soldier in the war.

John Jacko (Jacko Penaiswanquot's son) and his wife, Angeline, lived in Northport for about ten years. The couple had five children. Angeline died in 1885. Jacko farmed his land and periodically supplemented his income by fishing, loading cargo onto sailing ships, and working as a logger. He died in a lumber camp in 1907. After Jacko died, his second wife, Susan, made and sold baskets to support the family.

Thomas Kechittigo began a career in the lumber industry and was "quite an expert in riding logs through the turbulent waters." Several years after the war, tragedy struck his family. An outbreak

Thomas Kechittigo and his second wife, Mary, posed for this photo in 1915. Tom is wearing his GAR medal.

[Thomas Kechittigo pension file, National Archives]

of smallpox where they lived killed his wife and six children. Colonel DeLand had insisted that the First Michigan Sharpshooters be inoculated against smallpox. Ironically, Kechittigo's army service may have saved his life. He married again in 1875. He and his second wife, Mary, lived together for many years. After he died, in 1916, an organization called the Woodmen of America placed a memorial stone on his grave. It is shaped like a section of a tree trunk.

John Kedgnal remained in regular contact with his Company K friends and relatives. For several years, he lived next door to Amos Ashkebugnekay. After the war, he legally changed his last name to Duvernay, using that of his father, Charles. Eliza Duvernay, John's mother, often treated him with traditional medicines that she made from roots and herbs. They helped relieve John's pain from his war injuries and the symptoms of illnesses that stemmed from his imprisonment at Salisbury. He and his wife, Lucy, moved to Petoskey

John Kedgnal, who changed his last name to Duvernay after the war, enjoyed spending time with his son John Duvernay Jr. (on the right) and his granddaughter Betty. Kedgnal's son James is on the left.

[Thomas Duvernay]

(formerly Bear River), where they raised their family. Many of his descendants still live there and fondly remember family stories that say he was a storyteller with a good sense of humor.

Louis Miskoguon continued to suffer the effects of scurvy after he returned home to Charlevoix. He and his wife, Susan, had eight children, including a pair of twins. Two of their children died as infants. He and Payson Wolf remained close friends until Louis died in 1870, only five years after the war. Despite treatment, his health had steadily deteriorated.

Marcus Otto resumed civilian life at his home on the Isabella Reservation, where he inherited his brother Solomon's farm. Despite having lost an arm, he continued to work the land. He married his brother's widow, Mary, and they had ten children. In March 1904, Otto drove his wagon to town, fourteen or so miles from his home. It was unusually cold. On the way home, Otto's wagon veered off the road into a pool of water. He took off his coat and tried unsuccessfully to free the horse and wagon. Remaining with his wagon, he fell asleep and froze to death. He was fifty-six years old.

Thomas Smith was treated for severe eye infections at four different army hospitals before he returned home to Isabella. His eyes did not respond to treatment, and he became totally blind. Ten years after the war, he married his wife, Nancy. They did not have any children. Smith was a leader in his community and often advised people in the Isabella area on how to deal with land claims and government officials. Thomas Smith died April 22, 1909.

Joseph Wakazoo returned to Michigan after the war but moved to Minnesota, where he married his wife, Nesette, in 1884. Ordained as a deacon in the Episcopal Church in 1887, Wakazoo served as a teacher and missionary in the Anishinaabe community. When he died in 1910, he had been a pastor for twenty years at a mission on the White Earth Reservation in Minnesota.

Payson Wolf and his wife, Mary Jane, lived on their farm a short wagon ride from the Reverend George Smith's house. They had thirteen children. Wolf never regained the full use of his left arm and was unable to do the heavy farm work he had done before the war. Wolf regularly attended GAR meetings and decorated his star-shaped GAR medal by adding a pearl bead. Somehow, his medal was lost outdoors. Many years later, some children found it in the dirt near Wolf's Northport home. Now the medal is on loan to the Northport Area Museum. Wolf died in 1900.

AUTHOR'S NOTE

For the past few years, I've been on an amazing journey. Reading old documents and walking in places new to me, I have come to know the stories of a group of extraordinary men, their wives, sons, daughters, parents, in-laws, and neighbors. Telling the story of the Anishinaabe men who served in the First Michigan Sharpshooters has been an honor. Above all, I thank them for sharing their lives with me.

As I read the Company K pension files and military service records, it quickly became apparent that as the soldiers aged, most of them suffered increasingly from war-related concerns. While some were the result of wounds, others stemmed from harsh living conditions during the war. Many of the men suffered from tuberculosis, which may have been aggravated by exposure to unforgiving weather conditions and the stress of battle. The effects of scurvy, suffered by all who had been imprisoned, plagued them for the rest of their lives. And some unquestionably suffered from post-traumatic stress disorder, which has been identified only in modern times. These men, who struggled to resume civilian life, were war casualties too.

Telling this story would not have been possible without the help and support of many people.

My Sharpshooter journey began with a visit to Lake Forest Cemetery, in Grand Haven. *Miigwetch*, thanks, to Dennis Deverney, for driving there (despite a broken car window!) to show me the graves of his ancestors William Duvernay and Julia and Pierre Duvernay, and for telling me about their lives. Thanks also to David Schock for meeting with me and sharing his journey to Andersonville. The Grand Haven Public Library has lots of good material about the town's settlement and the Duvernay family.

Grand Haven is a short distance from the Old Wing Mission. The house where the Smiths lived still stands, and being there gave me a good perspective on where the Wakazoos, Kin-ne-quay and Payson Wolf, and others lived during their years at Old Wing.

The Ziibiwing Center of Anishinabe Culture & Lifeways, in Mount Pleasant, Michigan, is one of the state's shining stars and a must-see museum for anyone interested in Great Lakes Anishinabek cultures. My husband and I spent an entire day exploring its outstanding exhibits and learned a wealth of information about the ancient, the historic, and the modern lives of the Anishinaabek. *Miigwetch* to Anita Heard, the research center coordinator, for fielding my many questions.

The Eyaawing Museum and Cultural Center, in Suttons Bay, Michigan, is another lovely place to spend time learning about Anishinaabe culture. Cindy Winslow, the museum director, graciously showed us the amazing eagles and highlighted certain exhibits. Cindy, thanks especially for sharing the story of your ancestors Jacko Penaiswanquot and John Jacko.

The Northport Area Museum has an exhibit that includes Payson Wolf's GAR medal and a basket made by Kin-ne-quay. On loan from the Wolf family is a beautiful rolling pin that Payson carved for Mary Jane. Holding it was a privilege. Hiking around Elbridge, Pentwater, Northport, and Omena really allowed me to let my imagination roam so I could envision the land as the Company K families would have seen it. It was great to see the house where the Smiths lived and where Payson Wolf and his family spent many hours.

Thanks to Eric Hemenway, in Harbor Springs, at the Little Traverse Bay Bands of Odawa Indians, for sharing his knowledge of Company K and his journey to Petersburg. He suggested several helpful sources for information about Anishinaabe culture. And when he showed me Louis Miskoguon's photo—which I had never seen before—I almost fell off my chair! From the moment I first saw Miskoguon's name on the list of the *Sultana* survivors, I knew he had a story of his own to tell. Seeking his story led me to Company K and this book. So, a special *miigwetch* to Louis Miskoguon for leading me to Company K!

If it hadn't been for Thomas Duvernay, I wouldn't have learned how to load a Springfield rifle. My arms trembled after I held the

This monument, on the grounds of the Michigan State Capitol, in Lansing, honors the service of the Sharpshooters.

[Sally M. Walker]

rifle in the correct firing position for less than half a minute: It was way heavier than I thought! Thom showed me his reenactor's period-accurate Union uniform and told me about the required qualifying test for sharpshooters. He also shared his great-grandfather John Kedgnal's story. It was an honor to accompany Thom to Kedgnal's grave, where we paid our respects with an offering of *semaa*.

Many thanks to historian Chris Czopek for sharing his immense knowledge of Company K. He is a wonderful storyteller and a committed friend to all the Company K soldiers, especially those buried at Andersonville. Also thanks to Art Dembinski for sharing his knowledge of the Wakazoo family and his medical expertise on the symptoms of tuberculosis, which afflicted many Company K veterans after the war. Larry Wyckoff provided me with copies of the amazing petitions signed by Naishkaze (Moses Allen), Daniel Mwakewenah, and Jacko Penaiswanquot.

On the war's front in the east, I am especially grateful to Emmanuel Dabney, park curator at Petersburg National Battlefield, in Virginia. Although the visitors' center was closed due to an air-conditioner malfunction, he invited my husband and me in to see the park's not-to-be-missed video that provides an *excellent* overview of the Siege of Petersburg. The interpretation includes information about Company K. Emmanuel spent the whole morning escorting us to all the places where Company K fought: the area near Shand house, the Crater, Petersburg Courthouse, and the ruin of the trading post where Louis Marks and others were imprisoned before being transported to Andersonville. It was from Emmanuel that I first learned of the atrocity committed by some Union soldiers against their African American comrades in arms. While we were at the Crater, the weather was as hot as it was when Company K fought there. All the accounts of soldiers being thirsty are 100 percent accurate. The Crater is a powerful place, especially if you return for a visit just after sunrise, when no one else is there. The silence speaks louder than words.

The National Park Service staff at Chancellorsville and at Petersburg was very helpful. Greg Mertz and Grant Gates sent me documents about the Wilderness and Spotsylvania. Gary Castellino reviewed a battle map of the Wilderness with me and then told my husband and me exactly how to hike through the woods to reach the place where Company K was during the battle. The ankle-twisting terrain is indeed uneven, and even today it's hard to see any great distance through the undergrowth.

A very special thank-you to Dr. Troy Paino, president of the University of Mary Washington, for giving me permission to go onto the grounds of the Brompton house. My unexpected meeting and chat with his wife, Kelly, led to an informal tour of the house. Standing in Brompton's front hall, where surgeon William Reed saw wounded members of Company K, was one of the most memorable moments of my career. As I told Kelly about Charles Allen and his letters and how he was mortally wounded at the Wilderness and may have died where we stood, we both got goose bumps.

The National Archives is a national treasure. When I saw Charles Allen's letters in his pension file, I squealed out loud. Staff members looked up, but they didn't shush me. In fact, they became as interested in the letters as I was! So an extra thanks to Cherkea Howery and Jesse Wilinski, who went beyond the call of duty to find extra information about Charles Allen and to put those records digitally online in the NARA catalog.

Frustratingly, I could not read Charles Allen's letters. But an amazing chain of events, which began with Sara McLaughlin, the school liaison librarian at the Des Plaines Public Library in Illinois, ultimately led me to Dr. Richard Rhodes, a linguistics professor at the University of California, Berkeley. Dr. Rhodes specializes in Algonquian languages and has done extensive work translating historical documents written in the Odawa dialect, which was the language Charles Allen spoke and wrote. Dr. Rhodes's translations opened a personal window not only into Charles's family life but also into the unusual circumstance of being an American Indian who was called to testify in a trial where the man charged—Thomas Fitzpatrick—was white. *Miigwetch*, Rich!

Thanks to Eric Hemenway and Emmanuel Dabney for manuscript critique and corrections. Your helpful comments were much appreciated.

Last, but definitely not least, thanks to my husband, Jim, who treks with me on my research adventures. He doesn't mind sorting through old documents in archives, and he has keen eyes for spotting earthworks in the field and a good memory for recalling directions.

The story of Company K's soldiers goes beyond culture: It touches a deeply human place inside all people, regardless of our heritage. Their spirits speak and our hearts understand. We are angry that Tom Kechittigo was told he was not wanted. We cry at the deaths of Charles Allen and Daniel Mwakewenah. We feel relief that Louis Miskoguon and Amos Ashkebugnekay survived Andersonville and the *Sultana* disaster. We smile with Kin-ne-quay, Eliza Duvernay,

Mary Jane Wolf, and the other mothers, wives, and children who welcomed their loved ones home. Company K helps us better understand the risks and sacrifices that today's military men, women, and their families are making to keep us safe.

Getting to know Company K changed my life; now, I hope, it has changed yours. Carry their stories with you, and share them with others.

First Michigan Sharpshooters' Anishinaabe Soldiers and Age at Enlistment

COMPANY B

William Duvernay ★ 13

John Kedgnal ★ 18

COMPANY K

Agahgo, Charles ★ 24

Allen, Charles ★ 19

Amderling, Peter ★ 26

Anderson, Peter ★ 26

Andrew, John ★ 18

Aptargeshick, Oliver ★ 19

Arwonogezice, James ★ 25

Ashkanak, Joseph ★ 18

Ashkebug, George ★ 28

Ashkebugnekay, Amos ★ 32

Ashman, Daniel ★ 17

Awanakwad, Petros ★ 25

Battice, John ★ 19

Benasis, John ★ 22

Bennett, Louis ★ 31

Boushaw, Augustus ★ 20

Burns, Peter ★ 21

Cabecoung, William ★ 19

Carter, Charles ★ 21

Chamberlain, Amos ★ 22

Chatfield, Charles ★ 19

Chatfield, Samuel C. ★ 26

Church, Albert ★ 21

Collins, Jacob ★ 30

Collins, John ★ 21

Collins, William ★ 33

Corbin, George ★ 23

Crane, Amos ★ 28

Dabasequam, Jonah ★ 20

David, John ★ 21

Dutton, Luke ★ 19

Etarwegeshig, John ★ 26

Genereau, Louis Jr. ★ 18

George, David ★ 22

Gibson, Joseph Louis ★ 23

Going, Samuel ★ 20

Graveraet, Garrett A. ★ 23

Graveraet, Henry G. Jr. ★ 45

Greensky, Benjamin C. ★ 24

Greensky, Jacob ★ 18

Gruet, Peter ★ 21

Hall, Cornelius ★ 18

Hamlin, James H. ★ 22

Hannin, Joseph ★ 25

Hubert, Charles ★ 28

Isaacs, John ★ 21

Isaacs, William ★ 19

Jacko, John ★ 20

Jacko, Nattahmenoting ★ 24

Jackson, Edward A. ★ 27

Jackson, William ★ 26

Jeandron, Michael ★ 21

Johns, David ★ 19

Johns, William ★ 20

Kabaosa, Louis ★ 27

Kabayacega, George ★ 30

Kadah, Joseph ★ 21

Kakakee, Joseph ★ 35

Kaquatch, Samuel ★ 18

Kechittigo, Thomas ★ 27

Keeses, John ★ 30

Kejikowe, Simon ★ 23

Ketchebatis, Amable ★ 32

Kewaconda, Benjamin ★ 21

Kinewahwanipi, John ★ 20

Lamourandere, Thaddeus ★ 21

Lidger, David ★ 28

Light, Josiah ★ 18

Marks, Louis ★ 24

Marquette, Frank ★ 35

Mashkaw, James ★ 31

Mashkaw, John ★ 22

Miller, Thomas ★ 19

Misisaius, Edward ★ 25

Miskoguon, Louis ★ 30

Mixinasaw, William ★ 20

Mixonauby, Thomas ★ 39

Mogage, George W. ★ 23

Mwakewenah, Daniel ★ 40

Narquaquot, Joseph ★ 25

Narwegeshequabey, Jackson ★ 22

Naquam, Thompson ★ 23

Nelson, Thomas ★ 27

Nesogot, Joseph ★ 27

Neveaux, William ★ 18

Newton, William ★ 17

Ohbowakemo, James ★ 26

Otashquabono, Leon ★ 23

Otto, Marcus ★ 19

Otto, Solomon ★ 24

Pakemaboga, John ★ unknown

Pemassegay, Daniel ★ 24

Penaiswanquot, Jacko ★ 40

Peshekee, Mark ★ 30

Pesherbay, Albert ★ 25

Porcellay, Charles ★ 25

Prestawin, Jacob ★ 24

Quoboway, James ★ 32

Rubberdee, John ★ 25

Sahgahnahquato, Aaron ★ 21

Sanequaby, Simon ★ 25

Sashkobanquot ★ 45

Sawbequom, Adam ★ 28

Scott, Antoine ★ 22

Seymour, Joseph ★ 20

Shabena, Charles ★ 23

Shaw, Charles ★ 19

Shawanese, Joseph ★ 23

Shawonosang, Joseph ★ 18

Shegoge, John ★ 21

Shomin, John B. ★ 20

Shomin, John O. ★ 18

Shomin, Louis ★ 19

Smith, Thomas ★ 23

South, Peter ★ 18

Stoneman, George ★ 22

Sutton, Freeman ★ 32

Tabasash, Francis ★ 38

Tabyant, Antoine ★ 35

Tazhedewin, Joseph ★ 19

Thomas, Moses ★ 18

Valentine, Robert ★ 23

Wabano, Thomas ★ 24

Wabesis, Charles ★ 25

Wabesis, John ★ 23

Wakazoo, Joseph ★ 23

Wassagezic, Henry ★ 17

Watson, James V. ★ 44

Waubenoo, John ★ 22

Wayaubemind, Michael ★ 19

Waygeshegoing, William ★ 22

Wells, Peter ★ 18

Wesaw, Thomas ★ 22

Wesley, John ★ 28

Whiteface, Charles ★ 22

Williams, James ★ 18

Williams, Moses ★ 30

Williams, Samuel ★ 20

Wolf, Payson ★ 30

Sergeant Henry Graveraet, Lieutenant Garrett Graveraet's father, was killed at Spotsylvania.

[Emerson R. Smith Papers, Bentley Historical Library, University of Michigan]

APPENDIX B

Time Line of Company K
First Michigan Sharpshooters

1861—April 12, Confederate forces fire on Fort Sumter, South Carolina

1862—Colonel Charles DeLand forms First Michigan Sharpshooters

1862–1865—Anishinaabe men recruited and enlisted in Company K

1863—U.S. Arsenal at Dearborn, Michigan

1863–1864—August 16–March 17, Camp Douglas, Chicago

1864—Camp Parole, Annapolis, Maryland

1864—May 5–6, Battle of the Wilderness, Virginia

1864—May 12–18, Battle of Spotsylvania Court House, Virginia

1864—June 1–12, Battle at Cold Harbor, Virginia

1864–1865—June 9–April 2, Siege of Petersburg, Virginia

1864—June 17, Battle at Petersburg, fight near Shand house, Virginia

1864—July 30, Battle of the Crater, Virginia

1864—August 18–21, Battle at Weldon Railroad, Virginia

1864—September 30, Battle at Peebles' Farm, Virginia

1864—October 27, Battle at Hatcher's Run, Virginia

1865—March 25–April 2, Battles at Fort Stedman and Fort Mahone, assault on Petersburg

1865—April 9, General Lee surrenders, Appomattox, Virginia

1865—April 14, Abraham Lincoln is shot, dies next day, Washington, D.C.

1865—April 24, Second Brigade marches through Alexandria, Virginia

1865—April 28–July 28, Washington, D.C.

1865—July 28, mustered out of service

Treaties

These are excerpts from the 1836 and 1855 treaties between certain Anishinaabe bands and the U.S. government. Daniel Mwakewenah was one of the Anishinaabe leaders who signed the 1855 treaty. The complete text of the 1836 treaty may be found at: glifwc.org/TreatyRights/1836Treaty_SenateReport.pdf. The 1855 treaty may be found at: cmich.edu/hirary/clarke/ResearchResources/Native _American_Material/Treaty_Rights/

TREATY WITH OTTAWA AND CHIPPEWA NATIONS, 1836

Article 1.

The Ottawa and Chippewa nations of Indians cede to the United States all the tract of country within the following boundaries: Beginning at the mouth of Grand river of Lake Michigan on the north bank thereof, and following up the same to the line called for, in the first article of the treaty of Chicago of the 29th of August 1821, thence, in a direct line, to the head of Thunder-bay river, thence with the line established by the treaty of Saganaw of the 24th of September 1819, to the mouth of said river, thence northeast to the boundary line in Lake Huron between the United States and the British province of Upper Canada, thence northwestwardly, following the said line, as established by the commissioners acting under the treaty of Ghent, through the straits, and river St. Mary's, to a point in Lake Superior north of the mouth of *Gitchy Seebing*, or Chocolate river, thence south to the mouth of said river and up its channel to the source thereof, thence, in a direct line to the head of the *Skonawba* river of Green bay, thence down the south bank of said river to its mouth, thence, in a direct line, through the ship channel into Green bay, to the outer part thereof, thence south to a point in Lake Michigan west of the north cape, or entrance of Grand river, and thence east to the place of beginning, at the cape aforesaid, comprehending all the lands and islands, within these limits, not hereinafter reserved.

Article 2.

From the cession aforesaid the tribes reserve for their own use, to be held in common the following tracts for the term of five years from the date of the ratification of this treaty, and no longer; unless the United States shall grant them permission to remain on said lands for a longer period, namely: One tract of fifty thousand acres to be located on Little Traverse bay: one tract of twenty thousand acres to be located on the north shore of Grand Traverse bay, one tract of seventy thousand acres to be located on, or, north of the *Pieire Marquetta* river, one tract of one thousand acres to be located by Chingassanoo,—or the Big Sail, on the Cheboigan. One tract of one thousand acres, to be located by Mujeekewis, on Thunder-bay river.

Article 4.

In consideration of the foregoing cessions, the United States engage to pay to the Ottawa and Chippewa nations, the following sums, namely. 1st. An annuity of thirty thousand dollars per annum, in specie, for twenty years; eighteen thousand dollars, to be paid to the Indians between Grand River and the Cheboigun; three thousand six hundred dollars, to the Indians on the Huron shore, between the Cheboigan and Thunder-bay river; and seven thousand four hundred dollars, to the Chippewas north of the straits, as far as the cession extends; the remaining one thousand dollars, to be invested in stock by the Treasury Department and to remain incapable of being sold, without the consent of the President and Senate, which may, however, be given, after the expiration of twenty-one years. 2nd. Five thousand dollars per annum, for the purpose of education, teachers, school-houses, and books in their own language, to be continued twenty years, and as long thereafter as Congress may appropriate for the object. 3rd. Three thousand dollars for missions, subject to the conditions mentioned in the second clause of this article. 4th. Ten thousand dollars for agricultural implements, cattle, mechanics' tools, and such other objects as the President may deem proper. 5th. Three hundred dollars per annum for vaccine matter, medicines, and the services of physicians, to be continued while the Indians remain on their reservations. 6th. Provisions to the amount of two thousand dollars; six thousand five hundred pounds of tobacco; one hundred barrels of salt, and five hundred fish barrels, annually, for twenty years. 7th. One hundred and fifty thousand dollars, in goods and provisions, on the ratification of this treaty, to be delivered at Michilimackinac, and also the sum of two hundred thousand dollars, in consideration of changing the permanent reservations in article two and three to reservations for five years only, to be paid whenever their reservations shall be surrendered, and until that time the interest on said two hundred thousand dollars shall be annually paid to the said Indians.

Article 7.

In consideration of the cessions above made, and as a further earnest of the disposition felt to do full justice to the Indians, and to further their well being, the United States engage to keep two additional blacksmith-shops, one of which, shall be located on the reservation north of Grand river, and the other at the *Sault*

Ste. Marie. A permanent interpreter will be provided at each of these locations. It is stipulated to renew the present dilapidated shop at Michilimackinac, and to maintain a gunsmith, in addition to the present smith's establishment, and to build a dormitory for the Indians visiting the post, and appoint a person to keep it, and supply it with fire-wood. It is also agreed, to support two farmers and assistants, and two mechanics, as the President may designate, to teach and aid the Indians, in agriculture, and in the mechanic arts. The farmers and mechanics, and the dormitory, will be continued for ten years, and as long thereafter, as the President may deem this arrangement useful and necessary; but the benefits of the other stipulations of this article, shall be continued beyond the expiration of the annuities, and it is understood that the whole of this article shall stand in force, and inure to the benefit of the Indians, as long after the expiration of the twenty years as Congress may appropriate for the objects.

Article 8.

It is agreed, that as soon as the said Indians desire it, a deputation shall be sent to the southwest of the Missouri River, there to select a suitable place for the final settlement of said Indians, which country, so selected and of reasonable extent, the United States will forever guaranty and secure to said Indians. . . . When the Indians wish it, the United States will remove them, at their expence, provide them a year's subsistence in the country to which they go, and furnish the same articles and equipments to each person as are stipulated to be given to the Pottowatomies in the final treaty of cession concluded at Chicago.

Article 13.

The Indians stipulate for the right of hunting on the lands ceded, with the other usual privileges of occupancy, until the land is required for settlement.

In testimony whereof, the said Henry R. Schoolcraft, commissioner on the part of the United States, and the chiefs and delegates of the Ottawa and Chippewa nation of Indians, have hereunto set their hands, at Washington the seat of Government, this twenty-eighth day of March, in the year one thousand eight hundred and thirty-six.

TREATY WITH THE OTTAWA AND CHIPPEWA, 1855 (TREATY OF DETROIT)

Article 1.

. . . The United States will give to each Ottawa and Chippewa Indian being the head of a family, and to each single person over twenty-one years of age, 40 acres of land, and to each family of orphan children under twenty-one years of age containing two or more persons, 80 acres of land, and to each single orphan child under twenty-one years of age, 40 acres of land to be selected and located within the several tracts of land hereinbefore described, under the following rules and regulations. . . .

. . . All the land embraced within the tracts hereinbefore described, that shall not have been appropriated or selected within five years shall remain the property of the United States, and the same shall thereafter, for the further term of five years, be subject to entry in the usual manner and at the same rate per acre, as other adjacent public lands are then held, by Indians only; and all lands, so purchased by Indians, shall be sold without restriction, and certificates and patents shall be issued for the same in the usual form as in ordinary cases; and all lands remaining unappropriated by or unsold to the Indians after the expiration of the last-mentioned term, may be sold or disposed of by the United States as in the case of all other public lands. . . .

Article 5.

The tribal organization of said Ottawa and Chippewa Indians, except so far as may be necessary for the purpose of carrying into effect the provisions of this agreement, is hereby dissolved; and if at any time hereafter, further negotiations with the United States, in reference to any matters contained herein, should become necessary, no general convention of the Indians shall be called; but such as reside in the vicinity of any usual place of payment, or those only who are immediately interested in the questions involved, may arrange all matters between themselves and the United States, without the concurrence of other portions of their people, and as fully and conclusively, and with the same effect in every respect, as if all were represented.

The Eagle

Company K wasn't the only regiment to have an eagle as its mascot. Old Abe was the bald eagle mascot of Company C, Eighth Wisconsin Volunteer Infantry. Dubbed with the president's nickname, he had been captured by Chief Sky, a Chippewa Indian, who was a member of the Flambeau band, Wisconsin. Chief Sky sold the eagle to a white man for a bushel of corn. That man sold him to another, who gave him to Company C. Old Abe traveled with his company and lived through thirty-six battles. He survived two wounds, mustered out with the company in 1864, and died in March 1881.

On July 23, 1864, Constant Hanks, a soldier with the 80th New York Infantry, saw Company K's eagle. There has been discussion over whether Company K had an eagle mascot or whether Hanks had actually seen Old Abe. Several facts support Hanks's claim. The Eighth Wisconsin served in Mississippi, Louisiana, Missouri, Tennessee, and Arkansas. In June 1864, the regiment was in Arkansas and Mississippi. On July 4, 1864, Old Abe was in Chippewa

Old Abe, nicknamed in honor of the president, served as the mascot for Company C of the Eighth Wisconsin Volunteer Infantry. While he was the most famous eagle mascot, he wasn't the only one; Company K had one too. Unfortunately, its name has been lost over time.

[Library of Congress]

Falls, Wisconsin. Later that month, his "furlough" having ended, he traveled by train through Illinois, reuniting with the rest of his regiment in Memphis, Tennessee. Soon after, they were on their way south to Mississippi.

The eagle that Constant Hanks saw was in Petersburg, Virginia.

Further, in a letter to his sister Moll dated July 24, 1864, Hanks describes the eagle's platform and wrote that it belonged to "a company of Indians from Michigan. They are sharpshooters attached to Burnsides Corps." The Indians "have been all through the present campaign, was in the awful fight of the Wilderness, their eagle with them." And finally, "Their chief was wounded in the arm in one of the battles of the Wilderness, [he] went [to] Washington [and] died, his body embalmed sent to his tribe with all the honors."

Taken together, there seems little doubt that the eagle Hanks saw was, indeed, Company K's mascot and not Old Abe.

APPENDIX F

Complete Translation of Charles Allen's Letter Dated December 21, 1863

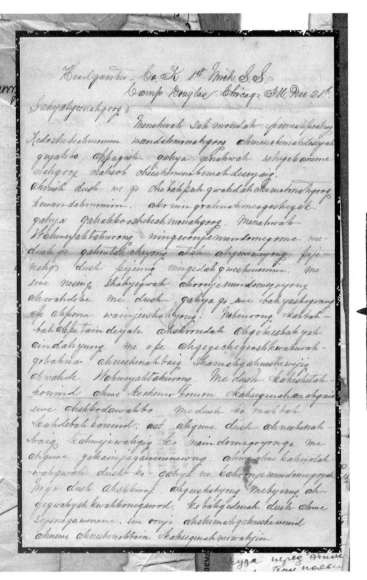

Charles Allen wrote this letter while stationed at Camp Douglas, in Chicago, Illinois. Two more of Allen's letters, written in Odawa, may be found online at the National Archives website: catalog.archives.gov /id/66390979.

Headquarters Co. K 1st Mich. S.S.
Camp Douglas Chicago, Ill. Dec 21st
Sahyahgeenahgoog
                    Menahwah sah mondah pemeahpechog
Kedoshebeahmonim weendahmonahgoog ahmenobemahdeseyah
gayahbe, ahpagish gahya genahwah eshegekaneme(–)
nahgoog nahsob cheeshemenobemahdeseyaig.
ahnish dush we go chebahpuhgwahdahchemotonahgoog
keweendahmonim. akoningoahnahmeagesheguk
gahya gahahkooshebeahmonahgoog. Menahwah
Wahweyahtahnoong ningeoonjenundomigome. Me—
dush go gahnetahcheyong atah ahgeneweyong peje—
nahgo dush pejinug ningedahgweshenomin. Me
ewe nesing shahyegwah ahoonjenundomegoyong
ahwahdebe. Me dush gahya go ewe bahyashigwung
ap ahpena wainjeeshahyong. Nebenoong okahbah—
bah ahpetaindeyah ahshoondah ahgebeeshahyah
aindahyung. Me ape ahgechegeoshkwabewah—
gebahne ahneshenahbaig shamahgahnesheweig
ahwahde Wahweyahtehnoong. Me dush kaheshetah—
konind ahwe kechemokomon kahsegenahonahgaid
ewe ahshkodawahbo. Me dush ko mahbah
kahdebahkonind. ast ahgewe dush ahneshenah—
baig kahwejewahgig ko naindomegoyonge me
ahgewe gekainjegawenenewug. ahwe ahne kahnotah—
nahgwah dush ko gahya ne kahonjemendomegoyah
Nogo dush ahshkwoj ahgeeshahyong mebejenug ah—
gegwahyah kwahkonegawod kebahgedenah dush ahwe
segenegawenene. ewe oonje ahshemahgahneshewenid
ahnewe ahneshenahbain kahsegenahmowahjin
Keeshpin dush bwahshemahgahneshewenepah ahpe—
je kagate tahgesahnahgese.
Mesahmondah menik enahjemoyah kedah–
nahmekonim aindahcheyaig wawane. Bosho
Bosho sah.
Neen Chas Allen

Headquarters Co. K 1st Mich. S.S.
    Camp Douglas Chicago, Ill. Dec 21st
    Dear loved ones,
                    Again at this point
I write to you all and tell you that I'm still doing well,
hoping to learn about you, too,
the same thing, that you are doing well.
Well, I have a wild story for you.
I'll tell it to you. A week ago
after I had written to you,
we were called to Detroit
It was just the four of us.
We had just gotten back the day before.
Three times already we were sent on assignment somewhere
or other. There was the one reason
we were always going. Last summer
while I was away from here having gone to where
we live. At that time they had gotten very drunk,
some Indian soldiers
in Detroit. An American bartender
had been arrested.
        And he was
on trial. The Indians involved were the Indians
that I accompanied whenever we were called on assignment.
There were these learned men. I was to speak to them one at a time
and for that reason I, too, was being accused.
Today finally we went.
The bartender was just acquitted and released.
because
the Indians he had served were soldiers.
If they had not been soldiers, it really
would have been trouble for him.
This is all I have to report.
My best wishes to everyone. Greetings.
Greetings.
I'm Chas Allen

GLOSSARY

Anishinaabek—the plural noun for the Odawa, Ojibwe, and Potawatomi people altogether

boon—the season of winter

boonishiwaaning—winter lodge

boozhoo—a greeting, similar to "hello"

cede—to give up

chevaux-de-frise—defensive structures with projecting spikes; in the Civil War, they were tall lines of sharply pointed logs crossed like an X, intended to block attackers on horseback

Chi Maawonidiwin—the Great Walk, the Anishinaabek's origin story of how they came to live in the Great Lakes region

clan—an extended family

company—a military unit usually made of 80–150 enlisted soldiers

desert—to leave the army without permission

digwaagi—the season of autumn

enlist—to enroll for service in the military

the front—the main area of a battle's action

giizhik—cedar

manoomin—wild rice

mashkodewashk—sage

mayagwewininiwag—foreigners

Mishigami—the Anishinaabe name for the area that is now Michigan

mitigwakik dewewigan—water drum, used in Anishinaabe ceremonies

mnookimi—the season of spring

muster in—the process of assembling soldiers together as a military unit

muster out—the process of disbanding a soldier from a military unit

niibing—the season of summer

Odoidaymiwan—a system of government based on clans (*odoidayiwug*)

ogitchedaw—Anishinaabe warriors

regiment—a military unit that usually contains about a thousand enlisted soldiers; it is subdivided into companies

semaa—tobacco

wiigwaam—a dwelling or lodge, usually with birchbark sheets as the roof; plural is *wiigwaaman*

wiigwaas—the bark from a birch tree

wiigwaasi-jiimaan—a birchbark canoe; plural is *wiigwaasi-jiimaanan*

wiingash—sweet grass

ziisibaakodokaaning—the camp made near or within a stand of sugar maples

PRIMARY SOURCES

Chadwick, Ransom. *Ransom Chadwick's Andersonville Prison Diary.* 2 vols. Saint Paul, MN: Minnesota Historical Society. www2.mnhs.org /library/findaids/00882-000006-1.pdf.

Farling, Amos. *Life in the Army: Recollections of Private Amos Farling of Company G, First Michigan Sharp Shooters 1863–1866.* Buchanan, MI, 1874. Reprint, Berrien Springs, MI: Berrien County Historical Association, 2005.

Pension files of various soldiers in Company K, First Michigan Sharpshooters, Civil War. Civil War and Later Pension Files, Records of the Department of Veterans Affairs, RG 15, National Archives Building, Washington, DC.

Smith, George Nelson. *George Nelson Smith Journals and Letters, 1840–1879.* Microfilm of the handwritten papers in the Manuscript Division, Library of Congress, Washington, DC. Read at Founders Library, Northern Illinois University, DeKalb, IL.

BOOKS

Adams, George Worthington. *Doctors in Blue: The Medical History of the Union Army in the Civil War.* New York: Henry Schuman, 1952.

Benton-Banai, Edward. *The Mishomis Book: The Voice of the Ojibway.* Minneapolis: University of Minnesota Press, 2010.

Blackbird, Andrew J. *History of the Ottawa and Chippewa Indians of Michigan.* Ypsilanti, MI, 1887.

Brooks, Stewart. *Civil War Medicine.* Springfield, IL: Charles C. Thomas, 1966.

Clark, Walter, ed. *Histories of the Several Regiments and Battalions from North Carolina in the Great War 1861-'65.* Vols. 1 (Raleigh, NC: E. M. Uzzell) and 3 (Goldsboro, NC: Nash Bros.), 1901.

Cleland, Charles E. *The Place of the Pike (Gnoozhekaaning).* Ann Arbor: University of Michigan Press, 2001.

Corrigan, Jim. *The 48th Pennsylvania in the Battle of the Crater: A Regiment of Coal Miners Who Tunneled Under the Enemy.* Jefferson, NC: McFarland & Co., 2006.

Cutcheon, Byron M. *The Story of the Twentieth Michigan Infantry.* Lansing: MI: Robert Smith, 1904.

Czopek, Chris. *Who Was Who in Company K.* Lansing, MI: Red Oak Research, 2015.

Densmore, Frances. *Chippewa Customs.* St. Paul: Minnesota Historical Society Press, 1979.

Dobson, Pamela J., ed. *The Tree That Never Dies: Oral History of the Michigan Indians.* Grand Rapids, MI: Grand Rapids Public Library, 1978.

Hauptman, Laurence M. *Between Two Fires: American Indians in the Civil War.* New York: Free Press, 1995.

Herek, Raymond J. *These Men Have Seen Hard Service: The First Michigan Sharpshooters in the Civil War.* Detroit: Wayne State University Press, 1998.

Johnson, Michael G. *Ojibwa: People of Forests and Prairies.* Richmond Hill, ON: Firefly, 2016.

Johnston, Basil. *Ojibway Ceremonies.* Toronto: McClelland and Stewart, 1982.

Kappler, Charles J., ed. *Indian Affairs: Laws and Treaties.* Washington, DC: Government Printing Office, 1904.

Karamanski, Theodore J. *Blackbird's Song: Andrew Blackbird and the Odawa People.* East Lansing: Michigan State University Press, 2012.

Levy, George. *To Die in Chicago: Confederate Prisoners at Camp Douglas, 1862–1865.* Evanston, IL: Evanston Publishing, 1994.

McClurken, James M. *Gah-Baeh-Jhagwah-Buk: The Way It Happened.* East Lansing: Michigan State University Museum, 1991.

Ransom, John L. *John Ransom's Diary.* New York: Paul S. Eriksson, 1963.

Reed, William Howell. *Hospital Life in the Army of the Potomac.* Boston, 1866. Sabin Americana, 1500–1926, Gale Digital Collection.

Rhea, Gordon C. *The Battle of the Wilderness: May 5–6, 1864.* Baton Rouge: Louisiana State University Press, 1994.

———. *The Battles for Spotsylvania Court House and the Road to Yellow Tavern: May 7–12, 1864.* Baton Rouge: Louisiana State University Press, 1997.

Schroeder-Lein, Glenna R. *The Encyclopedia of Civil War Medicine.* New York: M. E. Sharpe, 2008.

Shier, Quita V. *Warriors in Mr. Lincoln's Army.* Bloomington, IN: iUniverse, 2017.

Smith, W. A. *The Anson Guards: Company C, Fourteenth Regiment, North Carolina Volunteers, 1861–1865.* Charlotte, NC: Stone, 1914. Sabin Americana, 1500–1926, Gale Digital Collection.

Sutton, Robert K., and John A. Latschar, eds. *American Indians and the Civil War: Official National Park Service Handbook.* Fort Washington, PA: Eastern National, 2013.

Swierenga, Robert P., and William Van Appledorn, eds. *Old Wing Mission: Cultural Interchange as Chronicled by George and Arvilla Smith in Their Work with Chief Wakazoo's Otttawa Band on the West Michigan Frontier.* Grand Rapids, MI: William B. Eerdmans, 2008.

The War of the Rebellion: A Compilation of the Official Records of the Union and Confederate Armies. 70 vols. Washington, DC: Government Printing Office, 1880–1901.

Wright, John C. *The Crooked Tree: Indian Legends of Northern Michigan.* Harbor Springs, MI: John C. Wright, 1917.

ARTICLES

Bibbins, C. D. "The Indian Sharpshooters." *National Tribune* (Washington, DC), Oct. 16, 1913.

Bowley, Freeman S. "A Boy Lieutenant in a Black Regiment." *National Tribune* (Washington, DC), June 8 and June 29, 1899. The complete memoir was published in weekly installments April 20–Sept. 7, 1899.

Bump, Lucy. "A Short History of Petoskey County." *Petsokey (MI) Record,* Jan. 23, 1895, p. 5.

Campbell, George, W. "Old Choctaw: The 1st Mich. Chippewa Indian Sharpshooters and Their Methods." *National Tribune* (Washington, DC), Sept. 11, 1913.

Cassidy, Michelle. "'The More Noise They Make': Odawa and Ojibwe Encounters with American Missionaries in Northern Michigan, 1837–1871." *Michigan Historical Review* 38, no. 2 (Fall 2012): pp. 1–34.

Gray, Susan E. "Miengun's Children: Tales from a Mixed-Race Family." *Frontiers: A Journal of Women Studies* 29, no. 2/3 (2008): pp. 146–185.

Hemenway, Eric. "The Anishinaabek of Michigan's Company K: The Complexity of an Indigenous Population's Involvement in the Civil War." In National Park Service special issue, *The Sentinel: Overland Campaign 150th Anniversary 1864/2014,* pp. 36–38.

Wilson, Etta S. "Personal Recollections of the Passenger Pigeon." *Auk* 51, no. 2 (April 1934): pp. 157–168.

———. "Remembering Kin-ne-quay." *History Grand Rapids.* Grand Rapids Historical Commisssion. Accessed Jan. 21, 2017. historygrandrapids.org/article/2255/remembering-kinnequay.

VIDEO

Schock, David B., producer. *The Road to Andersonville: Michigan Native American Sharpshooters in the Civil War—Director's Cut.* penULTIMATE, Ltd, 2013. roadtoandersonville.com.

SUGGESTED FURTHER READING

Broker, Ignatia. *Night Flying Woman: An Ojibway Narrative.* St. Paul: Minnesota Historical Society Press, 1983.

Erdrich, Louise. Birchbark House novels chronicling generations of an Ojibwe family in nineteenth-century America.

Johnston, Basil H. *Tales the Elders Told: Ojibway Legends.* Toronto: Royal Ontario Museum, 1981.

Mitchell, John C. *Grand Traverse: The Civil War Era.* Suttons Bay, MI: Suttons Bay Publications, 2011.

Walker, Niki. *Life in an Anishinaabe Camp.* New York: Crabtree, 2003.

Walker, Sally M. *Sinking the* Sultana: *A Civil War Story of Imprisonment, Greed, and a Doomed Journey Home.* Somerville, MA: Candlewick Press, 2017.

Weeks, George. *Mem-ka-weh: Dawning of the Grand Traverse Band of Ottawa and Chippewa Indians.* Traverse City, MI: Village Press, 1992.

INTERNET

Bugle calls regulated a soldier's day. To hear a selection of the calls that Company K's men would have heard, visit bands.army.mil/music/buglecalls.

Drummers had a manual that contained the many rolls they had to learn. To see the musical notation online, visit nationalcivilwarfieldmusicschool.com/music/Klinehanse.pdf and nationalcivilwarfieldmusicschool.com/music/RudimentsandRudimentalDrumming Maling.pdf. To hear a selection of Civil War drum commands, visit youtube.com/watch?v=0fvkihdRV5g.

For more information about Anishinaabe culture:

Website of the Ziibiwing Center of Anishinabe Culture and Lifeways, Mount Pleasant, MI: sagchip.org/ziibiwing/ojibwere sources.weebly.com/the-clan-system.html.

The Grand Traverse Band of Ottawa and Chippewa Indians and the Eyaawing Museum and Cultural Center at gtbindians.org/eyaawing.asp.

The following website contains information about Anishinaabemowin: anishinaabemdaa.com.

PROLOGUE: JULY 30, 1864—PETERSBURG, VIRGINIA

xv The earth shook . . . into the air: William H. Randall, diary entry, July 30, 1864, Reminiscence 1867, p. 86, Bentley Historical Library, University of Michigan.

CHAPTER 1: A BROKEN COUNTRY

3 He issued . . . had seceded: Abraham Lincoln, Proclamation on State Militia, April 15, 1861, Abraham Lincoln Papers at the Library of Congress, ser. 1, General Correspondence, 1833–1916.

4 scouts . . . self-defense: "War News," *Altoona (PA) Tribune*, May 23, 1861, p. 2.

4 "They will be . . . to the army": "George Copway," *Detroit Free Press*, May 8, 1861, p. 1.

4 "the privilege" . . . "answer immediately": G. P. Miller to Simon Cameron, Oct. 30, 1861, "Letter from a Battle Creek, Michigan African American Physician to the Union Secretary of War," Letters Received, 3/1861–3/1866, Records of the Office of the Secretary of War, 1791–1948, RG 107, National Archives, catalog .archives.gov/id/3854722.

4 Kechittigo . . . "take Indians": Bernard F. Bourassa, deposition, May 26, 1920, pp. 2–3, in Thomas Kechittigo pension file.

4 He recalled . . . "womens and childrens": Perry Ostrander, "Biography of Thomas Ke-chit-ti-go," *Crawford Avalanche* (Grayling, MI), Feb. 4, 1915, p. 1.

5 Somehow . . . was accepted: B. F. Bourassa, 1910 U.S. census, Arenac County, MI, Indian population (enumeration district 30, sheet 14A, family 20, National Archives Publication T624, roll 635).

6 In 1860 . . . slaves: Morris Wardell, *A Political History of the Cherokee Nation, 1838–1907* (Norman: University of Oklahoma Press, 1938), pp. 116–117, in Laurence M. Hauptman, *Between Two Fires: American Indians in the Civil War* (New York: Free Press, 1995), p. 45.

7 whose ancestors had lived . . . of years: Saginaw Chippewa Indian Tribe, sagchip .org/ziibiwing/aboutus/history.htm.

7 In July 1863 . . . "will be *slaves, dogs*": *Detroit Advertiser and Tribune*, July 14, 1863, p. 1, in Raymond J. Herek, *These Men Have Seen Hard Service: The First Michigan Sharpshooters in the Civil War* (Detroit: Wayne State University Press, 1998), p. 59.

8 During the . . . Indian Territory: "Indian Treaties and the Removal Act of 1830," Office of the Historian, U.S. Department of State, accessed Aug. 28, 2017, history .state.gov/milestones/1830-1860/indian-treaties.

9 But under terms . . . federal government: Ratified Indian Treaty 208: Potowatomi—Near Yellow River, Indiana, August 5, 1836, National Archives, Record Group 11: General Records of the U.S. Government, 1778–2006, Series: Indian Treaties, 1722–1869, catalog.archives.gov/id/12013260.

9   "The president . . . about it": Daniel McDonald, *The Removal of the Pottawattomie Indians from Northern Indiana* (Plymouth, IN, 1898), p. 17, HathiTrust Digital Library, hdl.handle.net/2027/loc.ark:/13960/t7kp84f7s.

10   On September 4 . . . were dead: McDonald, *Removal of the Pottawattomie*, pp. 24–25.

10   In the early 1840s . . . could happen again: Chris Czopek, *Who Was Who in Company K* (Lansing, MI: Red Oak Research, 2015), p. 176; David B. Schock, *The Road to Andersonville: Michigan Native American Sharpshooters in the Civil War—Director's Cut* (penULTIMATE, Ltd., 2013), roadtoandersonville.com; Quita V. Schier, *Warriors in Mr. Lincoln's Army* (Bloomington, IN: iUniverse, 2017), pp. 447–448.

11   About thirty-nine hundred . . . in 1861: Hauptman, *Between Two Fires*, p. 127.

CHAPTER 2: CHI MAAWONIDIWIN

13   More than . . . (the Great Walk): Saginaw Chippewa Indian Tribe, sagchip.org /ziibiwing/aboutus/history.htm.

15   The name . . . called it Michigan: Dr. Richard Rhodes, personal communication to author, Aug. 14, 2017.

16   To bring strength . . . people spiritually: Edward Benton-Banai, *The Mishomis Book: The Voice of the Ojibway* (Minneapolis: University of Minnesota Press, 2010), pp. 74–78; and "The Clan System," *Anishinaabeg Bimaadiziwin: An Ojibwe Peoples Resource*, Georgian College Aboriginal Resource Centres, accessed April 15, 2018, ojibweresources.weebly.com/the-clan-system.html.

16   The words reminded . . . never-ending circle: Based on information provided in the permanent exhibit *Diba Jimooyung: Telling Our Story* at the Ziibiwing Center of Anishinabe Culture & Lifeways, Mount Pleasant, MI (hereafter cited as Ziibiwing Center).

20   When an object . . . with great care: Ziibiwing Center.

21   In 1615 . . . Odawa winter village: James M. McClurken, *Gah-Baeh-Jhagwah-Buk: The Way It Happened* (East Lansing: Michigan State University Museum, 1991), p. 3; and James M. McClurken, "We Wish to Be Civilized: Ottawa-American Political Contests on the Michigan Frontier" (PhD diss., Michigan State University, 1988), p. 12.

21   "They gave . . . very kindly": McClurken, "We Wish to Be Civilized," p. 13.

21   The Anishinaabek also . . . made in Europe: McClurken, "We Wish to Be Civilized," pp. 34–36.

21   Sometimes, an entire . . . disease: Eric Hemenway, personal communication to author, June 2, 2018.

22   "it is bent": Eric Hemenway, personal communication to author, June 12, 2018.

22   For generations . . . people lived there: John C. Wright, *The Crooked Tree* (Harbor Springs, MI: John C. Wright, 1917), pp. 7–8; McClurken, *Gah-Baeh-Jhagwah-Buk*, p. 4; and McClurken, "We Wish to Be Civilized," p. 49.

22   When *ogitchedaw* . . . shreds of *semaa* (tobacco): Frances Densmore, *Chippewa Customs* (St. Paul: Minnesota Historical Society Press, 1979), p. 132.

23   They helped . . . the *ogitchedaw*: *Patriot Nations: Native Americans in Our Nation's Armed Forces*, traveling exhibit, March 16, 2017, National Museum of the American Indian, Washington, DC; and Ziibiwing Center.

24   A man or woman . . . water or the air: Basil Johnston, *Ojibway Ceremonies* (Toronto: McClelland and Stewart, 1982), p. 169.

24   The Anishinaabek took . . . "person's integrity": Johnston, *Ojibway Ceremonies*, p. 80.

25   "in exchange for intoxicating drinks": Henry C. Gilbert, report no. 2, in *Annual Report of the Commissioner of Indian Affairs for the Year 1855*, 1855, ed. George W. Manypenny (Washington, DC: Office of the Commissioner of Indian Affairs, 1855), p. 31.

25   "to enjoy . . . lands ceded": "Treaty Between the Ottawa, Chippewa, Wyandot, and Potawatomi Indians," Nov. 17, 1807, Indian Treaties, 1722–1869, General Records of the United States Government, 1778–2006, RG 11, National Archives, catalog .archives.gov/id/596331.

25   "enjoy the privilege . . . waste upon the trees": "Treaty with the Chippewa, 1819," in *Indian Affairs: Laws and Treaties*, ed. Charles J. Kappler (Washington, DC: Government Printing Office, 1904), vol. 2, pp. 185–186, dc.library.okstate.edu /digital/collection/kapplers/id/25853.

25   remained the property of the United States: "Treaty Between the Ottawa Chippewa, Wyandot, and Potawatomi Indians," 1807.

CHAPTER 3: SURVIVING A CHANGING WORLD

30   "the Ottawa" . . . "for the object": "Treaty with the Ottawa, Etc., 1836," in Kappler, *Indian Affairs: Laws and Treaties*, vol. 2, p. 452, under Article Fourth.

31   "agricultural implements" . . . "mechanic arts": "Treaty with the Ottawa, Etc., 1836," p. 453.

31   whose ancestors came from Europe did: "Treaty with the Ottawa, Etc., 1836," pp. 450–456.

31   In 1837 . . . (now Lake Macatawa): Robert P. Swierenga and William Van Appledorn, eds., *Old Wing Mission: Cultural Interchange as Chronicled by George and Arvilla Smith in Their Work with Chief Wakazoo's Otttawa Band on the West Michigan Frontier* (Grand Rapids, MI: William B. Eerdmans, 2008), p. 5.

32   The mission . . . (the Wing): Swierenga and Van Appledorn, *Old Wing Mission*, p. 5.

32   forty-one Anishinaabe students: Swierenga and Van Appledorn, pp. 230–231.

32   One day . . . twenty miles: Swierenga and Van Appledorn, p. 301.

33   He lived . . . his father's name: Wolf's parents' names are spelled several different ways. Wolf's daughter Etta Wilson spelled her grandparents' names as "Kin-ne-quay" and "Mi-in-gun." I chose to use her spelling. Etta S. Wilson, "Personal Recollections of the Passenger Pigeon," *Auk* 51, no. 2 (April 1934): p. 160.

34   "All the Indians . . . sugar camps yesterday": Swierenga and Van Appledorn, p. 265.

35 In 1845 . . . $1,200 in cash: Swierenga and Van Appledorn, p. 33. The cash equivalent in purchasing power is from Official Data Foundation, officialdata.org /1845-dollars-in-2018?amount=1200.

36 "a place the Dutchman couldn't find": Swierenga and Van Appledorn, p. 47.

37 "I solemnized" . . . barely sixteen: George Nelson Smith, *George Nelson Smith Journals and Letters, 1840–1879* (microfilm of the handwritten papers in the Manuscript Division, Library of Congress, Washington, DC), read at Founders Library, Northern Illinois University, DeKalb, IL (hereafter cited as Smith papers).

37 As the years . . . accompanied him: Smith papers, various dates, 1851–1863.

37 "was the champion" . . . "anyone else": Wilson, "Personal Recollections of the Passenger Pigeon," pp. 159–163.

38 During his time . . . letters to each other: Swierenga and Van Appledorn, p. 347.

38 When Louis . . . many occasions: Payson Wolf, affidavit, 1894, in Louis Miskoguon pension file.

39 With the approval . . . if they wished: Peter Dougherty to Daniel Wells, July 9, 1839, Presbyterian Historical Society, digital.history.pcusa.org/islandora:89408.

39 log homes . . . on the outside: Ruth Craker, *The First Protestant Mission in the Grand Traverse Region* (East Jordan, MI, 1932; repr., Mount Pleasant, MI: Rivercrest House, 1979), p. 65.

40 "a great interest" . . . "blessed Savior": Peter Dougherty to Walter Lowrie, July 26, 1842, Presbyterian Historical Society, digital.history.pcusa.org/islandora/object /islandora:89418.

41 "white men looking about" . . . "suspicious": Peter Dougherty letter, May 23, 1850, Presbyterian Historical Society, digital.history.pcusa.org/islandora/object /islandora:88540.

41 "You know . . . the American people": Letter to the U.S. president and Congress, Oct. 1843, from Chief Aish-qua-go-na-be et al., *Letters Received by the Office of Indian Affairs, 1824–1881* (National Archives Microfilm Publication M234, roll 425, pp. 516–523), Records of the Bureau of Indian Affairs, 1801–1952, RG 75, National Archives Building, Washington, DC.

42 Moses Allen . . . eldest son, Charles: Annie Allen, claimant's testimony, June 10, 1885, in Charles Allen pension file.

42 by the time . . . helped his family: Peter Dougherty, "Report of Expenses at Grove Hill from Jan. 1 to July 1, 1862," Presbyterian Historical Society, digital.history .pcusa.org/islandora/object/islandora:89447.

42 In 1862 . . . in 2018: Purchasing power equivalent found at Official Data Foundation, officialdata.org/1862-dollars-in-2018?amount=50.

43 Mwakewenah, an Odawa . . . helped build the school: Michelle Cassidy, "'The More Noise They Make': Odawa and Ojibwe Encounters with American Missionaries in Northern Michigan, 1837–1871," *Michigan Historical Review* 38, no. 2 (Fall 2012): pp. 14–15.

43 "We love . . . beside theirs also": Delegation of Chippewa and Ottawa to George

Manypenny, Jan. 16, 1855, from Nisawakwatt et al., *Letters Received by the Office of Indian Affairs, 1824–1881* (National Archives Microfilm Publication M234, roll 404, pp. 561–566), RG 75.

44 Joseph Nabawnayasang . . . name Joseph Gibson: Simon Petasigay and Joseph Petasigay, affidavit, July 11, 1866, in Joseph [Gibson] Nabawnayasang pension file.

45 While they were . . . on their shoulders: Lucy Bump, "A Short History of Petoskey," *Petoskey (MI) Record*, Jan. 23, 1895, p. 5.

CHAPTER 4: AIM FOR THE BULL'S-EYE

47 Gray clouds drizzled snow: Local and News Items, *Grand Haven (MI) News*, Dec. 10, 1862, p. 3.

47 a sure-shot hunter: Dennis Deverney, personal communication to author, June 28, 2016.

49 She treated her patients . . . strapping good health: Eliza Deverney, affidavit, Dec. 5, 1888; William Sly, affidavit, Oct. 27, 1897; and Watson B. Weeks, affidavit, Nov. 29, 1889; all three documents are in John Kedgnal pension file.

50 Charles V. DeLand . . . the Union cause: Herek, *These Men Have Seen Hard Service*, pp. 2–3.

50 In July 1862 . . . First Michigan Sharpshooters: M. A. Leeson, *History of Saginaw County, Michigan* (Chicago, 1881), pp. 465–466, HathiTrust Digital Library, hdl .handle.net/2027/miun.bad1164.0001.001.

51 By the end . . . begin recruiting: Austin Blair to Edward J. Buckbee, Nov. 18, 1862, *Civil War Letters and Related Materials, 1862–1926*, Buckbee Family Papers, Bentley Historical Library, University of Michigan.

51 The would-be . . . passed the test: Thomas Duvernay, personal communication to author, July 12, 2017.

52 Sunrise . . . bed: Orders no. 3, April 26, 1863, Regimental Letter, Order, and Courts-Martial Book, First Michigan Sharpshooters, Book Records of Volunteer Union Organizations, Records of the Adjutant General's Office, RG 94, National Archives Building, Washington, DC (hereafter cited as Regimental Letter Book).

53 He practiced . . . on one of his fingers: Erin Walker Bliss, personal communication to author, Oct. 13, 2017.

54 Whether they . . . dug in the ground: Battalion orders no. 2, April 25, 1863, Regimental Letter Book.

55 When smallpox . . . vaccinated: Herek, *These Men Have Seen Hard Service*, p. 30.

55 In April, Kedgnal . . . as a deserter: Register of Deserters, no date, Regimental Letter Book; Thomas Duvernay, personal communication to author, August 12, 2017.

55 By that time . . . arrested deserters: "Arsenal at War," July 4, 2013, Dearborn Historical Museum, thedhm.com/2013/07/04/arsenal-at-war/; and "The Sharpshooters," *Detroit Free Press*, April 24, 1863, p. 1.

CHAPTER 5: NEW *OGITCHEDAW*

57 In these . . . in action: "16th Regiment Michigan Volunteer Infantry," Michigan Genealogy on the Web, migenweb.org/michiganinthewar/infantry/16thinf.htm.

58 On August 30 . . . reported missing: Department of the Interior, Bureau of Pensions, Nov. 4, 1893, in Joseph Wakazoo pension file.

58 "there will be . . . the graves of our friends": *Detroit Advertiser and Tribune*, July 14, 1863, in Herek, *These Men Have Seen Hard Service*, p. 59.

58 Despite treaty . . . Mississippi River: Eric Hemenway, personal communications to author, July 13, 2017, and April 19, 2018.

61 army's terms . . . in the army: Special orders no. 24, June 1, 1863, Regimental Letter Book.

61 He did not . . . with his left hand: Elijah Pelcher, affidavit, March 10, 1894, in Thomas Smith pension file.

63 In May 1861 . . . to miss: Smith papers, May 20, 1861.

64 "German, French" . . . "every new word": *The Andress Family: A Centennial Tribute*, July 5, 1981, Genealogy Collection, Chesaning Public Library, Michigan, accessed Sept. 3, 2017, onedrive.live.com/?id=9050D7B45491601F%211961&cid =9050D7B45491601F.

64 After Andress . . . to volunteer: Louis M. Hartwick and William H. Tuller, *Oceana County Pioneers and Business Men of To-Day: History, Biography, Statistics and Humorous Incidents* (Pentwater, MI, 1890; repr., Salem, MA: Higginson, 1998), p. 46, HathiTrust Digital Library, hdl.handle.net/2027/mdp.39015071216843.

65 "healthy athletic . . . every day": Joseph Hall and Isaac Bennett, affidavit, n.d., in Amos Ashkebugnekay pension file.

65 "The word Ashkebugnekay" . . . "when I die": Amos Ashkebugnekay, affidavit, n.d., in Amos Ashkebugnekay pension file.

66 Yet everyone . . . and good wishes: Hartwick and Tuller, *Oceana County Pioneers and Business Men of To-Day*, p. 46.

66 "recall white soldiers" . . . "than white troops": No title, editorial, *Detroit Free Press*, July 9, 1863, p. 2.

68 The six-month-old . . . one month later: Smith papers, Sept. 6, 1863.

68 Amable Ketchebatis . . . he enlisted: Elizabeth Ketchebatis, claim for widow's pension with minor children, Jan. 17, 1870, in Amable Ketchebatis pension file.

69 Amable Ketchebatis . . . seven different ways: Lizette Ketchebatis, deposition, March 23, 1869, in Amable Ketchebatis pension file.

70 Gibson's father . . . farming and fishing: Lilla Na-baw-na-ya-sang, claim for mother's pension, Oct. 1, 1866, in Joseph [Gibson] Nabawnayasang pension file.

70 Before Garrett left . . . would be fine: Henry Graveraet, 1850 and 1860 U.S. censuses, Michilimackinac County, MI, population schedules (dwelling 265, family 270, National Archive Publication M432, roll 357; dwelling 785, family

424, M653, roll 542); Summary of Material Facts, March 12, 1877; and affidavit by Joseph Pyant, April 14, 1877, in Henry and Garrett Graveraet pension files. (Garrett Graveraet's first name is spelled Gerrett on his pension file, but documents within the file spell it as Garrett or Garret. For uniformity, I use Garrett.)

71 By the end . . . 102 men: Czopek, *Who Was Who in Company K*, pp. 214–215.

CHAPTER 6: RIFLES AND RULES

74 First he took . . . without the grooves: Thomas Duvernay, personal communication to author and a lesson loading a Springfield, July 12, 2017.

75 On average . . . in the teens: Thomas Duvernay, personal communication to author, July 12, 2017.

76 Allen called . . . leaves of absence: William Watson, *Life in the Confederate Army* (London, 1887), pp. 140–141.

76 One day . . . trial for December: "Local Intellignece [*sic*]," *Detroit Free Press*, Dec. 18, 1863, p. 1, and Dec. 15, 1863, p. 1.

77 More than 2,933 . . . the city: George Levy, *To Die in Chicago: Confederate Prisoners at Camp Douglas, 1862–1865* (Evanston, IL: Evanston Publishing, 1994), p. 6.

78 Flat, open land . . . supply of water: Dennis Kelly, *A History of Camp Douglas, Illinois, Union Prison, 1861–1865* (U.S. Department of the Interior, National Park Service, Southeast Region, 1989), p. 4, nps.gov/parkhistory/online_books/ande /douglas.pdf.

78 An inspector . . . rotting garbage: Levy, *To Die in Chicago*, p. 59.

78 The Union soldiers . . . deplorable conditions: "The City: Fires at Camp Douglas," *Chicago Daily Tribune*, Oct. 18, 1862, p. 4.

79 "Camp Douglas . . . 8,000 prisoners": Levy, *To Die in Chicago*, p. 118.

79 When Payson Wolf . . . tall board fence: Edward J. Buckbee, memoir, "The Story I Tell My Children, Being a True Story of Capture, Prison Pen, and Escape," ca. 1886, p. 15, Buckbee Family Papers.

80 Before sunset . . . the day after: Levy, *To Die in Chicago*, p. 51.

80 A newspaper reporter . . . "breaking away": "The City: Camp Douglas Prisoners of War," *Chicago Daily Tribune*, Aug. 24, 1863, p. 4.

80 The next day . . . miming the capture of an enemy: "An Indian on Copper," *Daily Pantagraph* (Bloomington, IL), Aug. 24, 1863, p. 2.

81 "At this place . . . behind trees & bushes": George Harry Weston, diary, Sept. 27, 1863, Rubenstein Rare Book and Manuscript Library, Duke University.

82 Perhaps he was . . . snakes, and turtles: Robert D. Graham, "Fifty-Sixth Regiment," in *Histories of the Several Regiments and Battalions from North Carolina in the Great War 1861–'65*, ed. Walter Clark, vol. 3 (Goldsboro, NC: Nash Bros., 1901), pp. 361–362.

82 "I just received . . . I love you": Payson Wolf to Mary Jane Wolf, Jan. 16, 1864,

Wolf family collection. Copy of letter shown to author by Art Dembinski, June 2018.

83 In September . . . at the same time: Smith papers, Sept. 5, 1863.

83 He wrote . . . "as we are paid": Joseph Gibson to Richard Cooper, February 22, 1864, in Joseph [Gibson] Nabawnayasang pension file.

83 "One soldier who . . . in one time": Payson Wolf to Mary Jane Wolf, Jan. 16, 1864.

83 Charles Allen usually . . . in a letter: Charles Allen to Suhyahgeenahgoog (Dear loved ones, translated by Dr. Richard Rhodes), Feb. 28, 1864, in Charles Allen pension file. Letter also available online at Archival Research Catalog (66390979) archives.gov.

84 "wild story" . . . "trouble for him": Special orders no. 84, Nov. 17, 1863, Regimental Letter Book; Charles Allen to Suhyahgeenahgoog, Dec. 21, 1863, translated by Dr. Richard Rhodes, in Charles Allen pension file.

84 Payson Wolf's family . . . for the trips: Smith papers, Oct. 15 and 29, Nov. 13, 22, and 25, 1863.

86 On September 9 . . . in November: Smith papers, Sept. 10, 1863; and Department of the Interior, Bureau of Pensions, Nov. 4, 1893, in Joseph Wakazoo pension file.

87 "The court is thus . . . of the U.S. Service": Court-martial ruling, n.d., Regimental Letter Book.

88 Bitter-cold . . . coldest winter ever: William H. Randall, diary entry, Jan. 1, 1864, *Reminiscence 1867*, p. 55, Bentley Historical Library, University of Michigan (hereafter cited as Randall diary).

88 On the night . . . charged with murder: "The Moynihan Murder," *Chicago Daily Tribune*, March 19, 1864, p. 4.

88 (worth about three dollars in 2018): Purchasing power equivalent found at Official Data Foundation, officialdata.org/1864-dollars-in-2018?amount=0.20.

89 (His service records . . . still unknown): Department of the Interior, Bureau of Pensions, Feb. 24, 1896, in Charles Wabesis pension file.

89 "The Indian Company . . . have ever seen": Edward Buckbee, memoir, p. 7, Buckbee Family Papers.

CHAPTER 7: THE ROAD TO BATTLE

91 *Suhyahgeenahgoog* . . . "in the spring": Allen to Suhyahgeenahgoog, Feb. 28, 1864.

91 an offensive . . . thousand volunteers: Abraham Lincoln, "Proclamation 116—Calling for 500,000 Volunteers," July 18, 1864, in The American Presidency Project, ed. Gerhard Peters and John T. Woolley, presidency.ucsb.edu/ws/?pid=69996.

92 On March 17, . . . of the Potomac: [George H. Turner, ed.], *Record of Service of Michigan Volunteers in the Civil War 1861–1865* (Kalamazoo, MI: Ihling Bros. & Everard, n.d.), vol. 44, p. 2.

92 "any stimulating drinks . . . walk on air": Buckbee, memoir, p. 17.

92 The next day . . . a warm supper: "City and Suburban," *Daily Pittsburgh Gazette*, March 22, 1864, p. 4.

92 ten to twelve thousand soldiers: "From the 2d Cavalry," *Western Reserve Chronicle* (Warren, OH), April 13, 1864, p. 3.

92 An eagle traveled . . . the eagle went too: Constant Hanks to his sister Moll, July 24, 1864, Rubenstein Rare Book and Manuscript Library, Duke University.

92 A story passed . . . revered the bird: Benton-Banai, *The Mishomis Book*, pp. 80–82.

93 Many of the soldiers . . . offered before battle: Eric Hemenway, personal communication to author, April 3, 2018.

94 Joseph Gibson . . . loading wagons: Regimental Letter Book, various dates, April 1864.

94 "Lee's Army . . . will go also": John Y. Simon, ed., *The Papers of Ulysses S. Grant* (Carbondale: Southern Illinois University Press, 1972), vol. 10, pp. 273–274.

95 Within a few weeks . . . at Camp Parole: "Burnside's Second Eppedition [*sic*]": *Memphis (TN) Daily Appeal*, April 9, 1864, p. 1.

95 The general commanded . . . the Third Division: Herek, *These Men Have Seen Hard Service*, pp. 98–99.

96 The Ninth Corps was completely . . . to mend harnesses: Randall diary, May 5, 1864, p. 65.

97 On April 23 . . . to strike tents: Amos Farling, *Life in the Army: Recollections of Private Amos Farling of Company G, First Michigan Sharpshooters 1863–1866* (Buchanan, MI, 1874; repr., Berrien Springs, MI: Berrien County Historical Association, 2005), p. 9.

97 Each Sharpshooter carried . . . of a long walk: Farling, *Life in the Army*, p. 9.

98 Just before . . . their appearance: Byron M. Cutcheon, *The Story of the Twentieth Michigan Infantry* (Lansing, MI: Robert Smith, 1904), p. 99.

98 There is . . . of the earth: Abraham Lincoln, "Speech to Indians," March 27, 1863, in *The Collected Works of Abraham Lincoln*, ed. Roy P. Basler (New Brunswick, NJ: Rutgers University Press, 1953), vol. 6, pp. 152–153.

100 "The president . . . careworn": Randall diary, April 22, 1864, p. 63.

100 Ladies waved . . . "Remember Fort Pillow": "From Washington: Military Matters," *Cleveland Morning Leader*, April 27, 1864, p. 1.

100 A Confederate force . . . specifically targeted: "Fort Pillow," National Park Service, nps.gov/abpp/battles/tn030.htm; and John Cimprich and Robert C. Mainfort Jr., "The Fort Pillow Massacre: A Statistical Note," *Journal of American History* 76 (1989): pp. 836–837.

101 Company K . . . farther southwest: Amos Chamberlin, affidavit, Jan. 12, 1895, in Edwin Andress pension file.

CHAPTER 8: INTO THE WILDERNESS

103 At noon . . . way across: Buckbee, memoir, p. 19.

104 A company on picket . . . main forces: Hauptman, *Between Two Fires*, p. 127.

104   By nightfall . . . cannon fire: Randall diary, May 5, 1864, p. 65.

105   "We slept . . . that night": Byron M. Cutcheon, report no. 244, Aug. 7, 1864, in *The War of the Rebellion: A Compilation of the Official Records of the Union and Confederate Armies*, ser. 1, vol. 36, pt. 1 (Washington, DC, 1891), p. 975 (hereafter cited as *WOR*).

106   They noticed . . . camouflage: Buckbee, memoir, p. 8; as George Campbell, "Old Choctaw: The 1st Mich. Chippewa Indian Sharpshooters and Their Methods," *National Tribune* (Washington, DC), Sept. 11, 1913, p. 7; and C. D. Bibbins, "The Indian Sharpshooters," *National Tribune*, Oct. 16, 1913, p. 7.

107   so dense . . . fifty yards separated them: A. B. Williams, "Additional Sketch Tenth Regiment: Company C—Light Battery," in Clark, *Histories of the Several Regiments*, vol. 1, p. 547.

107   Daniel Mwakewenah . . . he shot: Campbell, "Old Choctaw."

108   Fire at will . . . a rebel soldier: Buckbee, memoir, p. 19.

109   cloud of white smoke: Chris Czopek, personal communication to author, Oct. 2017.

109   buzzing . . . mosquitoes: Homer B. Sprague, *History of the 13th Infantry Regiment of Connecticut Volunteers, During the Great Rebellion* (Hartford, CT, 1867), p. 142.

110   Everyone tried to move . . . his skin bruised: Louis Meichaba, deposition, Sept. 20, 1892, in George Ashkebug pension file.

110   In their haste . . . Ojibwe dialect: "Desperate Fighting of N.C. Troops," *Western Democrat* (Charlotte, NC), May 31, 1864, p. 2; R. T. Bennett, "Fourteenth Regiment," in Clark *Histories of the Several Regiments*, vol. 1, pp. 721–722; and "From the Diary of a Confederate Officer: Experiences with the Army of Virginia," *Our Living and Our Dead* (New Bern, NC), Feb. 4, 1874, p. 2.

110   "fought a regiment" . . . "sent home and prized": W. A. Smith, *The Anson Guards, Company C, Fourteenth Regiment, North Carolina Volunteers, 1861–1865* (Charlotte, NC: Stone, 1914), p. 235.

110   The 20th Michigan . . . to their own earthworks: Byron M. Cutcheon, report no. 242, Oct. 23, 1864, *WOR*, ser. 1, vol. 36, pt. 1, pp. 966–967.

111   A bullet . . . was serious: Annie Allen, Declaration for an Original Pension of a Mother, Feb. 21, 1881, in Charles Allen pension file.

112   "The blaze ran . . . glare of the flames": Henry C. Houston, *The Thirty-Second Maine Regiment of Infantry Volunteers: An Historical Sketch* (Portland, ME: Southworth Bros., 1903), p. 101, HathiTrust Digital Library hdl.handle.net/2027 /hvd.hx2nbu.

113   Two hundred . . . to death: George Worthington Adams, *Doctors in Blue: The Medical History of the Union Army in the Civil War* (New York: Henry Schuman, 1952), p. 99.

113   Before he settled . . . represented officers: "The Patriotic Offering of the Ottawas," *Evening Star* (Washington, DC), June 16, 1864, p. 2.

113 When Colonel DeLand . . . and Charles Allen: Charles DeLand, report, May 26, 1864, Regimental Letter Book.

113 Six hundred . . . Union wounded: Adams, *Doctors in Blue*, p. 97.

115 Of eleven thousand . . . performed surgeries: Jenny Goellnitz, "Civil War Battlefield Surgery," Ehistory, Ohio State University, accessed Oct. 10, 2017, ehistory.osu.edu/exhibitions/cwsurgeon/cwsurgeon/amputations.

115 The surgeon probed . . . ceramic-tipped probe: Glenna R. Schroeder-Lein, *The Encyclopedia of Civil War Medicine* (New York: M. E. Sharpe, 2008), p. 121.

115 the surgeon located . . . in Allen's chest: Charles Allen Carded Medical Records, n.d., National Archives building, RG94.

115 A nurse . . . dressing in place: Stewart M. Brooks, *Civil War Medicine* (Springfield, IL: Charles C. Thomas, 1966), p. 86.

116 On May 7 . . . from the Wilderness: Randall diary, May 7, 1864, p. 67.

CHAPTER 9: GALLANTRY UNSURPASSED

120 Confusion reigned . . . Sharpshooters to retreat: DeLand report, May 26, 1864.

120 Captain Edwin Andress . . . two months later: Surgeon General's Office, Nov. 2, 1881, and Military Department, Michigan, Adjutant General's Office, Dec. 24, 1875, in Edwin Andress pension file.

120 A bullet struck . . . the field hospital: Buckbee, memoir, pp. 20–21.

121 "left us standing . . . knee-deep": Farling, *Life in the Army*, p. 12.

121 Battle-smoke . . . filled the air: Randall diary, May 12, 1864, p. 68.

122 Then the three . . . from the enemy's sight: Cutcheon, report no. 242, Oct. 23, 1864, *WOR*, ser. 1, vol. 36, pt. 1, p. 969.

123 Hearing the whistle . . . He collapsed: Joseph Wakazoo statement, June 11, 1889, and Interior Department document, Nov. 28, 1881, in Joseph Wakazoo pension file.

124 "a murderous crossfire . . . and canister": DeLand report, May 26, 1864.

124 A piece of shell . . . left side: James Arwonogezice, affidavit, 1896; John H. Thomas, affidavit, 1884; Interior Department document, May 2, 1884; and Surgeon General's Office document, Aug. 25, 1884; all documents found in George Ashkebug pension file.

124 But he'd been . . . reload his rifle: Herek, *These Men Have Seen Hard Service*, p. 155; and Surgeon General's Office, April 20, 1865, in Daniel Mwakewenah pension file.

124 Marcus Otto . . . excruciating: Sources differ on the date of Marcus Otto's wound. A duplicate of his Certificate of Disability for Discharge notes he received the wound "in action at the Wilderness." At that time, some army recorders grouped the battles at Spotsylvania and the Wilderness together, generally calling them the Wilderness. A document in Otto's pension file, written by James DeLand, certifies that Otto was "present at the battle of

Spotsylvania on May 12" and was wounded in his right arm while in action there. A copy of this document can be viewed on the blog *Company K First Michigan Sharpshooters*, Jan. 22, 2018, nativesharpshooters.blogspot.com/2018 /01/. *The Medical and Surgical History of the War of the Rebellion* (Washington, DC, 1877), vol. 2, pt. 2, p. 757, also lists the date of his injury as May 12, 1864. This can be viewed at resource.nlm.nih.gov/14121350R. Unlike the certificate, these two documents give a specific date. I have chosen to accept them as the date of Otto's injury. Regardless, the severity of Otto's wound and the amputation of his right arm are indisputable.

124 "Advance was impossible" . . . "gallantry unsurpassed": DeLand report, May 26, 1864.

125 Colonel DeLand was twice . . . hospital for treatment: DeLand report, May 26, 1864.

127 A large white . . . the tree fell: David Holt, *A Mississippi Rebel in the Army of Northern Virginia: The Civil War Memoirs of Private David Holt*, eds. Thomas D. Cockrell and Michael B. Ballard (Baton Rouge: Louisiana State University Press, 2001), p. 257.

128 "seething . . . hate and murder": John West Haley, diary entry, May 12, 1864, *Rebel Yell and Yankee Hurrah*, ed. Ruth L. Silliker (Camden, ME: Down East Books, 1985), p. 157, quoted on historical marker at Spotsylvania Battlefield, Fredericksburg and Spotsylvania National Military Park, Virginia, June 10, 2017.

128 "We halted . . . and wept": Holt, *A Mississippi Rebel*, p. 263.

129 Poor road conditions . . . up to their hubs: William Howell Reed, *Hospital Life in the Army of the Potomac* (Boston, 1866), p. 14.

129 The ambulances . . . yelled with pain: Adams, *Doctors in Blue*, pp. 99–100.

130 "In a group . . . for our care": Reed, *Hospital Life*, p. 27.

132 A steamboat . . . leg wound healed: Various documents in Louis Genereau Jr. pension file.

133 In fact, Kechittigo's . . . Colored Sharpshooters: Thomas Kechittigo, hospital record card, Military Service Records, RG94, National Archives Building, Washington, DC.

133 By then . . . remain a mystery: Czopek, *Who Was Who in Company K*, p. 132.

133 Approximately thirty-six thousand . . . missing in action: Historical marker, Spotsylvania Battlefield; and *WOR*, ser. 1, vol. 36, pt. 1, pp. 132, 149.

134 "after he was wounded" . . . "days thereafter": Antoine Scott, testimony, Oct. 23, 1873, in John Etarwegeshig pension file.

134 Garrett Graveraet reported . . . Beverly family: Internment records at Fredericksburg National Cemetery, read by author June 11, 2017.

134 He carefully noted . . . in Michigan: Buckbee, memoir, p. 20.

135 "in a handsome coffin . . . it was received": "The Patriotic Offering of the Ottawas," *Evening Star* (Washington, DC), June 16, 1864, p. 2.

135 "He was a brave and good soldier": Lemuel Nichols, sworn statement, May 4 (or 8), 1865, in Daniel Mwakewenah pension file.

CHAPTER 10: THE CONTINUING FIGHT

137 "profoundly ignorant" . . . over a month: Edward J. Buckbee to his mother, June 7, 1864, Buckbee Family Papers.

138 New Hampshirite . . . he had received: Wyman S. White, *The Civil War Diary of Wyman S. White, First Sergeant of Company F. 2nd United States Sharpshooter Regiment, 1861–1865* (Baltimore: Butternut and Blue, 1991), p. 250.

138 After a barrage . . . that pulled them: Campbell, "Old Choctaw."

139 Twenty-six horses . . . at the other: Campbell, "Old Choctaw."

140 En masse . . . June 14: The description of the June 12–16 march is summarized in Cutcheon, *Story of the Twentieth Michigan*, pp. 131–132.

142 Hours before . . . fifteen hundred rifles: Description of Shand House and the attack based on Leander W. Cogswell, *A History of the Eleventh New Hampshire Regiment, Volunteer Infantry in the Rebellion War, 1861–1865* (Concord, NH, 1891), pp. 378–381, HathiTrust Digital Library, hdl.handle.net/2027/ucl.$b61724.

143 They were . . . in that area: Herek, *These Men Have Seen Hard Service*, p. 178.

143 Captain Rhines . . . charge the salient: Leverette Case to Mollie Church, June 19, 1864, Buckbee Family Papers.

143 As the evening . . . repulsed them: Case to Church, June 19, 1864.

143 When a cannon . . . grew silent: George H. Murdoch, "Bivouac and Battlefield," *Detroit Free Press*, May 9, 1886, p. 9.

143 A minié ball . . . his left arm: Garrett Graveraet to his mother and sister, June 22, 1864, in Garrett A. Graveraet pension file.

143 The surgeon . . . amputated it: Graveraet to mother and sister, June 22, 1864.

144 "We surrender, don't shoot": Case to Church, June 19, 1864.

144 "the fire . . . clothing of the men": Randall diary, June 17, 1864, p. 79.

145 Buckbee wisely . . . his sword: Case to Church, June 19, 1864.

145 At first light . . . toward Petersburg: Herek, *These Men Have Seen Hard Service*, pp. 396–399.

145 Their captors . . . close of the war: Robert D. Graham, "Fifty-Sixth Regiment," in Clark, *Histories of the Several Regiments*, vol. 3, p. 362.

145 Louis Genereau . . . to the Sharpshooters: Pamela J. Dobson, *The Tree That Never Dies: Oral History of the Michigan Indians* (Grand Rapids, MI: Grand Rapids Public Library, 1978), p. 129; and Case to Church, June 29, 1864.

146 Fifteen . . . Company K: Czopek, *Who Was Who in Company K*, p. 222.

146 Charles Campbell and his children . . . "nothing to say": Charles Campbell, diary entry, June 18, 1864, "Diary of the War," Various Journals, Diaries, and an Index, William & Mary Libraries Transcription, transcribe.swem.wm.edu/items/show /1779.

148 Fifteen men had died . . . prisoners of war: Herek, *These Men Have Seen Hard Service*, pp. 394–399.

148 Genereau told . . . he'd seen him: Case to Church, June 29, 1864.

148 Because the regiment's . . . Companies I and K: Regimental orders no. 19, Date June 30, 1864, Regimental Letter Book.

148 Lieutenant William Randall . . . "names to write out": Randall diary, June 28, 1864, p. 81.

149 John Kedgnal . . . spent bullet: Deposition by Charles Stafford, Oct. 12, 1897, in John Kedgnal pension file.

149 As Asher Huff . . . Huff's knee: Randall diary, June 26, 1864, p. 80; and Surgeon General's Office, Sept. 20, 1883, in John Andrew pension file.

149 On June 22 . . . "to my senses": Graveraet to mother and sister, June 22, 1864.

150 "A letter from you . . . Garret A Graveraet": Graveraet to mother and sister, June 22, 1864.

150 William Driggs's father . . . "all the men": Joseph Finch (assistant ward master Armory Square Hospital) to Sophia Graveraet, July 26, 1864, in Garrett A. Graveraet pension file.

150 Still mourning . . . his body home: Richard Cooper (at Sophia Graveraet's request) to D. M. Bess (or Best), July 25, 1864, Garrett A. Graveraet Military Service Records, RG94, National Archives Building, Washington, DC.

CHAPTER 11: EXPLOSION!

153 Thomas Smith . . . almost blind: Brv Lt. Colonel Bontecon, Harewood General Hospital, September 6, 1865, in Thomas Smith pension file.

154 annoyed them at night: John H. Thomas, deposition, Oct. 13, 1892, in George Ashkebug pension file.

154 ripe berries . . . back in Michigan: Andrew J. Blackbird, *History of the Ottawa and Chippewa Indians of Michigan* (Ypsilanti, MI, 1887), p. 11.

156 "a peculiar whirring" . . . "15 minutes": Randall diary, July 24, 1864, p. 85.

157 On June 25 . . . were helping: Jim Corrigan, *The 48th Pennsylvania in the Battle of the Crater* (Jefferson, NC: McFarland & Co., 2006), p. 21.

158 Men from the . . . "the mined fort": Cutcheon, *Story of the Twentieth Michigan*, p. 138.

160 "They were a new" . . . "could be relied upon": *Report of the Committee on the Conduct of the War on the Attack on Petersburg, on the 30th Day of July, 1864* (Washington, DC, 1865), pp. 4–5.

161 But now . . . as attendants: Charles DeLand, orders, July 28, 1864, Regimental Letter Book.

161 "Everything indicates" . . . in case they died: Randall diary, July 29, 1864, p. 85.

162 Byron Cutcheon . . . "hid it from view": Cutcheon, *Story of the Twentieth Michigan*, p. 139.

164 Ledlie's First . . . the men inside: William Humphrey, report no. 204, *WOR*, ser. 1, vol. 40, pt. 1, pp. 586–587.

165 "We started on . . . our works": Farling, *Life in the Army*, p. 15.

165 As Colonel DeLand prepared . . . assumed command: Randall diary, July 30, 1864, p. 88; and Herek, *These Men Have Seen Hard Service*, p. 220.

166 Several soldiers . . . "Surrender or die!": Freeman S. Bowley, *Honor in Command: Lt. Freeman S. Bowley's Civil War Service in the 30th United States Colored Infantry*, ed. Keith Wilson (Gainesville: University Press of Florida, 2006), p. 131.

166 "Every man that" . . . U.S. Colored Infantry: George S. Bernard, ed., *War Talks of Confederate Veterans* (Petersburg, VA, 1892), p. 162.

167 General Willcox . . . of ammunition: O. B. Willcox, report, Aug. 6, 1864, *WOR*, ser. 1, vol. 40, pt. 1, p. 575.

167 They heaved them . . . "riddled with bullets": John C. Featherston, "Graphic Account of Battle of Crater," in *Southern Historical Society Papers*, ed. R. A. Brock (Richmond, VA: Southern Historical Society, 1905), vol. 33, pp. 363–364.

167 "great coolness": Randall diary, July 30, 1864, p. 92.

167 "to the very top" . . . "quickly down again": Freeman S. Bowley, "A Boy Lieutenant in a Black Regiment," *National Tribune* (Washington, DC), June 29, 1899.

167 Freeman Bowley . . . "waste no bullets": Freeman S. Bowley, "The Crater," *National Tribune* (Washington, DC), Nov. 6, 1884.

167 Bowley saw . . . death song: Bowley, "A Boy Lieutenant."

168 "The slaughter was . . . eight bodies deep": Featherston, "Graphic Account," p. 365.

168 Without water . . . were unusable: Randall diary, July 30, 1864, p. 92.

168 they were enraged by . . . "having them there": Featherston, p. 364.

168 "arms against . . . of the court": Joint Resolution on the Subject of Retaliation, sec. 4, May 1, 1863, *The Statutes at Large of the Confederate States of America, Passed at the Third Session of the First Congress, 1863*, in E. A. Hitchcock to Edwin M. Stanton, Nov. 22, 1865, *WOR*, ser. 2, vol. 8, p. 800.

169 they turned and . . . "Confederate vengeance": George L. Kilmer, "The Dash into the Crater," *Century Illustrated Monthly Magazine* 34, no. 5 (Sept. 1887): p. 776, HathiTrust Digital Library, hdl.handle.net/2027/ucl.b2922243.

169 But Scott didn't join . . . "shell and escaped": John G. Parke, Medal of Honor recommendation, Feb. 21, 1865, in Antoine Scott compiled military service record, Carded Records Showing Military Service of Soldiers Who Fought in Volunteer Organizations During the American Civil War, 1890–1912, Records of the Adjutant General's Office, 1762–1984, RG 94, National Archives.

171 By August 5 . . . was essential: Charles DeLand, report, Aug. 5, 1864, Regimental Letter Book.

172 Less than a week . . . for DeLand's regiment: James B. Fry to Michigan governor, Aug. 9, 1864, *WOR*, ser. 3, vol. 4, pp. 597–598.

172 Fifteen Anishinaabe men . . . September: Czopek, *Who Was Who in Company K*, pp. 215–216.

174 One soldier . . . "End the war": Joseph C. Snyder (Company K, 132nd Pennsylvania Volunteer Infantry), diary entry, Sept. 18, 1862, unpublished diary in possession of author's family.

174 In November . . . "in the presidential election": Joseph Wakazoo to Honorable Commissioner of pensions, Washington, DC., Dec. 13, 1880, in Joseph Wakazoo pension file.

175 When the regiment's . . . margin: Herek, *These Men Have Seen Hard Service*, p. 270.

CHAPTER 12: THE GATES OF HELL

178 1,620 feet long by 779 feet wide: "History of the Andersonville Prison," April 14, 2015, Andersonville National Historic Site, National Park Service, nps.gov/ande /learn/historyculture/camp_sumter_history.htm.

178 Between April . . . them died: Michael Dougherty, diary entry, April 12, 1864, *Prison Diary of Michael Dougherty, Late Co. B, 13th Pa., Cavalry* (Bristol, PA: Chas. A. Dougherty, 1908), p. 39.

178 More than . . . June 27: Ransom Chadwick, diary, June 27, 1864, *Ransom Chadwick's Andersonville Prison Diary*, vol. 1 (St. Paul, MN: Minnesota Historical Society), www2.mnhs.org/library/findaids/00882/pdfa/00882-000006-1.pdf.

178 By then . . . twenty-five thousand prisoners: Herek, *These Men Have Seen Hard Service*, p. 289.

178 By August . . . intended population: "Where We Held Each Other Prisoner," *Andersonville* brochure, Andersonville National Historic Site, National Park Service, nps.gov/ande/planyourvisit/upload/ANDE_mapandguide-2013.pdf.

178 fifteen of them from Company K: Czopek, *Who Was Who in Company K*, p. 222.

178 "Raiders about . . . believe possible": Henry W. Tisdale, diary, June 21, 1864, *Civil War Diary of Henry W. Tisdale, Company I, Thirty-Fifth Regiment, Massachusetts Volunteer Infantry*, civilwardiary.net/diary1864b.htm.

178 "Raiders going on . . . put them down": John L. Ransom, diary, June 27, 1864, *John Ransom's Diary* (New York: Paul S. Eriksson, 1963), pp. 98–99.

180 "The Indians, back . . . quit the fight": Bibbins, "The Indian Sharpshooters."

180 "Battese has . . . self protection": Ransom diary, June 27, 1864, pp. 98–99.

180 On June 28 . . . the Raiders' possession: Tisdale diary, June 28 and 30, 1864.

181 On July 5 . . . were dead: Ransom diary, July 3, 5, 7, and 11, 1864, pp. 105–108, 112–105.

182 "Lice by the" . . . correctly won: Ransom diary, June 15, 1862, p. 92.

183 Often the men . . . ate the vomit: Smith papers, Dec. 28 and 30, 1864.

184 "Dead bodies lay" . . . "live in it": Ransom diary, July 10, 1864, pp. 111–112.

184 During the day . . . each trench: Ransom diary, July 12, 1864, p. 117.

185 Amos Ashkebugnekay's gums . . . blanket shelter: Edgar Baker, deposition, n.d., in Amos Ashkebugnekay pension file.

185 William Newton . . . reduce the swelling: William Newton, deposition, February 5, 1887, in Amos Ashkebugnekay pension file.

185 Louis Miskoguon had seen . . . his friend die: Lewis Miscogwan [*sic*], affidavit, Oct. 31, 1865, in Joseph [Gibson] Nabawnayasang pension file.

185 By October 20 . . . how Ashkebugnekay fared: William Newton, deposition, Feb. 5, 1887, in Amos Ashkebugnekay pension file.

187 While in prison . . . head north: George P. Miller, affidavit, n.d., in Amos Ashkebugnekay pension file.

187 Mixinasaw died on October 26: Document from Surgeon General's Office, March 24, 1866, in William Mesenasaw pension file.

187 Four-inch-deep . . . he slept: Smith papers, Dec. 28, 1864.

187 The only way . . . lost several teeth: Application for the Increase of an Invalid Pension, June 6, 1878, and George N. Smith, document, May 1866; both in Payson Wolf pension file.

188 She and Amable . . . if he could: Lizette Ketchebatis, deposition, March 23, 1869, in Amable Ketchebatis pension file.

188 "marched . . . to Danville": James I. Robertson, "Houses of Horror: Danville's Civil War Prisons," *Virginia Magazine of History and Biography* 69, no. 3 (July 1961): p. 335.

189 "a meal of corn . . . two inches wide": Robertson, "Houses of Horror," p. 336.

189 "rat dung . . . in the cabbage soup": Robertson, "Houses of Horror," p. 337.

189 At one point . . . in Building 3: Homer B. Sprague, *Lights and Shadows in Confederate Prisons* (New York: G. P. Putnam's Sons, 1915), pp. 78, 129.

189 Before Ketchebatis . . . who did: Robertson, "Houses of Horror," p. 335.

189 "i am a prisnor" . . . in Building 3: Amable Ketchebatis to Lizette Ketchebatis, Aug. 5, 1864, in Amable Ketchebatis pension file.

190 "The negro soldiers" . . . "seven survivors": Sprague, *Lights and Shadows in Confederate Prisons*, p. 129.

190 He told her . . . first day of March 1865: Louis Shomin, testimony, Dec. 3, 1866, in Amable Ketchebatis pension file.

190 Recent investigations . . . late February: Hospital and cemetery records are confusing about Amable Ketchebatis's death and burial. It appears that hospital people unfamiliar with Anishinaabe names wrote his name as Amiab J. After he died, his body was taken to the dead house, where it was mistakenly tagged as J. Amos. This name was subsequently misidentified as Ketchebatis's Company K comrade Amos Ashkebugnekay, who was temporarily at Danville Prison but survived the war. The hospital and cemetery note that the death was in February. Amos Ashekbugnekay listing, National Cemetery Administration, U.S. Department of Veterans Affairs, m.va.gov/gravelocator/index.cfm#N841; and Shier, *Warriors in Mr. Lincoln's Army*, pp. 218–219.

191 He had no blanket . . . no shoes: John Kedgnal, deposition, Feb. 11, 1897, in John Kedgnal pension file.

191 Union officers . . . dead in the prison yard: Sprague, *Lights and Shadows in Confederate Prisons*, pp. 52–56.

191 His gums ached . . . with similar ailments: John Kedgnal, deposition, Feb. 11, 1897, in John Kedgnal pension file.

192 One day . . . on a stretcher: Ezra Faunce, deposition, Feb. 11, 1897, and John Kedgnal to P. J. Lockwood, Sept. 6, 1889; both documents in John Kedgnal pension file.

193 No one from Company K . . . early November: Amos Ashkebugnekay, affidavit, n.d., and Payson Wolf, affidavit, n.d.; both in William Newton pension file.

193 The prison, which . . . in shanties: Ransom diary, Nov. 1, 1864, pp. 163–165.

194 On December 15 . . . "hear of him again": Smith papers, Dec. 15, 1864.

195 Nine years . . . front of Smith: George Smith, sworn statement, Jan. 26, 1865, in William Mixinasaw pension file.

CHAPTER 13: A WILD CRY OF JOY

199 After his capture . . . promoted to major: Herek, *These Men Have Seen Hard Service*, p. 283; and obituary clippings for Julian Edward Buckbee, newspaper names not included, Buckbee Family Papers.

200 With his furlough . . . in Company K: Payson Wolf, compiled military service record, Carded Records Showing Military Service of Soldiers Who Fought in Volunteer Organizations During the American Civil War, 1890–1912, Records of the Adjutant General's Office, 1762–1984, RG 94, National Archives; Smith papers, March 23, 1865.

201 The surprised Union . . . any given night: Herek, *These Men Have Seen Hard Service*, p. 302.

202 "the soldiers in the fort" . . . "Rebs on the run": Edward J. Buckbee to Mollie Church, March 25, 1865, Buckbee Family Papers.

202 Before morning's end . . . Fort Stedman: Ira Evans, report no. 138, March 27, 1865, *WOR*, ser. 1, vol. 46, pt. 1, p. 327. While the report cites Companies I and H, Company K was the second company under James DeLand's command.

203 "about 2,000 prisoners . . . plenty of dead": Buckbee to Church, March 25, 1865.

203 At ten o'clock . . . "Take the enemy's line": Buckbee to Church, March 25, 1865.

204 an advance guard . . . perpendicular to the Union line: Herek, p. 316.

205 A bullet . . . joined his shoulder: Miraculously, James DeLand survived. Colonel Charles DeLand was with him in the hospital within forty-eight hours and cared for his younger brother day and night. The constant care was probably one reason that James survived. Charles DeLand to his parents, April 18, 1865, DeLand Family Papers, 1811–1943, Bentley Historical Library Civil War Collections Online, quod.lib.umich.edu/cgi/t/text/idx/b/bhlcivilwar/2011341.0002.001/38.

205 "We could have . . . fought splendidly": Edward Buckbee to Charles DeLand, April 2, 1865, DeLand Family Papers, quod.lib.umich.edu/cgi/t/text/idx/b/bhlcivilwar/2011341.0002.001/25.

205 The Sharpshooters lost . . . later died: Herek, *These Men Have Seen Hard Service*, pp. 406–407.

206 Earlier, they'd also . . . "distant thunder": Cutcheon, *Story of the Twentieth Michigan*, p. 166.

206 Before the sun rose . . . into the air: Buckbee to Church, March 25, 1865.

209 On April 8 . . . Thomas Wesaw's hand: Anthony Foerster, interviewed in Schock, *The Road to Andersonville*.

209 "What it meant" . . . with happiness: Farling, *Life in the Army*, p. 20.

CHAPTER 14: HOMEWARD BOUND

212 Noting that . . . "could have asked": Edward J. Buckbee to Mollie Church, April 24, 1865, Buckbee Family Papers.

212 Four days later . . . village of Tennallytown: Herek, *These Men Have Seen Hard Service*, p. 337.

214 "returned home . . . savage cruelty": George Smith, certified statement, Dec. 20, 1866, in Payson Wolf pension file.

216 Jesse Huffaker . . . "He will be alright": Elsie Huffaker, unpublished reminiscences about her father, Jesse Huffaker, Sultana Disaster Museum; and Gene Eric Salecker, personal communication to author, July 3, 2017.

216 Amazingly . . . to his home: Payson Wolf, affidavit, Jan. 22, 1894, in Amos Ashkebugnekay pension file.

216 "Louis Muskoguan . . . that he is alive": Smith papers, July 2, 1865.

217 Twenty-four hours . . . a meal: "Passed Through," *Daily Pittsburgh Gazette*, July 31, 1865, p. 1.

218 On July 31 . . . Lake Erie to Detroit: "City News: Troops in Transit," *Cleveland Leader*, July 31, 1865, p. 4.

219 Five First Michigan . . . were still alive: Herek, *These Men Have Seen Hard Service*, p. 368.

220 "On the advice" . . . governor of Michigan: "Congress's Findings on 'The Burt Lake Band of Ottawa and Chippewa Indians Reaffirmation Act,'" March 19, 2007, House Report 1575, sec. 2, Findings, burtlakeband.org/Media/Docs/Congress.pdf, accessed June 30, 2018.

220 One day . . . for themselves: Richard Wiles, "Burt Lake Native Lands Seized in 1900," *Mackinac Journal*, Nov. 2013, pp. 12–15.

220 "They were good . . . their rights": Thomas Eagleson to General Black, Sept. 9, 1887, in George Kabayacega pension file.

221 Daniel Mwakewenah's . . . their guardian: To Anne Rood, letter of guardianship, Denis Downing, Jan. 1868 (exact date not given), and Margaret Ogishia, medical statement, July 2, 1868; both found in Daniel Mwakewenah pension file.

222 In May 2010 . . . by their people: Schock, *The Road to Andersonville*.

EPILOGUE

227 The GAR . . . Omer, Michigan: Czopek, *Who Was Who in Company K*, pp. 100, 126, 182.

227 When Ashkebug died . . . to bury George in: John A-gatch-ie, deposition, Oct. 12, 1892, in George Ashkebug pension file.

228 Amos Ashkebugnekay . . . funeral: Austin Kibber, medical affidavit, Feb. 20, 1887, in Amos Ashkebugnekay pension file; and Amos Ashkebugnekay obituary, *Ludington (MI) Chronicle*, June 27, 1906, p. 5.

228 "the man who was . . . the third finger": William Duvernay, affidavit, March 31, 1891, in William Duvernay pension file.

228 By 1881 . . . with tuberculosis: William Duvernay, affidavit, Feb. 1, 1892, in William Duvernay pension file.

229 "I am going to die . . . my poor little boy:" Johnstone Ojigokey, deposition, Jan. 24, 1874, in Louis Genereau Jr. pension file.

229 John Jacko . . . support the family: "Jacko Is Dead!," *Charlevoix (MI) Sentinel*, April 25, 1907; Chris Czopek, personal communication to author, June 24, 2017; and Shier, *Warriors in Mr. Lincoln's Army*, p. 168.

229 "quite an expert . . . turbulent waters": Ostrander, "Biography of Thomas Ke-chit-ti-go."

229 An outbreak of smallpox . . . six children: H. F. Gloetzner to commissioner of pensions, May 31, 1920, and Mary Kechittigo, deposition, April 28, 1920; both in Thomas Kechittigo pension file.

231 He married . . . fifty-six years old: Czopek, *Who Was Who in Company K*, p. 131; and "Two Indians Frozen to Death," *Isabella County Enterprise* (Mount Pleasant, MI), April 1, 1904, p. 1.

231 Thomas Smith . . . April 22, 1909: Thomas Smith, Declaration for an Original Invalid Pension, Aug. 20, 1890; B. C. Shaw, physician's affidavit, 1904; and Jacob Tip-si-coe, affidavit, March 28, 1904; all three documents in Thomas Smith pension file; and Chris Czopek, personal communication to author, June 24, 2017.

232 They had thirteen . . . before the war: Payson Wolf, Application for an Increase of Invalid Pension, Sept. 21, 1867, and Bureau of Pensions, Jan. 15, 1898, in Payson Wolf pension file.

232 Wolf regularly . . . Area Museum: Sue Hanson and Dick Hanson, "Medal of Civil War Sharpshooter Wolfe Lost and Then Found," *Leelanau (MI) Enterprise*, Jan. 8, 2015.

APPENDIX C: TREATIES

244 The complete text of the Treaty with the Ottawa and Chippewas, 1836, can be accessed online via Readex, NewsBank, U.S. Congressional Serial Set, and at Kappler's Indian Affairs: Laws and Treaties, Digital Collections at Oklahoma State University Library, dc.library.okstate.edu/digital/collection/kapplers/id/26291.

246 The complete text of the 1855 Treaty of Detroit can be found at Clarke Historical Library, Central Michigan University, Mount Pleasant, MI, cmich.edu/library /clarke/ResearchResources/Native_American_Material/Treaty_Rights/Text_of _Michigan_Related_Treaties/Pages/default.aspx and at Kappler's, dc.library.okstate .edu/digital/collection/kapplers/id/26567.

APPENDIX D: THE EAGLE

248 Dubbed with . . . in March 1881: "Civil War Eagle," *St. Joseph (MI) Saturday Herald*, March 5, 1904, p. 1.

248 On July 4, 1864 . . . south to Mississippi: J. O. Barrett, *"Old Abe:" The Live War-Eagle of Wisconsin* (Madison, WI, 1876), pp. 81–84, archive.org/stream /04237218.3392.emory.edu/04237218.

249 "a company of Indians . . . all the honors": Constant Hanks, July 24, 1864, Rubenstein Rare Book and Manuscript Library, Duke University

(Page references in *italic* refer to illustrations.)

Index